GROWTH
MARKETING
UNLOCKED

GROWTH MARKETING
UNLOCKED

THE PLAYBOOK
FOR STARTUPS AND BEYOND

MARCOS G. FIGUEIRA

MARCIA BERARDINELLI

Growth Marketing Unlocked: The Playbook for Startups and Beyond

Figueira, Marcos G., & Berardinelli, Marcia.

Growth Marketing Unlocked: The Playbook for Startups and Beyond

Edition: 1st ed.

Publication: USA: Independently published, 2024.

ISBN: 9798394155734

1. Marketing. 2.Growth Marketing. 3.Growth Hacking. 4.Marketing Strategy. 5. Growth Strategy. 6.Exponential Growth. 7 Business Growth.

Foreword

Welcome to **Growth Marketing Unlocked: The Playbook for Startups and Beyond** – a roadmap designed to demystify the world of growth marketing and equip you with the strategies to thrive in an ever-changing business landscape.

In today's fast-paced, digitally-driven economy, traditional marketing strategies simply aren't enough. Businesses are scaling faster than ever, and the ones that succeed have cracked the code on growth marketing. This book is here to help you do just that. Whether you're an ambitious startup founder, a seasoned marketer at a scaling business, or a curious entrepreneur eager to unlock the secrets of exponential growth, you're in the right place.

Why this book matters

The relevance of **Growth Marketing Unlocked** lies in its ability to guide readers through the jungle of modern marketing by offering practical strategies that actually work. We live in a world of information overload, where businesses are bombarded with the latest buzzwords – from "AI-driven" this to "automated" that — and marketers struggle to sift through what's hype and what's truly valuable.

This book doesn't just recycle trendy marketing jargon. It provides concrete, actionable insights into how businesses – from scrappy startups to established enterprises – can identify, acquire, and retain customers in ways that scale.

The methodologies and tactics in this book are battle-tested by leading companies that have used growth marketing to outpace competitors, scale globally, and dominate their industries. But more than just offering cookie-cutter solutions, this book arms you with a playbook of growth strategies that can be tailored to your unique business goals and audience.

Who should read this book?

If you're reading this, chances are you fall into one of two camps: you're either trying to grow something new or you're trying to break through a plateau and push your business to the next level. Either way, you'll find value here.

This book is for:

Startup founders who are trying to move quickly, disrupt markets, and make their mark.
Entrepreneurs who want to break away from slow growth and ignite a period of rapid expansion.
Marketers in established companies who are tired of the traditional playbook and are ready to embrace innovative approaches.
Product managers who know their product has potential but need a roadmap to get it in front of the right people.
Business owners at any stage of growth looking to build a sustainable, scalable marketing machine.

Whether you're in SaaS, e-commerce, B2B, or B2C, growth marketing principles can help you accelerate results, improve customer retention, and ultimately, scale your business in ways you didn't think were possible.

What you'll gain from reading this book

Reading Growth Marketing Unlocked will provide you with a comprehensive toolkit to tackle the full spectrum of growth challenges. The pages that follow are packed with tried-and-tested methods, from the foundational strategies that every business needs, to cutting-edge technologies that are transforming the way we approach marketing.

Here's what you can expect:

Clarity: We break down complex concepts and demystify buzzwords. You'll understand what growth markcting really means and how to implement it.

Practical tactics: This isn't just theory. Every chapter provides actionable insights and real-world case studies from companies that have mastered growth marketing.

Adaptable strategies: Whether you're a bootstrapped startup or a scaling enterprise, the strategies in this book can be tailored to fit your unique context.

Cutting-edge technology: You'll gain a deep understanding of how to leverage marketing automation and artificial intelligence to scale your efforts without burning out your team.

Data-driven decision making: Discover how to harness analytics to refine your growth strategy and make informed decisions that deliver results.

So, whether you're a growth marketer with years of experience under your belt or just stepping into the role of chief marketer for your business, Growth Marketing Unlocked will empower you with the insights, tools, and strategies to drive sustainable, exponential growth.

Get ready to dive into a world where marketing is more than just clever ads and email blasts. Growth marketing is about creating systems, using data to fuel your decision-making, and experimenting constantly to find what really works.

Now let's get started – the journey to unlocking your growth begins here.

About the 1st author
MARCOS G. FIGUEIRA

Marcos Figueira has spent over 30 years devoted to marketing, working across various industries, from finance to publishing, and ultimately finding his passion in growth marketing, performance marketing, and branding. His journey began in the financial sector at ABN AMRO Bank, where he honed his marketing skills, before moving to Los Angeles to work in the publishing industry, gaining a deeper understanding of storytelling and brand building.

Since the early 1990s, Marcos has been a partner at WYSE, an agency that specializes in growth marketing and strategic branding. Over the years, he has consulted for a wide range of companies, from startups to medium-sized businesses, helping them navigate their growth challenges.

For the past 12 years, Marcos has also shared his knowledge as a professor in MBA programs at Fundação Getúlio Vargas (FGV) in Brazil. With an MBA from PUC, an MSc. from FGV, and a PhD from Rennes Business School in France, his approach to marketing blends practical experience with academic insight.

Currently, Marcos balances his roles as a consultant, speaker, professor, and author. In Growth Marketing Unlocked, he draws on his experiences to offer straightforward, practical strategies for anyone looking to grow their business. This book isn't about big promises or flashy tricks—it's about sharing what he's learned through years of hands-on work, teaching, and a lot of listening.

About the 2nd author
MARCIA BERARDINELLI

Marcia Berardinelli is a partner and founder at **Wyse**, a leading marketing consultancy known for helping businesses accelerate growth and scale effectively in today's competitive landscape. With a Master's degree in Customer Experience and a specialization in Growth Marketing, Marcia brings a wealth of knowledge and expertise to every project she undertakes.

Over her career, she has helped hundreds of companies across diverse industries to not only escalate their sales but also build strong, resilient brands. Her approach combines data-driven insights with customer-centric strategies, empowering businesses to optimize their marketing efforts and connect more deeply with their target audiences.

At Wyse, Marcia has been at the forefront of the marketing industry's evolution, embracing innovative technologies and growth strategies to deliver measurable results for her clients. She is passionate about transforming the way companies approach growth, always striving to unlock their full potential through a blend of creativity, data, and customer empathy.

As an expert in her field, Marcia shares her insights in this playbook, providing readers with the tools, tactics, and inspiration needed to thrive in the ever-changing world of marketing. Whether you're a startup founder, a marketing professional, or a business leader, Marcia's guidance will help you navigate the complexities of growth marketing with confidence and clarity.

Table of Contents

CHAPTER 4

Demand generation and marketing funnels   95

Creating demand in saturated markets

Building and optimizing marketing funnels

From awareness to purchase: mapping the customer journey

CHAPTER 5

Account-based marketing for hyper-targeted growth   115

What is ABM and why it matters for B2B growth

Developing personalized strategies for high-value accounts

Tools and techniques to implement ABM at scale

CHAPTER 6

Customer-centric growth: putting the customer at the heart of your strategy   137

The importance of customer centricity in growth marketing

Building strategies around customer feedback, needs, and desires

Creating emotional connections and building brand loyalty

CHAPTER 7

Customer experience (CX) and user experience (UX) as growth drivers   159

The role of CX in customer retention and advocacy

Optimizing the digital experience: from websites to apps

User experience principles that drive conversions

CHAPTER 8

Retention is the new acquisition   181

The power of customer retention in sustainable growth

Creating loyalty programs and customer engagement loops

Using email and in-app notifications to keep users engaged

CHAPTER 9

Revenue and monetization strategies   203

INTRODUCTION
Unlocking the potential of growth marketing

What is Growth Marketing?

Growth marketing is not just another term for "marketing with a twist." It's a paradigm shift that flips traditional marketing on its head. While traditional marketing relied on broad strategies—billboards, TV commercials, and endless email blasts—growth marketing is the equivalent of a sniper's aim: precise, data-driven, and obsessed with optimization at every stage of the customer journey.

At its core, growth marketing is about **experimentation** and **iteration**. It's like running a series of scientific experiments on your marketing strategies, collecting data, and then tweaking your approach to get even better results. Imagine you're building a rocket. The traditional marketer would build it, launch it, and cross their fingers that it reaches the moon. A growth marketer, on the other hand, builds a prototype, runs test flights, learns from each crash, and iterates until they have a spaceship that soars. That's the beauty of growth marketing: it's a constant cycle of learning, adjusting, and optimizing.

Growth marketing vs. traditional marketing

Now, let's tackle the obvious question: *How is growth marketing different from traditional marketing?* Traditional marketing can be compared to fishing with a large net—you cast it wide and hope you catch something worthwhile. Growth marketing, however, is like spearfishing: you target specific fish based on data and insights, adapting your approach to each situation. It's not about getting as many leads as possible; it's about acquiring the right leads, keeping them engaged, and turning them into loyal customers.

While traditional marketing often focuses on the **top of the funnel**—awareness and acquisition—growth marketing takes a full-funnel approach. It's not just about getting customers in the door; it's about guiding them through every stage, from awareness to acquisition, activation, retention, referral, and revenue (often called the **AAARRR** or "Pirate" metrics). A growth marketer obsesses over each part of this funnel, tweaking it to boost conversion rates, customer retention, and ultimately, revenue.

Think of traditional marketing as a one-night stand—flashy, immediate, but often lacking substance. Growth marketing, on the other hand, is a committed relationship: you're not just wooing the customer; you're investing in them, understanding their needs, and nurturing that bond for the long haul. In a world where customers are bombarded with options, creating a lasting relationship is what sets successful companies apart.

The elements of growth marketing

So, what exactly makes growth marketing tick? **Experimentation, data, and a customer-centric mindset** are at the heart of it all.

1. **Experimentation:** Growth marketing is a playground for creative experimentation. Remember the rocket analogy? Every experiment is a test flight. Growth marketers run A/B tests on landing pages, try out different content strategies, and test new channels to find what resonates

with their audience. It's about running small, controlled experiments to see what works and scaling those strategies once they've proven successful.

For instance, Dropbox's famous referral program was born out of a growth experiment. They didn't just guess that a referral program would work—they tested, iterated, and found that offering extra storage space in exchange for referrals skyrocketed their user base. The lesson? Growth marketing is about embracing failure as part of the learning process.

2. **Data-Driven:** Numbers don't lie, and growth marketers are data addicts. Unlike traditional marketing, where gut feelings and intuition often drive decisions, growth marketing leans on analytics, metrics, and KPIs. Growth marketers track every interaction, analyze customer behavior, and use this data to refine their strategies. It's not about spraying and praying; it's about using insights to make informed decisions.

   Take Airbnb as an example. The company used data to identify what was stopping users from completing bookings. By introducing professional photography services for hosts, they significantly improved listing quality and increased booking rates. This data-driven tweak transformed Airbnb's growth trajectory, showing how small, informed changes can have a massive impact.

3. **Customer-Centric:** Growth marketing places the customer at the heart of every strategy. It's not about pushing products; it's about solving customer problems and creating value. Growth marketers listen to customer feedback, analyze user behavior, and adapt their approach to meet customer needs. It's why you'll often find growth marketing tied closely with product development—because the best growth strategies enhance the customer experience.

   Think about Slack. The company didn't just promote its product; it built a community around it. By listening to users, refining its features, and ensuring that every interaction with the product was seamless, Slack didn't just gain users—it gained advocates. This customer-centric approach is a cornerstone of growth marketing.

Growth marketing in action: examples from the trenches

Growth marketing is not just theory—it's practiced daily by companies that have cracked the code of sustainable growth. Look at companies like HubSpot and Spotify. They've mastered the art of creating personalized, data-driven experiences that keep users coming back.

- **HubSpot:** Recognizing the power of inbound marketing, HubSpot offered free tools and valuable content to attract potential customers. They didn't just sell a product; they built a resource hub that answered their audience's questions and solved their problems. HubSpot's growth strategy wasn't just about acquiring leads; it was about nurturing those leads through valuable content until they were ready to become paying customers.

- **Spotify:** Spotify leveraged data and user behavior analysis to create personalized playlists like "Discover Weekly." This feature didn't just keep users engaged; it became a key differentiator in the crowded music streaming market. By focusing on customer experience and personalization, Spotify transformed casual listeners into loyal subscribers.

These companies didn't rely on traditional, static marketing tactics. They employed growth marketing—using data, running experiments, and prioritizing the customer journey—to drive their success.

The growth marketing toolkit

Growth marketing isn't just a mindset; it's a toolbox filled with various techniques and strategies, from **SEO** to **content**

marketing, email campaigns, social media engagement, and **paid advertising**. It involves tracking **North Star metrics**(the single most important metric that captures the core value your product delivers) and other key performance indicators to gauge success.

A growth marketer's toolkit is constantly evolving, incorporating new technologies like **AI** and **machine learning** to gain deeper insights into customer behavior. It's not about sticking to one tried-and-true method; it's about being flexible, adapting, and learning from every campaign.

The impact: why growth marketing matters

In today's landscape, where customer attention is a scarce commodity, growth marketing offers a pathway to not just survive but thrive. It's the difference between a startup that fades into obscurity and one that scales into a household name. Growth marketing matters because it is a **holistic, adaptable approach** that evolves with customer needs and market shifts. It's about finding that sweet spot where your product, message, and customer experience align to drive sustainable, long-term growth.

Growth marketing isn't a silver bullet, nor is it a quick fix. It's a disciplined, iterative process—a commitment to ongoing learning, customer understanding, and data-driven decision-making. In the chapters that follow, we'll delve deeper into the strategies, mindsets, and tools that form the backbone of growth marketing. This is your playbook to unlocking exponential growth. Let's dive in.

The evolution from traditional marketing to growth marketing

Marketing has come a long way since the days of newspaper ads, billboards, and jingles. The landscape has evolved at breakneck speed, and with it, the strategies and tools marketers use to capture the hearts and minds of consumers. Traditional marketing was once king, but the throne now belongs to growth marketing, a dynamic approach that combines creativity, data, and a relentless focus on the customer. To understand how we got here, let's take a trip down marketing's memory lane and explore how growth marketing emerged from the shadows of traditional tactics.

The old guard: traditional marketing's one-way street

For decades, traditional marketing dominated the scene. Think back to the Mad Men era of advertising, where brands relied on TV commercials, radio spots, billboards, and print ads to broadcast their message. These methods were expensive, one-size-fits-all, and built on the principle of interruption. Brands interrupted your favorite TV show or magazine to deliver their pitch, hoping that something would stick.

The problem? This approach was a one-way street. Brands talked, and customers were expected to listen. The marketer's job was essentially to shout the loudest and most creatively, trying to grab the consumer's attention. The impact of these campaigns was hard to measure beyond surface-level metrics like impressions or reach. Sure, companies could conduct surveys or focus groups, but these methods provided limited insights into what customers truly wanted or how they engaged with a brand.

In short, traditional marketing was all about *casting a wide net*. If you were lucky, you might catch some fish. If not, well, you threw more money at the problem, hoping for a better outcome. While this approach worked to some extent in the pre-digital era, it had one glaring flaw: it treated all consumers as a monolithic group, ignoring the nuances of individual behavior, preferences, and needs.

The cracks begin to show

By the early 2000s, the digital revolution had begun to poke holes in traditional marketing's armor. The rise of the internet, social media, and mobile technology shifted the power dynamic between brands and consumers. Suddenly, people had more choices and more control over how they consumed information. They could skip ads, block pop-ups, and ignore cold calls. With information at their fingertips, consumers started demanding more personalized, relevant interactions with brands.

Marketers began to realize that the old playbook was becoming less effective. Throwing money at blanket advertising campaigns no longer guaranteed results. Brands needed to connect with consumers in more meaningful ways, creating tailored experiences that resonated on a personal level.

At the same time, the digital age introduced a game-changer: **data**. For the first time, marketers could track user behavior online, from clicks and conversions to customer journeys across multiple touchpoints. This data opened up a treasure trove of insights, enabling brands to make more informed decisions. The question was no longer, "Did our billboard work?" but rather, "How many users clicked our ad, signed up, and made a purchase?"

The birth of growth marketing

Enter growth marketing: a response to the changing tides of consumer behavior and technology. Unlike traditional marketing, which was primarily focused on acquisition, growth marketing adopts a **full-funnel approach**. It's not just about attracting new customers; it's about nurturing them, keeping them engaged, and turning them into loyal advocates for your brand. This holistic strategy acknowledges that customer acquisition is only the beginning of a much longer journey.

Growth marketing isn't just a set of tactics; it's a mindset shift. Instead of relying on gut feelings or past practices, growth marketing uses data and experimentation to drive decision-making. It treats every aspect of the customer lifecycle—acquisition, activation, retention, referral, and revenue—as an opportunity for growth. Rather than shouting into the void, growth marketers listen to their customers, test different approaches, and optimize based on what works.

Take the example of Netflix. In its early days, Netflix relied on traditional marketing tactics like mail-order DVDs and TV commercials. But as the company transitioned into the digital realm, it pivoted towards a growth marketing approach. By analyzing user data, Netflix was able to understand viewing habits and preferences, leading to personalized recommendations that keep viewers hooked. This data-driven strategy not only improved user experience but also significantly increased customer retention. Today, Netflix's growth is fueled by a combination of personalized content, seamless user experience, and targeted marketing efforts—all hallmarks of growth marketing.

Why the evolution matters

The shift from traditional marketing to growth marketing is more than just a change in tactics; it's a change in philosophy. Growth marketing acknowledges that the customer is in control and that successful marketing requires meeting customers where they are. It's not enough to blast your message to the masses; you need to tailor your approach based on individual behaviors and preferences. This evolution matters for several key reasons:

1. **Customer-Centricity:** Growth marketing places the customer at the center of every strategy. In a world where customers are bombarded with options, creating personalized, meaningful experiences is what sets brands apart. It's about understanding the customer's journey and using that knowledge to provide value at every touchpoint.

2. **Agility:** Unlike traditional marketing, which often involved long planning cycles and rigid campaigns,

growth marketing is agile. It encourages rapid experimentation and iteration. A campaign didn't work? No problem—analyze the data, learn from it, and pivot. Growth marketing thrives on this cycle of constant improvement, allowing brands to adapt quickly to market changes.

3. **Data-Driven Decisions:** Traditional marketing was notorious for its guesswork. Growth marketing, however, leverages data to drive decisions. It's not about gut feelings; it's about using metrics like customer lifetime value, churn rate, and acquisition cost to optimize strategies. This data-driven approach leads to more effective marketing efforts and better ROI.

4. **Full-Funnel Focus:** Traditional marketing primarily concentrated on the top of the funnel—awareness and acquisition. Growth marketing, however, understands that true growth happens when you nurture customers throughout their entire lifecycle. This full-funnel approach involves acquiring new customers, activating them, retaining them, and turning them into advocates who refer others to your brand.

Real-world transition: HubSpot's story

To see this evolution in action, let's look at HubSpot. In its early years, HubSpot relied on outbound marketing tactics like cold calling and direct mail. But as digital marketing gained momentum, they recognized the limitations of traditional methods and pivoted to a growth marketing approach. HubSpot began focusing on **inbound marketing**, creating valuable content that attracted prospects organically. They used data to understand what content resonated with their audience and optimized their strategy accordingly.

By adopting a growth marketing mindset, HubSpot transformed from a company that chased leads into one that drew customers in through valuable interactions. Today, their growth is fueled by a combination of content marketing, SEO, social media, and targeted campaigns—supported by data-driven decision-making and a relentless focus on the customer journey.

Where do we go from here?

The evolution from traditional marketing to growth marketing is an ongoing process. As technology continues to advance and consumer behaviors evolve, growth marketing will adapt and expand. What's clear is that the days of shouting your message from the rooftops are over. In their place, a new era of marketing has emerged—one that values experimentation, data, and customer-centricity above all else.

Growth marketing isn't a fad; it's the future. As we continue our journey through this playbook, we'll explore the strategies, tools, and mindsets that define this evolution. We'll dive into the nitty-gritty of building a growth foundation, acquiring the right customers, driving retention, and much more. Get ready to embrace the next chapter in marketing's evolution.

Why growth marketing matters for startups and beyond

If you've ever watched a startup pitch, you've probably heard the phrase, "We're looking to scale quickly." Scaling quickly is the dream, right? It's what separates a startup from just another small business. But here's the catch: scaling isn't about growth for growth's sake. It's about sustainable, smart growth. This is where growth marketing comes into play. It's not just a buzzword or a trendy approach; it's the lifeblood of success for startups and established companies alike.

Growth marketing isn't some magic bullet that will skyrocket your business overnight. Instead, it's a strategic, holistic method that focuses on long-term success. It's about optimizing every stage of the customer lifecycle—acquisition, activation, retention, revenue, and referral—to build a growth engine that scales. For startups clawing for market share or established companies seeking to avoid stagnation, growth marketing matters now more than ever.

The startup game: survival of the nimblest

In the world of startups, growth marketing is often the difference between making it big and becoming a cautionary tale. Why? Because startups operate in a reality where resources are limited, competition is fierce, and every dollar counts. They don't have the luxury of throwing massive budgets at traditional advertising campaigns hoping something sticks. They need to be nimble, innovative, and laser-focused on acquiring the right customers at the right time.

Take Airbnb, for example. In its early days, the company faced a daunting challenge: how to get people to trust and use their platform. They could have poured money into traditional advertising, but instead, they adopted a growth marketing mindset. One of their pivotal growth hacks involved posting their listings on Craigslist, piggybacking off an already established user base. By doing so, they reached their target audience in a cost-effective, scalable way. This experiment-driven approach, coupled with data analysis, allowed Airbnb to rapidly acquire users and grow into the global behemoth it is today.

For startups, growth marketing is more than just a strategy—it's a survival mechanism. When every customer counts and budgets are tight, startups must focus on acquiring high-quality leads, optimizing conversions, and building long-term relationships. Growth marketing provides the framework to do exactly that, using data-driven tactics to maximize ROI and build a sustainable path to scale.

Beyond the startup: avoiding stagnation in established companies

You might think that once a company has "made it," growth marketing takes a backseat. Not so fast. Even well-established companies face the ever-present threat of market saturation, changing consumer behaviors, and agile new competitors ready to disrupt the status quo. Growth marketing is just as vital for these companies as it is for startups, if not more so.

Think of companies like Slack or Spotify. Both began as scrappy startups but have since grown into household names. Yet, they didn't rest on their laurels once they reached a certain level of success. Instead, they embraced growth marketing as a continuous process. For instance, Spotify leverages user data to continuously refine its recommendations, improving customer retention and creating an ever-evolving product experience. Similarly, Slack listens to user feedback and regularly rolls out updates to meet customer needs, enhancing the product while deepening user engagement.

For established companies, growth marketing is about **avoiding stagnation**. The market is filled with cautionary tales of companies that failed to adapt—Blockbuster, Kodak, Nokia. These giants dominated their industries but were ultimately dethroned because they clung to outdated strategies while the world around them changed. Growth marketing keeps established companies nimble and customer-focused, allowing them to pivot, innovate, and explore new channels for growth.

A customer-centric approach in a crowded market

Today's consumers have more choices than ever before. They're bombarded with advertisements, content, and offers at every turn. In such a crowded market, the brands that win are the ones that **truly understand their customers** and deliver value at every interaction. This is where growth marketing's customer-centric approach shines.

Unlike traditional marketing, which often treats customers as mere numbers on a spreadsheet, growth marketing puts the customer at the heart of every strategy. It's not about shouting the loudest or having the flashiest ad; it's about listening to customers, understanding their pain points, and delivering solutions tailored to their needs. When done right, growth marketing turns customers into advocates who promote the brand organically.

Look at how Dropbox used a customer-centric growth strategy to explode in popularity. Instead of relying on expensive ads, Dropbox focused on creating a seamless, valuable experience for its users. The company introduced a referral program, offering free storage space to both the referrer and the referee. This program incentivized existing users to spread the word, turning satisfied customers into brand ambassadors. It wasn't just about acquiring more users; it was about delivering a value-driven experience that resonated with customers and encouraged them to engage.

For established companies, the customer-centricity of growth marketing can be the antidote to the impersonal, cookie-cutter campaigns of the past. By leveraging data to understand customer behavior and preferences, companies can create personalized, relevant experiences that foster loyalty and drive repeat business. In an era where customer loyalty is often fleeting, growth marketing provides the tools to build lasting relationships that translate into long-term growth.

Data and agility: the competitive edge

The rise of digital platforms has created a sea of data, and growth marketing is about harnessing this data to make **smart, informed decisions**. Startups and established companies alike can benefit from tracking metrics such as customer acquisition cost (CAC), customer lifetime value (CLV), churn rate, and conversion rates to fine-tune their strategies. In this data-driven landscape, gut feelings and guesswork are replaced by experimentation and analysis.

Consider how Amazon uses data to drive its growth. From analyzing customer purchase history to tracking browsing behavior, Amazon gathers a wealth of data to optimize its product recommendations, pricing, and marketing efforts. This data-centric approach has allowed Amazon to continually refine its customer experience, maintain its dominance, and expand into new markets.

But data is only part of the equation. Growth marketing also requires **agility**. The market changes fast, consumer preferences shift, and new competitors emerge. Companies that rely solely on static, long-term campaigns risk becoming obsolete before they even launch. Growth marketing, with its emphasis on rapid experimentation and iteration, enables companies to pivot quickly and adapt to market changes. This agility is a competitive edge that allows companies to seize new opportunities and address challenges in real-time.

Building a growth culture

One of the most overlooked aspects of growth marketing is its potential to shape company culture. When a company adopts a growth marketing mindset, it creates a culture that values experimentation, learning, and customer-centricity. This culture permeates every department, from product development to customer support, fostering a shared commitment to growth.

For startups, building this growth culture from day one can set the foundation for long-term success. For established companies, adopting a growth mindset can be the key to breaking down silos and encouraging cross-functional collaboration. When everyone is aligned around a shared goal—driving growth through customer value—the entire organization becomes more focused, innovative, and resilient.

The bottom line: growth marketing is not optional

In today's hyper-competitive market, growth marketing isn't just a nice-to-have; it's a necessity. For startups, it's the roadmap to scaling effectively, acquiring the right customers, and building a brand that resonates. For established companies, it's the safeguard against stagnation, the engine for innovation, and the means to maintain customer loyalty in an ever-changing landscape.

Growth marketing matters because it acknowledges that success isn't just about acquiring customers—it's about keeping them, delighting them, and turning them into advocates. It's about using data to make smart decisions, experimenting to find what works, and constantly optimizing for better results. In short, growth marketing is the sustainable path to building and scaling a business in the modern world.

As we move forward in this playbook, we'll dive deeper into the mechanics of growth marketing, from building a solid foundation to unlocking acquisition, driving retention, and scaling effectively. Whether you're a scrappy startup or a seasoned enterprise, the principles of growth marketing will be your guide to achieving—and sustaining—success.

C H A P T E R 1

Building the foundation for growth

Understanding your target audience

Every successful growth marketing strategy starts with a fundamental question: *Who are we trying to reach?* It might sound obvious, but you'd be surprised how many companies dive into marketing without a clear understanding of their target audience. They throw money at ads, churn out content, and run campaigns, hoping something sticks. But growth isn't about hope; it's about precision. If you want to grow effectively, you need to know exactly who your audience is, what they care about, and how to connect with them on a deeper level.

Think of it this way: marketing without a defined target audience is like trying to sell snow shovels in the desert. You might be putting in tons of effort, but it's wasted because you're speaking to the wrong people in the wrong context. To unlock real growth, you need to zero in on your target audience and understand their needs, desires, and behaviors. This is your growth marketing GPS —it helps you navigate the complexities of customer acquisition, retention, and revenue generation.

Why knowing your audience is critical

Understanding your audience is the cornerstone of growth marketing for several reasons:

1. **Personalized Experiences:** In today's market, customers expect personalization. They don't want to be treated as faceless transactions; they want experiences tailored to their needs and preferences. When you know your audience, you can create content, products, and campaigns that speak directly to them, increasing engagement and conversion rates.

2. **Efficient Resource Allocation:** When you know who you're targeting, you can allocate your marketing resources more effectively. Instead of spreading your budget thin across multiple channels and campaigns, you can focus on the platforms and tactics that resonate most with your audience. This laser-focused approach leads to a higher ROI and better use of your time and budget.

3. **Product-Market Fit:** Your audience insights can guide product development and innovation. By understanding your customers' pain points, you can refine your product to better meet their needs, enhancing your value proposition. This alignment is crucial for achieving product-market fit, the bedrock of any successful growth strategy.

4. **Retention and Loyalty:** Knowing your audience goes beyond acquisition; it also plays a key role in retention. When you understand what keeps your customers engaged and satisfied, you can build strategies to foster loyalty and encourage repeat business. In growth marketing, retention is just as important—if not more so—than acquisition.

Defining your target audience: the basics

So, how do you go about defining your target audience? It starts with creating **customer personas**, which are detailed profiles of your ideal customers. A persona typically includes demographic information (age, gender, location), psychographic details (interests, values, lifestyle), behavior patterns (buying habits, online activity), and pain points.

For example, let's say you're a B2B SaaS company offering a project management tool. Your target persona might be "Sarah, the Mid-Level Project Manager," a 35-year-old woman working in a tech company. She values efficiency, struggles with team communication, and spends a lot of time on LinkedIn. This persona provides a snapshot of your ideal customer, guiding your marketing efforts toward addressing her specific needs and preferences.

However, personas alone are just the beginning. You also need to understand your audience's **customer journey**—the path they take from awareness to purchase to retention. What triggers their interest in a product like yours? What information do they seek during the decision-making process? By mapping out the customer journey, you can identify touchpoints where your marketing can make the most impact.

Digging deeper: audience research methods

Understanding your target audience requires more than just guesswork or broad assumptions. It demands in-depth research and analysis. Here's how to get started:

1. **Surveys and Interviews:** One of the most direct ways to understand your audience is to ask them. Conduct surveys and interviews with your existing customers to gather insights into their preferences, challenges, and motivations. Open-ended questions like "What problem does our product solve for you?" or "What would improve

your experience?" can reveal valuable information that guides your marketing strategy.

2. **Social Listening:** Social media is a goldmine for understanding your audience's sentiments and behaviors. Use social listening tools to monitor conversations around your brand, competitors, and industry. What are people saying about products like yours? What questions or concerns do they have? This real-time feedback can shape your messaging and product development.

3. **Analytics:** Website and app analytics provide a wealth of data about how users interact with your brand. Track metrics like user demographics, traffic sources, and behavior flow to understand who's visiting your site, what content they engage with, and where they drop off. This data helps you refine your marketing funnels and create more targeted campaigns.

4. **Competitor Analysis:** Sometimes, understanding your audience involves studying your competitors. Who are they targeting? How are they positioning their products? By analyzing your competitors' audience and strategies, you can identify gaps in the market and uncover opportunities to differentiate your brand.

5. **Customer Feedback:** Reviews, support tickets, and customer success calls are rich sources of insights. Pay attention to what customers love and what frustrates them. Are there common themes in their feedback? Use this information to improve your product and tailor your marketing to address their concerns.

Creating value: speaking your audience's language

Understanding your audience isn't just about gathering data; it's about using that data to **speak your audience's language**. This means crafting messages, content, and offers that resonate with their unique needs and aspirations. If your target persona is a busy project manager struggling with team coordination, your messaging should focus on how your product simplifies communication and saves time, not on technical jargon or features that aren't relevant to their pain points.

The key here is empathy. When you understand your audience's challenges and desires, you can position your brand as the solution they've been searching for. This approach builds trust and establishes a connection, setting the stage for long-term engagement and loyalty.

Take Nike, for example. The brand doesn't just sell shoes; it sells empowerment, strength, and the pursuit of greatness. Nike understands its audience—athletes and fitness enthusiasts—and crafts messages that speak directly to their mindset: *"Just Do It."* This deep understanding of their audience's psyche is what makes Nike's marketing so effective and enduring.

Using audience insights to drive growth

Once you have a clear understanding of your target audience, you can use these insights to drive growth in several ways:

1. **Content Creation:** Knowing your audience's interests and pain points helps you create content that resonates. Whether it's blog posts, videos, or social media content, tailor your messaging to address the specific challenges and desires of your target personas. This targeted content attracts the right visitors, engages them, and guides them further down the marketing funnel.

2. **Product Development:** Audience insights can inform your product roadmap. By understanding what features your customers value most, you can prioritize development efforts and build a product that better meets their needs. A product that aligns with your audience's

preferences is more likely to achieve product-market fit and drive customer retention.

3. **Channel Selection:** Not every channel is right for every audience. Your research will reveal where your audience spends their time—whether it's Instagram, LinkedIn, email, or niche forums. By focusing your marketing efforts on the platforms where your audience is most active, you increase the chances of reaching and engaging them effectively.

4. **Personalized Campaigns:** Use audience data to create personalized campaigns. Segment your audience based on behavior, demographics, and preferences to deliver targeted messages. For instance, if you know a segment of your audience is price-sensitive, tailor your email campaigns to highlight discounts or value-added offers.

The bottom line: audience understanding is your growth engine

Understanding your target audience isn't just a checkbox on your marketing to-do list; it's the engine that drives growth. When you know who your customers are, what they want, and how they behave, you can create experiences that resonate, build products that solve real problems, and develop campaigns that convert.

In growth marketing, success is not about being everything to everyone. It's about being *exactly what your target audience needs*. As you move forward in your growth journey, keep your audience insights at the forefront of every strategy, campaign, and product decision. This audience-first approach is what will set you apart, fuel your growth, and transform your customers into advocates for your brand.

Product-market fit: The bedrock of growth

In the world of startups and growth marketing, few concepts carry as much weight as **product-market fit**. It's often described as the holy grail, the tipping point where a product meets the market's needs so perfectly that it practically sells itself. But product-market fit isn't just about creating a product that people want; it's about crafting a solution that resonates so deeply with your target audience that they can't imagine living without it.

Finding product-market fit is the bedrock of any growth strategy. Without it, all the marketing hacks, ad spend, and customer acquisition efforts will fall flat. It's like building a house on quicksand—no matter how fancy the house is, it's bound to collapse. When you achieve product-market fit, you lay a solid foundation that supports long-term, sustainable growth.

What exactly is product-market fit?

The term "product-market fit" was popularized by Marc Andreessen, co-founder of Netscape and a prominent venture capitalist. He described it as "being in a good market with a product that can satisfy that market." Simply put, it means your product perfectly matches the needs and desires of a large enough customer segment to support business growth.

Achieving product-market fit is often characterized by several signs:

- **High demand:** Customers actively seek out your product and are willing to pay for it.

- **Positive feedback:** Users love your product, talk about it, and recommend it to others.

- **Rapid adoption:** New users flock to your product, and existing customers stick around.

- **Market pull:** Instead of pushing your product onto customers, you experience a pull from the market where demand drives growth.

Think about Uber in its early days. It wasn't just another ride-sharing app; it was a solution to a very real problem—convenient, reliable, and accessible transportation. Uber didn't need to convince people they needed its service; people immediately saw the value and spread the word. This is the power of product-market fit: it transforms your product from a nice-to-have into a must-have.

The road to product-market fit

Achieving product-market fit isn't a linear journey; it's an iterative process that requires deep customer understanding, experimentation, and constant refinement. Here's how to navigate the path to product-market fit:

1. **Identify a real problem:** The starting point of product-market fit is understanding a genuine problem that your target audience faces. The more specific and pressing this problem is, the better. For instance, Slack identified the pain point of fragmented workplace communication and built a tool to streamline team collaboration. Before building your product, conduct extensive market research, interviews, and surveys to uncover unmet needs within your target market.

2. **Build a Minimum Viable Product (MVP):** Don't waste resources building a full-fledged product right away. Instead, create an MVP—a simplified version of your product that addresses the core problem. The MVP allows you to test your hypothesis, gather user feedback, and validate whether there is a real demand for your solution. Dropbox, for example, initially launched as a simple video explaining the concept of cloud storage. This helped

gauge interest before they invested in building a robust platform.

3. **Test and iterate:** After launching your MVP, collect feedback from early users. What do they like? What frustrates them? Are they willing to pay for your product? Use this feedback to iterate on your product, refining it to better fit your audience's needs. Airbnb went through several iterations before finding product-market fit, experimenting with different website designs, features, and user experiences to meet both hosts' and guests' needs.

4. **Measure engagement:** One of the clearest indicators of product-market fit is user engagement. Look at metrics such as customer retention, churn rate, and Net Promoter Score (NPS) to gauge how well your product resonates with your audience. High retention and a strong NPS indicate that users find real value in your product and are likely to recommend it to others.

5. **Adapt based on feedback:** Sometimes, achieving product-market fit requires a pivot. You may discover through user feedback and market analysis that your initial product concept doesn't quite hit the mark. In these cases, be willing to adapt. Instagram, for example, started as a location-based check-in app called Burbn. After noticing that users were primarily using the app to share photos, the team pivoted to focus solely on photo-sharing, leading to the birth of Instagram as we know it.

How to know when you've achieved product-market fit

Recognizing product-market fit can be tricky. It's not always a clear-cut moment but rather a culmination of several positive signals. Here are a few telltale signs that you've hit the sweet spot:

1. **Explosive demand:** When you achieve product-market fit, you'll notice a surge in demand. Customers start coming to you through word-of-mouth and organic channels rather than solely through paid advertising. This demand often translates into a spike in user sign-ups, downloads, or sales.

2. **Customer love:** Customers don't just use your product; they rave about it. You start receiving unsolicited positive feedback, testimonials, and referrals. People talk about your product on social media, and reviews consistently highlight the value your product provides.

3. **High retention:** Users don't just try your product once and disappear; they keep coming back. A high retention rate indicates that customers find ongoing value in your product, a strong indicator that you've aligned with their needs.

4. **Pricing power:** When customers perceive your product as valuable and essential, they're willing to pay a premium for it. If you can increase prices without significant pushback, it's a sign that you've achieved product-market fit.

5. **Consistent growth:** Growth becomes more predictable and less reliant on aggressive marketing. Instead of feeling like you're constantly pushing a boulder uphill, you experience a more natural, organic growth curve driven by satisfied customers.

Product-market fit is not static

Here's a crucial point: product-market fit isn't a "set it and forget it" milestone. Markets evolve, customer preferences change, and new competitors emerge. What works today may not work tomorrow. Even if you've achieved product-market fit, you need to continuously listen to your customers, monitor market trends, and adapt your product accordingly.

Netflix is an excellent example of a company that continuously adapts its product-market fit. Initially, Netflix achieved product-market fit by offering DVD rentals by mail, disrupting the traditional video rental model. However, as streaming technology advanced and consumer preferences shifted, Netflix pivoted to a streaming service, constantly refining its content offerings and user experience to match evolving market demands. Today, Netflix's ongoing success hinges on its ability to remain aligned with its audience's changing tastes.

Why product-market fit matters for growth

Product-market fit is the foundation upon which all growth strategies are built. Without it, efforts to acquire customers, drive engagement, and generate revenue are akin to filling a leaky bucket—you can pour in resources, but they'll quickly drain away. Here's why product-market fit is so vital for growth:

1. **Efficient marketing:** When you achieve product-market fit, marketing becomes more effective. You know exactly who your audience is, what pain points you're solving, and how to communicate your value proposition. This clarity allows you to craft more targeted campaigns, reducing customer acquisition costs and improving conversion rates.

2. **Retention and loyalty:** A product that truly fits the market doesn't just attract customers; it keeps them. High retention rates and loyal customers are the cornerstones of sustainable growth. When customers are satisfied, they're more likely to become repeat buyers and advocates for your brand, fueling organic growth through referrals.

3. **Scalability:** With product-market fit, you have a validated product and a receptive market. This gives you the

confidence to scale up marketing efforts, expand into new markets, and explore new revenue streams. Scaling without product-market fit, on the other hand, is a recipe for wasted resources and potential failure.

4. **Foundation for innovation:** Achieving product-market fit provides a deep understanding of your audience's needs, setting the stage for future innovation. It allows you to identify additional features, services, or products that can further enhance your value proposition and drive continued growth.

The bottom line: your north star for growth

Product-market fit is not just a box to check off; it's the **north star** that guides your entire growth strategy. Without it, growth efforts become a struggle, like trying to push water uphill. But when you align your product perfectly with market demand, you create a powerful growth engine fueled by customer satisfaction, loyalty, and advocacy.

As you continue building your growth marketing playbook, keep product-market fit at the forefront of every decision, experiment, and strategy. Listen to your customers, iterate based on feedback, and remain adaptable in the face of changing market dynamics. Remember, growth marketing isn't just about growing fast; it's about growing *right*. And that journey begins and thrives on the bedrock of product-market fit.

Setting up growth-driven goals (North Star metrics, OKRs)

In growth marketing, setting the right goals is like charting a course for a long voyage. Without a clear destination, you're left adrift in an ocean of data, channels, and tactics, with no way to measure progress or success. That's where **growth-driven goals** come in. By establishing specific, measurable, and aligned objectives, you set a compass for your team, guiding every decision, strategy, and experiment toward sustainable growth.

Effective growth marketing is not just about trying random tactics to see what sticks; it's about being **deliberate**. It's about understanding your business objectives and translating them into actionable goals that drive meaningful outcomes. Two of the most powerful frameworks for setting and achieving these goals are **North Star metrics** and **Objectives and Key Results (OKRs)**. Together, they provide a strategic approach to measuring progress and keeping your growth efforts on track.

The importance of goal-setting in growth marketing

Before diving into the specifics of North Star metrics and OKRs, let's explore why goal-setting is so critical in growth marketing:

1. **Alignment:** Goals ensure that everyone on the team is working toward a common purpose. When you define clear, growth-driven objectives, you align marketing, product development, customer success, and other departments around shared priorities. This alignment minimizes wasted effort and fosters collaboration.

2. **Focus:** In the world of growth marketing, it's easy to get distracted by shiny new tactics or the latest growth hacks. Clear goals help you maintain focus, ensuring that your efforts are directed toward strategies that move the needle. They act as guardrails, keeping you from veering off course and chasing unproductive endeavors.

3. **Measurement:** Growth is all about experimentation, but not all experiments are created equal. By setting measurable goals, you establish criteria for success, making it easier to evaluate the impact of your strategies. This data-driven approach enables you to double down on what works and pivot away from what doesn't.

4. **Motivation:** Ambitious yet attainable goals serve as motivation for your team. They provide a sense of purpose and progress, encouraging everyone to push the boundaries and strive for continuous improvement.

The North Star metric: your guiding light

One of the most effective ways to focus your growth efforts is by identifying your **North Star metric**. This metric is the single, most important measure that captures the core value your product delivers to customers. It serves as a guiding light for your growth strategy, ensuring that all marketing, product, and customer success activities are directed toward enhancing this key outcome.

The North Star metric is not about tracking vanity metrics like social media followers or website traffic; it's about focusing on a metric that directly correlates with customer value and business growth. For example:

- **Airbnb:** Their North Star metric is "Nights Booked." This metric reflects the core value Airbnb delivers—providing unique accommodations—and is closely tied to both customer satisfaction and revenue.

- **Spotify:** Spotify's North Star metric is "Time Spent Listening." This metric highlights the value users derive from the platform (music and audio content) and is a strong indicator of user engagement and retention.

- **Dropbox:** Dropbox's North Star metric is "Number of Files Uploaded." This metric showcases the value users find in storing and sharing files, aligning directly with customer satisfaction and long-term retention.

Choosing your North Star metric: To identify your own North Star metric, ask yourself: *What is the key action or outcome that represents the value my product provides to customers?* Your metric should be specific, measurable, and closely linked to both customer success and revenue growth.

Once you've identified your North Star metric, use it to guide all your growth activities. Every campaign, feature release, and product improvement should ultimately contribute to enhancing this metric. This focus creates a sense of unity across teams, ensuring that everyone is working toward a common, value-driven goal.

OKRs: breaking down growth into actionable steps

While the North Star metric provides an overarching direction, **Objectives and Key Results (OKRs)** break down your growth strategy into more specific, actionable goals. OKRs are a goal-setting framework popularized by companies like Google, Intel, and LinkedIn, designed to create alignment, clarity, and focus.

Here's how OKRs work:

- **Objectives:** These are ambitious, qualitative goals that describe what you want to achieve. Objectives should be inspiring and set a clear direction. For example, an objective might be, "Expand our user base in key markets."

- **Key Results:** These are specific, measurable outcomes that indicate progress toward your objective. Each objective typically has 3-5 key results. For the example above, key results might include:

    o   Increase monthly active users (MAUs) in North America by 25%.

    o   Achieve a 15% conversion rate from free to paid plans in Europe.

    o   Launch a localized marketing campaign in Asia, reaching 1 million new users.

The beauty of OKRs lies in their clarity and measurability. They not only define *what* you want to achieve (the objective) but also lay out the *how* (the key results). This approach ensures that your goals are both ambitious and grounded in tangible outcomes.

Implementing OKRs for growth marketing

To effectively use OKRs in your growth marketing strategy, follow these steps:

1. **Set quarterly OKRs:** OKRs are typically set on a quarterly basis, providing a balance between short-term focus and long-term vision. Begin by defining high-level objectives that align with your North Star metric and overall growth strategy.

2. **Define key results:** For each objective, identify 3-5 key results that are specific, measurable, and achievable within the quarter. Key results should be challenging but realistic, pushing your team to strive for improvement.

3. **Align across teams:** Share your OKRs with the entire company, ensuring that each department's goals align with the overall growth objectives. For instance, if your marketing team's objective is to "Increase customer acquisition," the product team might have a complementary objective to "Improve onboarding to boost conversion rates."

4. **Track progress:** Regularly review your OKRs to track progress and make adjustments as needed. Use tools like dashboards, spreadsheets, or project management software to monitor key results, providing visibility for the entire team.

5. **Reflect and learn:** At the end of each quarter, reflect on your OKRs to evaluate what worked, what didn't, and why. This retrospective analysis is crucial for learning and adapting your growth strategy for future success.

The synergy between North Star metrics and OKRs

North Star metrics and OKRs work hand-in-hand to create a cohesive growth strategy. The North Star metric sets the overarching direction, ensuring that all efforts contribute to delivering core customer value. OKRs, on the other hand, break this vision into specific, actionable steps that drive progress toward that ultimate goal.

For example, if your North Star metric is "Nights Booked" (like Airbnb), your OKRs might include objectives such as "Increase host listings in top markets" with key results like "Onboard 500 new hosts in New York and Los Angeles this quarter." This synergy ensures that every effort, from marketing campaigns to product features, aligns with and accelerates your progress toward achieving product-market fit and sustainable growth.

Common pitfalls to avoid

While setting up growth-driven goals is essential, there are common pitfalls to be aware of:

1. **Chasing vanity metrics:** Not all metrics are created equal. Avoid the trap of focusing on metrics that look good on paper but don't drive real growth (e.g., social media followers, website traffic). Always link your goals to metrics that reflect customer value and business outcomes.

2. **Setting too many goals:** It's tempting to set numerous goals, but doing so dilutes focus. Keep your OKRs concise, prioritizing the objectives that will have the most significant impact on your North Star metric.

3. **Lack of flexibility:** While it's important to have clear goals, be flexible and willing to adapt based on market conditions, customer feedback, and data insights. Growth marketing thrives on experimentation and iteration, so be prepared to pivot if something isn't working.

The bottom line: goals as your growth compass

Setting up growth-driven goals through North Star metrics and OKRs is like building a compass for your marketing journey. The North Star metric provides a clear direction, focusing your team on delivering core customer value. OKRs break this vision into concrete, measurable steps, driving your growth strategy forward with purpose and clarity.

In the fast-paced world of growth marketing, success isn't about luck; it's about deliberate, data-driven action. By setting the right goals and aligning your team around them, you create a powerful framework for scaling your business, experimenting with new tactics, and achieving long-term, sustainable growth.

As we continue into the next chapters, keep this goal-setting foundation in mind. Every strategy, experiment, and campaign should trace back to your North Star and OKRs, ensuring that your growth efforts are not just busywork but purposeful strides toward success.

CHAPTER 2

The growth marketer's mindset

Data-driven decision-making

In the digital age, data is everywhere. From website traffic to social media interactions, product usage patterns, customer feedback, and beyond, companies have access to more information than ever before. But having data is not enough; the key lies in **what you do with it**. This is where **data-driven decision-making** becomes the backbone of effective growth marketing.

Growth marketing without data is like sailing without a compass. Sure, you might catch a gust of wind now and then, but you're essentially navigating blind. Data-driven decision-making shifts the focus from guesswork and gut feelings to informed strategies. It's about using data to understand your customers, optimize marketing efforts, and fuel continuous growth. Growth marketers who embrace this mindset are equipped to make smarter choices, pivot quickly, and maximize ROI.

Why data matters in growth marketing

In traditional marketing, success was often measured by surface-level metrics: ad impressions, TV ratings, or the number of flyers handed out. But these metrics don't tell the full story. They don't reveal whether your campaigns are driving real value, if you're reaching the right audience, or how effectively you're converting prospects into loyal customers. Data-driven marketing, on the other hand, opens the door to **insightful analysis**, allowing you to answer critical questions:

- Which channels are delivering the highest-quality leads?

- What content resonates most with your target audience?

- How do changes in user behavior correlate with retention rates?

- Which growth experiments are actually moving the needle?

By analyzing data, growth marketers can fine-tune their strategies, identify areas for improvement, and optimize every stage of the customer journey. Data provides clarity and direction, turning marketing from a shot in the dark into a precise, effective practice.

Building a data-driven growth framework

Implementing data-driven decision-making in your growth strategy requires more than just collecting numbers. It involves building a **data-driven framework** that guides how you gather, analyze, and act on information. Here's how to set up a robust framework:

1. **Identify key metrics:** Not all data points are relevant to your growth strategy. Start by identifying the **key metrics**that align with your North Star metric and growth goals. Common growth metrics include:

   o **Customer Acquisition Cost (CAC):** How much does it cost to acquire a new customer?

o   **Customer Lifetime Value (CLV):** What is the total revenue you can expect from a customer over their relationship with your brand?

o   **Churn Rate:** How many customers are leaving your service over a specific period?

o   **Conversion Rate:** What percentage of website visitors or leads convert into paying customers?

2.   These metrics provide a snapshot of your growth health and help you assess the effectiveness of your marketing efforts.

3.   **Set up tracking tools:** To gather data, you need the right tools in place. **Analytics platforms** like Google Analytics, Mixpanel, and Amplitude can track user behavior on your website and app. For marketing data, tools like HubSpot, Marketo, and Facebook Analytics provide insights into campaign performance. Implement **CRM systems** to track customer interactions, segment your audience, and measure engagement.

4.   **Create data dashboards:** Data is only valuable if it's accessible and understandable. Create **data dashboards** that visualize your key metrics in real-time, making it easy for your team to monitor performance and spot trends. Tools like Tableau, Google Data Studio, and Power BI are excellent for building customized dashboards tailored to your specific growth goals.

5.   **Regularly analyze data:** Set up regular intervals to analyze your data—whether it's weekly, monthly, or quarterly. During these reviews, look for patterns, anomalies, and trends. Which campaigns are driving the most conversions? Where are customers dropping off in

the funnel? This analysis is crucial for identifying what's working and what needs adjustment.

Leveraging data for growth experiments

In growth marketing, experimentation is the name of the game. But how do you know which experiments are worth pursuing? Data is your guide. **A/B testing** (split testing) and **multivariate testing** are common practices that rely on data to optimize campaigns and user experiences.

For example, let's say you're testing two different landing page designs. With A/B testing, you split your audience into two groups, directing one to the original page (control) and the other to the new variation. By tracking metrics like conversion rates, time on page, and bounce rate, you gather data on which design performs better. This data-driven approach removes guesswork from the equation, allowing you to make decisions based on evidence rather than intuition.

Beyond A/B testing, data can fuel more sophisticated experiments. For instance:

- **Personalization:** Use customer data to personalize your marketing campaigns, such as sending tailored email recommendations based on past purchases. Track how personalized content impacts metrics like open rates, click-through rates, and customer retention.

- **Pricing strategies:** Experiment with different pricing models or discount strategies. Use data to analyze how changes in price affect sales volume, customer acquisition cost, and customer lifetime value.

- **Product features:** Leverage data to identify which product features drive the most user engagement. This insight guides product development, helping you focus on features that enhance the customer experience and contribute to growth.

Data-driven content marketing

Content marketing is one area where data can have a transformative impact. Rather than creating content based on hunches, use data to inform your content strategy. Here's how:

1. **Keyword research:** Tools like Ahrefs, SEMrush, and Moz provide insights into what keywords your target audience is searching for. Use this data to create content that addresses relevant topics, driving organic traffic to your website.

2. **Content performance analysis:** Track metrics like page views, time on page, bounce rate, and social shares to gauge how well your content resonates with your audience. Identify high-performing content pieces and look for patterns — do certain formats (e.g., blogs, videos) perform better? What topics drive the most engagement?

3. **Conversion tracking:** Measure how your content influences conversions. For example, use UTM parameters in URLs to track which blog posts or social media shares lead to sign-ups or purchases. This data helps you identify the types of content that are most effective in moving prospects through the funnel.

By harnessing data, you can refine your content strategy to focus on creating pieces that resonate with your audience and drive meaningful results.

The human element: data-informed, not data-obsessed

While data is a powerful tool in growth marketing, it's important to strike a balance. Data-driven decision-making should be **data-**

informed rather than **data-obsessed**. In other words, use data to guide your strategy, but don't lose sight of the human element.

Numbers tell you what is happening, but they don't always explain why it's happening. For instance, a drop in user engagement might be due to a poor user experience, changing customer preferences, or seasonal factors. To fully understand the context, you need to combine data analysis with qualitative insights, such as customer feedback, surveys, and user interviews.

Airbnb is a prime example of this balanced approach. While the company heavily relies on data to optimize its platform, it also values customer feedback to guide its product development. By blending quantitative data with qualitative insights, Airbnb creates an experience that aligns with both user behavior and customer needs.

Common pitfalls to avoid in data-driven marketing

Using data to drive decisions is not without its pitfalls. Here are some common mistakes to avoid:

1. **Chasing vanity metrics:** Vanity metrics, like social media likes or website traffic, may look impressive but don't necessarily correlate with growth. Focus on metrics that reflect customer value and impact your bottom line, such as conversion rates, retention, and customer lifetime value.

2. **Data overload:** It's easy to get overwhelmed by the sheer volume of data available. Avoid "analysis paralysis" by concentrating on a select set of key metrics that directly align with your growth goals.

3. **Ignoring context:** Data doesn't exist in a vacuum. Always consider the context behind the numbers. For example, a sudden spike in website traffic could be due to external factors like a mention in a popular publication. Analyzing data in isolation can lead to misguided decisions.

4.   **Assuming correlation equals causation:** Just because two metrics move in tandem doesn't mean one causes the other. Be cautious when interpreting data relationships and use controlled experiments to validate assumptions.

The bottom line: using data as your growth compass

In growth marketing, data-driven decision-making is your **compass**. It points you in the right direction, guides your experiments, and helps you navigate the complexities of customer behavior, market trends, and campaign performance. By leveraging data effectively, you transform growth marketing from a game of chance into a strategic, informed practice.

However, remember that data is a tool, not a crutch. Use it to inform your decisions, but don't lose sight of the human element — the emotions, desires, and experiences of your customers. The most successful growth marketers are those who blend data with empathy, creating strategies that resonate with people while driving measurable results.

As we continue through this playbook, we'll explore more aspects of the growth marketer's mindset, from embracing experimentation to building the right team. Keep your data compass handy; it's an essential guide on your path to growth.

Embracing experimentation and iteration

In the world of growth marketing, **experimentation** isn't just a tactic; it's a mindset. It's about being open to new ideas, testing hypotheses, learning from failures, and continually iterating to find what works. The days of setting up a marketing campaign, running it for months, and hoping for the best are long gone. Modern growth marketing thrives on agility, constant learning, and the willingness to embrace change. This is where experimentation and iteration become the engine that powers innovation and sustainable growth.

Why experimentation is at the heart of growth marketing

Growth marketing is a field where **certainty** is rare. Consumer behavior evolves, new competitors emerge, and what worked yesterday may not work tomorrow. In this dynamic environment, the only way to stay ahead is through continuous experimentation. Testing new ideas allows you to explore opportunities, understand your audience better, and optimize your strategies based on real data.

Experimentation in growth marketing is not about taking wild risks; it's about making informed bets. It's a process of generating hypotheses, running tests, analyzing results, and using those insights to guide future actions. This approach enables you to:

- **Identify opportunities:** Experiments help uncover what resonates with your audience, revealing opportunities to refine your product, messaging, or marketing channels.

- **Reduce risk:** By testing ideas on a small scale, you can identify potential pitfalls before rolling out strategies on a larger scale, minimizing the risk of costly failures.

- **Maximize ROI:** Iterative testing and optimization ensure that your marketing spend is directed toward tactics that deliver the highest returns.

The experimentation process: building a growth engine

Embracing experimentation involves establishing a structured process that drives systematic learning and growth. Here's a step-by-step breakdown of how to build an effective experimentation framework:

1. **Generate hypotheses:** Start by identifying areas of your marketing strategy that you want to improve. This could be anything from increasing landing page conversions to boosting customer retention. Then, generate hypotheses about what changes might lead to better outcomes. A hypothesis should be specific, testable, and focused on a measurable outcome. For example, "If we add customer testimonials to our landing page, it will increase sign-up rates by 15%."

2. **Prioritize experiments:** Not all experiments are created equal. Use a prioritization framework to determine which tests to run first. One popular method is the **ICE framework**, which scores experiments based on three factors:

    o **Impact:** How significant will the outcome be if the experiment is successful?

    o **Confidence:** How confident are you in the hypothesis and its potential results?

    o **Ease:** How easy is it to implement the experiment? Does it require minimal resources?

3. Prioritize experiments that have high impact, high confidence, and low effort. This approach allows you to quickly test ideas with the potential for meaningful results.

4. **Design the experiment:** Plan the specifics of your experiment, including the variables, audience segments, timeline, and metrics you'll use to measure success. For example, if you're A/B testing two versions of a landing page, decide how you'll split your audience, which performance metrics (e.g., conversion rate, bounce rate) to track, and how long the test will run.

5. **Run the test:** Implement the experiment using your selected tools and platforms. During the test, monitor performance in real-time to ensure everything runs smoothly. However, resist the urge to make changes mid-experiment, as this can compromise the integrity of your results.

6. **Analyze the results:** Once the test concludes, dive into the data to assess the outcome. Did the new variation outperform the control? Were the results statistically significant? Go beyond the surface metrics to understand why the experiment succeeded or failed. This analysis will inform your next steps.

7. **Iterate and implement:** Use the insights from your experiment to iterate on your strategy. If the experiment was successful, consider rolling out the change more broadly. If it wasn't, refine your hypothesis and test a new variation. Remember, the goal of experimentation is continuous improvement, so each test is a stepping stone toward a more optimized strategy.

Examples of experimentation in action

Experimentation can take many forms in growth marketing, depending on your goals and customer journey stage. Here are a few examples:

1. **A/B testing landing pages:** A/B testing is a classic experimentation method where you create two variations of a landing page to determine which one performs better. Elements you might test include headlines, call-to-action (CTA) buttons, images, or page layout. By experimenting with different elements, you can identify the most effective design and messaging for driving conversions. **Example:** When Buffer was optimizing its landing page, they ran A/B tests comparing different headlines. By testing variations such as "Save Time with Your Social

Media Management" versus "The Smart Way to Share on Social Media," they identified the messaging that resonated most with their audience, leading to a significant increase in sign-ups.

2. **Optimizing email campaigns:** Experimentation in email marketing can involve testing subject lines, send times, content length, personalization tactics, or CTA placement. By systematically testing different aspects of your emails, you can increase open rates, click-through rates, and conversions.
   Example: Spotify frequently experiments with personalized email recommendations. By using customer data to tailor suggestions, they can identify the types of music and playlists that lead to higher engagement, iterating their email strategy to keep users actively engaged with the platform.

3. **Testing product features:** Growth marketing isn't just about acquisition; it's also about optimizing the product experience. Experimentation extends to product features, user interfaces, onboarding flows, and pricing models. Testing different product iterations allows you to refine the user experience and boost retention.
   Example: Slack has continually experimented with its product features, focusing on user feedback and behavior data. One experiment involved simplifying the onboarding process for new users. By iterating on the onboarding flow and reducing friction, they improved user activation rates, driving long-term growth.

Embracing failure: the key to iteration

One of the most challenging aspects of experimentation is learning to **embrace failure**. Not every experiment will succeed —and that's okay. In fact, failure is an essential part of the learning process. When an experiment doesn't yield the desired results, it provides valuable insights into what doesn't work, guiding you toward more effective strategies.

Iteration is the natural follow-up to experimentation. It's the process of refining, tweaking, and improving your strategies based on data and feedback. Each experiment, regardless of its outcome, contributes to a cycle of continuous learning and growth. This iterative approach ensures that your marketing strategy evolves over time, adapting to changes in consumer behavior, market conditions, and competitive dynamics.

Take **Facebook** as an example. The platform didn't achieve success overnight. It constantly tested features, interfaces, ad placements, and algorithms, learning from both successes and failures. This commitment to experimentation and iteration allowed Facebook to create a product experience that resonates with billions of users worldwide.

Building a culture of experimentation

For experimentation to thrive, it must be ingrained in your company culture. A culture of experimentation encourages **curiosity**, **creativity**, and a willingness to question the status quo. Here's how to foster this mindset within your team:

1. **Encourage idea generation:** Create an environment where team members feel comfortable sharing ideas, no matter how unconventional they may seem. The best experiments often arise from diverse perspectives and outside-the-box thinking.

2. **Normalize failure:** Reinforce the idea that failure is a natural part of experimentation. Celebrate the learnings from failed experiments just as much as the successes. This mindset reduces the fear of taking risks and encourages bold, innovative testing.

3. **Share learnings:** Encourage transparency by sharing the results and insights from experiments across teams. This knowledge exchange prevents siloed efforts and ensures that everyone benefits from the lessons learned, driving a collective effort toward growth.

4. **Invest in the right tools:** Equip your team with the tools and platforms necessary for effective experimentation, such as A/B testing software, analytics platforms, and customer feedback tools. The easier it is to run and analyze experiments, the more likely your team is to embrace a test-and-learn mindset.

The bottom line: test, learn, iterate, grow

In growth marketing, experimentation and iteration are the engines that drive innovation and progress. By adopting a test-and-learn approach, you move beyond guesswork, using data and insights to guide your strategies. This mindset allows you to explore new opportunities, optimize your marketing efforts, and continuously improve the customer experience.

The journey of growth is not a straight line. It's a cycle of testing, learning, iterating, and refining. The marketers who succeed are those who embrace this cycle, viewing each experiment as a stepping stone toward a more effective, optimized strategy. So, be bold in your experiments, learn from every outcome, and iterate with purpose. The path to growth is paved with curiosity and the willingness to embrace change.

The growth marketing team: who do you need?

Behind every successful growth marketing strategy is a talented and versatile team. Growth marketing is a multidisciplinary effort that requires a blend of creativity, data analysis, technical skills, and strategic thinking. It's not a solo endeavor; it's a team sport where every member plays a unique role in achieving the ultimate goal: growth.

Building an effective growth marketing team is more than just filling roles; it's about assembling the right mix of skills, mindsets, and collaboration dynamics to tackle the challenges of acquisition, activation, retention, and revenue generation. The best growth teams are agile, data-driven, and always experimenting. They operate at the intersection of marketing, product, sales, and customer success, working cohesively to drive sustainable, scalable growth.

The anatomy of a growth marketing team

While the specific composition of a growth marketing team can vary depending on the company's size, industry, and goals, there are several key roles that are commonly found in successful growth teams. Let's break down these roles and the unique value each one brings to the table.

1. **Growth Lead / Growth Marketing Manager:** The quarterback of the growth team, the Growth Lead (or Growth Marketing Manager) is responsible for setting the overall growth strategy, identifying key metrics (like the North Star metric), and leading the team in executing growth initiatives. This role requires a mix of strategic thinking, project management, and a deep understanding of marketing channels, user behavior, and data analysis. **Key responsibilities:**

    - Define growth goals and KPIs in alignment with the company's objectives.

    - Oversee experimentation processes, from ideation to implementation.

   o   Collaborate cross-functionally with product, sales, and customer success teams to drive cohesive growth efforts.

   o   Analyze performance data to optimize marketing strategies and identify new growth opportunities.

2. The Growth Lead must have a blend of creativity, analytical skills, and leadership capabilities. They act as the driving force behind the team, keeping everyone aligned and focused on the end goal.

3. **Data Analyst / Data Scientist:** Growth marketing is driven by data, and the Data Analyst is the team's compass, providing insights that guide decision-making. This person is responsible for collecting, processing, and interpreting data to measure the performance of marketing efforts, identify trends, and uncover actionable insights. **Key responsibilities:**

   o   Set up tracking and analytics tools (e.g., Google Analytics, Mixpanel, Amplitude) to monitor key metrics.

   o   Analyze user behavior, segmentation, and funnel performance to inform marketing strategies.

   o   Run A/B tests and interpret results to identify what's working and where improvements are needed.

   o   Create data dashboards to provide real-time visibility into growth performance.

4. A solid Data Analyst has strong analytical skills, proficiency in data visualization tools, and a knack for turning complex data into clear, actionable insights. They

play a critical role in ensuring that the team's efforts are data-informed rather than guesswork-driven.

5. **Content Marketer:** Content is the fuel that powers many growth strategies, from SEO to social media to email marketing. The Content Marketer creates valuable, engaging content that attracts, educates, and nurtures prospects through the customer journey. This role requires a deep understanding of the target audience and the ability to produce content that resonates with their needs and preferences.
   Key responsibilities:

   - Develop a content strategy aligned with the company's growth goals.

   - Create high-quality content, including blog posts, ebooks, infographics, videos, and social media posts.

   - Optimize content for SEO to drive organic traffic and improve search engine rankings.

   - Collaborate with the rest of the growth team to support campaigns, product launches, and user education.

6. A successful Content Marketer is not only a skilled writer but also has a strategic mindset. They understand how to craft content that aligns with the broader growth strategy, whether it's driving traffic, generating leads, or improving retention.

7. **Paid Acquisition Specialist:** Acquiring new customers through paid channels, such as Google Ads, Facebook Ads, and other PPC platforms, requires a specific skill set. The Paid Acquisition Specialist manages the paid media

strategy, optimizing ad campaigns to reach the target audience and drive conversions.

Key responsibilities:

- ○ Develop and execute paid advertising campaigns across various platforms.

- ○ Perform keyword research, audience targeting, and ad creative testing to optimize campaign performance.

- ○ Monitor key metrics like Cost Per Acquisition (CPA), Return on Ad Spend (ROAS), and conversion rates.

- ○ Run A/B tests on ad copy, creatives, and landing pages to identify what works best.

8. This role demands a data-driven mindset, analytical skills, and an in-depth understanding of digital advertising platforms. The Paid Acquisition Specialist ensures that the company's marketing budget is allocated effectively to maximize ROI and growth.

9. **SEO Specialist:** Organic traffic is a vital component of growth marketing, and the SEO Specialist is the expert in driving visibility through search engines. They focus on optimizing the company's website, content, and online presence to improve search rankings and attract high-quality leads.

Key responsibilities:

- ○ Conduct keyword research to identify high-value search terms relevant to the target audience.

- Optimize website content, meta tags, and structure for search engine visibility.

- Build backlinks and improve the site's domain authority to boost organic rankings.

- Monitor SEO performance using tools like Ahrefs, Moz, and SEMrush, adjusting strategies as needed.

10. The SEO Specialist must stay up-to-date with the latest search engine algorithms and best practices to keep the company ahead in the organic search game. They work closely with content marketers to ensure that the content strategy aligns with SEO objectives.

11. **Product Marketer:** The Product Marketer bridges the gap between product development and marketing. They focus on positioning the product in a way that resonates with the target audience, communicating its value, and driving user adoption. This role requires a deep understanding of both the product and the market.

Key responsibilities:

- Develop product messaging and positioning that align with customer needs and market trends.

- Plan and execute product launches, working closely with the marketing, sales, and product teams.

- Gather and analyze customer feedback to refine the product and marketing strategy.

- Create product-focused content, such as feature guides, case studies, and product demos.

12. Product Marketers need strong communication skills, market research abilities, and a knack for translating complex product features into clear, customer-centric benefits.

13. **UX/UI Designer:** The user experience is a crucial element of growth. The UX/UI Designer ensures that every interaction a customer has with the company's product, website, or marketing assets is seamless and engaging. They work on creating user-friendly interfaces that drive conversions and improve customer satisfaction.

Key responsibilities:

- Design intuitive and aesthetically pleasing product interfaces and website layouts.

- Collaborate with the growth team to optimize landing pages, onboarding flows, and user journeys.

- Conduct user testing to gather feedback and iterate on design elements.

- Implement design best practices to enhance usability, accessibility, and overall user experience.

14. A skilled UX/UI Designer combines creative flair with a user-centric approach, playing a key role in boosting activation and retention rates.

Cross-functional collaboration: the secret sauce

While each role in the growth marketing team has a specific focus, success hinges on **cross-functional collaboration**. Growth marketing is inherently multidisciplinary, and the team must work closely with other departments, such as product development, sales, customer success, and engineering, to drive cohesive efforts.

For example, the Data Analyst may uncover insights about user behavior that inform the Content Marketer's strategy. The Product Marketer might work with the UX/UI Designer to refine the onboarding experience, while the Growth Lead coordinates with the sales team to align on lead generation and qualification criteria. This collaborative dynamic ensures that every experiment, campaign, and product feature is optimized for growth.

Building your dream growth team

Whether you're a scrappy startup building your first growth team or an established company scaling up your marketing efforts, assembling the right mix of talent is essential. Here's how to approach building your dream growth marketing team:

1. **Start small and scale:** If you're early in your growth journey, start with a **Growth Lead** who can wear multiple hats and drive the initial strategy. As you identify key areas for growth, gradually bring in specialists, such as a Data Analyst or Content Marketer, to support specific needs.

2. **Hire for mindset:** Beyond technical skills, look for team members who embody a **growth mindset**—those who are curious, data-driven, open to experimentation, and comfortable with ambiguity. Growth marketing is fast-paced and ever-changing, so adaptability is a must.

3. **Foster a culture of learning:** Encourage continuous learning and skill development within your team. Growth marketing requires staying ahead of trends, adopting new tools, and exploring innovative tactics. Create an

environment where team members can experiment, share insights, and learn from both successes and failures.

The bottom line: the sum of the parts

Building an effective growth marketing team is about more than just filling roles; it's about creating a **cohesive unit** that works together to drive growth. Each member brings a unique set of skills, from data analysis to content creation to design, but it's the collaboration, experimentation, and shared vision that turn individual efforts into impactful results.

As you move forward with your growth marketing journey, invest time in building a team that embodies the growth mindset, embraces data, and is constantly iterating. The team is your growth engine, and when all parts work in harmony, there's no limit to what you can achieve.

CHAPTER 3
Acquisition unlocked: capturing the right audience

Organic vs. paid acquisition: when to use which

Capturing the right audience is the first step in building a successful growth marketing strategy. But with an ever-growing list of acquisition channels available, deciding where to focus your efforts can be a daunting task. The debate often comes down to two key approaches: **organic acquisition** and **paid acquisition**. Each has its unique strengths, and understanding when to use which is crucial for maximizing your growth potential.

Organic acquisition and paid acquisition are two sides of the same coin, each serving different purposes within a holistic marketing strategy. Organic channels, like SEO, content marketing, and social media, build long-term brand visibility and authority. Paid channels, on the other hand, like PPC advertising, social media ads, and sponsored content, offer speed, scalability, and precise targeting. Knowing when to leverage each approach allows you to create a balanced acquisition strategy that aligns with your growth goals and market dynamics.

Organic acquisition: the slow-burn powerhouse

Organic acquisition refers to the traffic, leads, and customers you gain without paying for direct placements. It includes tactics like content marketing, search engine optimization (SEO), social media engagement, email marketing, and community building. While organic growth doesn't come overnight, its long-term benefits can be game-changing.

Pros of organic acquisition:

1. **Cost-effectiveness:** Organic marketing efforts like blogging, SEO, and social media engagement often have lower upfront costs compared to paid advertising. While they require time and effort, their impact can be felt long after the initial investment.

2. **Sustainable growth:** Organic channels are built on providing value to your audience. When you create high-quality content, optimize your website for SEO, or foster community engagement, you lay the groundwork for sustainable, long-term growth. Content and SEO-driven traffic, in particular, continue to attract and convert users even after campaigns end.

3. **Trust and credibility:** Organic content, such as blogs, videos, and social media posts, helps establish your brand as an authority in your niche. Customers are more likely to trust brands that provide valuable, educational content rather than those solely pushing advertisements.

4. **Audience building:** Organic acquisition allows you to build a community of loyal followers. By engaging with your audience on social media, through newsletters, or in forums, you nurture relationships that lead to higher customer retention and advocacy.

Cons of organic acquisition:

1. **Time-consuming:** Building organic traction takes time. SEO, for example, can take months to show results, as it requires consistent content creation, link-building, and optimization.

2. **Less control:** Unlike paid ads, organic reach is often at the mercy of algorithms (think Google's search rankings or social media feeds). Changes in these algorithms can affect your visibility and traffic, making organic acquisition somewhat unpredictable.

Paid acquisition: the fast-track to visibility

Paid acquisition involves spending money to drive traffic, leads, and sales through channels like pay-per-click (PPC) advertising, social media ads, sponsored content, influencer partnerships, and display ads. The key advantage of paid acquisition is its speed and precision. You can quickly launch campaigns, target specific audiences, and measure results in real-time.

Pros of paid acquisition:

1. **Immediate results:** Paid advertising provides instant visibility. Whether you're running Google Ads, Facebook campaigns, or sponsored posts, you can start generating traffic and leads as soon as your campaigns go live. This speed is invaluable, especially for new products, time-sensitive promotions, or short-term growth targets.

2. **Scalability:** Paid channels are highly scalable. As long as you have the budget, you can expand your reach to target new audiences, test different markets, and drive more traffic. This scalability is particularly beneficial for companies looking to grow quickly or enter new markets.

3. **Precise targeting:** One of the biggest strengths of paid acquisition is the ability to target specific demographics,

interests, behaviors, and even lookalike audiences. Platforms like Facebook, Google, LinkedIn, and TikTok offer advanced targeting options, allowing you to tailor your campaigns to reach the right people at the right time.

4. **Data and insights:** Paid campaigns come with a wealth of data. You can track performance metrics like click-through rates, conversion rates, cost per acquisition (CPA), and return on ad spend (ROAS) in real-time. This data allows for quick optimization, enabling you to refine your campaigns and improve ROI.

Cons of paid acquisition:

1. **Costly:** Paid acquisition can become expensive, particularly in competitive industries or during peak seasons. Ad costs fluctuate based on demand, bidding strategies, and targeting parameters. Without careful budget management, it's easy to overspend and reduce your campaign ROI.

2. **Short-term impact:** Paid campaigns generate results quickly, but their impact diminishes once the budget runs out. Unlike organic content, which can continue to attract traffic over time, paid ads require ongoing investment to maintain visibility and drive conversions.

When to use organic acquisition

Organic acquisition is best suited for scenarios where you want to build a **long-term foundation** for growth, nurture customer relationships, and enhance brand credibility. Here's when to prioritize organic strategies:

1. **Early-stage startups:** If you're in the early stages of building your brand, organic acquisition is a cost-effective way to gain visibility and establish credibility. By creating valuable content, optimizing your website, and engaging

with your audience, you lay the groundwork for sustainable growth. For example, many SaaS startups use content marketing to educate their audience and drive organic sign-ups, building a loyal user base over time.

2. **Nurturing customer relationships:** Organic channels like email marketing, social media, and community building are ideal for nurturing relationships with your existing customers. By providing valuable content, updates, and support, you foster customer loyalty and encourage advocacy, leading to word-of-mouth referrals.

3. **Building authority:** If your goal is to position your brand as an industry authority, focus on organic content strategies such as blogging, podcasting, video content, and social media engagement. Providing valuable insights and information helps you gain the trust of your audience, making it easier to convert them into customers.

4. **SEO and long-tail growth:** Organic acquisition through SEO is particularly effective for driving long-tail traffic. If your business revolves around niche products, services, or topics, creating optimized content can attract highly targeted users actively searching for solutions.

When to use paid acquisition

Paid acquisition is the go-to strategy when you need **immediate results** and have a specific budget to invest in quick wins. Here's when to prioritize paid acquisition:

1. **Launching a new product or service:** When you're launching a new product, service, or feature, paid ads can quickly generate awareness and drive traffic. A well-crafted advertising campaign with targeted messaging ensures that your product gets in front of the right audience at the right time.

2. **Testing and market validation:** Paid ads are excellent for testing product-market fit or validating new markets. You can use small-budget campaigns to gauge demand, test different messaging, and identify which audience segments respond best. This data can then inform your broader marketing strategy.

3. **Seasonal or time-sensitive promotions:** For time-sensitive promotions like holiday sales, product launches, or event registrations, paid acquisition offers the speed and control needed to capitalize on the opportunity. Paid ads can amplify your reach, driving traffic and conversions during peak times.

4. **Scaling quickly:** If your growth goal is to scale rapidly, paid acquisition provides the scalability you need. With the right budget and targeting, you can expand your reach, attract new customers, and boost sales in a short period.

Combining organic and paid acquisition: a balanced approach

The most effective growth strategies often involve a **combination** of organic and paid acquisition. Each approach has its unique strengths, and when used together, they can complement each other to create a balanced, robust marketing funnel.

- **Kick-start with paid, sustain with organic:** For startups or new product launches, use paid ads to gain initial traction and generate leads quickly. Simultaneously, invest in organic channels like content marketing, SEO, and social media to build a sustainable pipeline of traffic and leads. As your organic presence grows, you can gradually reduce reliance on paid ads, optimizing your budget allocation.

- **Use paid to boost organic:** Paid advertising can amplify your organic efforts. For instance, you can use paid social ads to promote high-performing content, increasing its reach and engagement. This boost not only drives traffic but also signals to algorithms (like Facebook or LinkedIn) that your content is valuable, potentially enhancing its organic visibility.

- **Leverage retargeting:** Retargeting ads allow you to re-engage users who have interacted with your brand organically (e.g., visited your website, engaged with social posts). By combining organic and paid efforts, you nurture leads through multiple touchpoints, increasing the likelihood of conversion.

The bottom line: finding the right mix

The choice between organic and paid acquisition is not an either/or decision; it's about finding the right mix for your growth goals, budget, and market conditions. Organic acquisition provides the foundation for long-term, sustainable growth, while paid acquisition offers speed, scalability, and precision targeting. By understanding the strengths and limitations of each, you can strategically allocate resources to maximize impact and drive continuous growth.

SEO, content marketing, and social media mastery

In the growth marketer's playbook, **SEO (Search Engine Optimization)**, **content marketing**, and **social media** are three cornerstones of organic acquisition. They are not standalone tactics; when integrated effectively, they create a powerful, cohesive strategy that drives brand visibility, attracts high-quality leads, and nurtures relationships with your target audience. Mastering these components is key to building a sustainable growth engine that continues to fuel your business over the long term.

SEO: the art of being found

SEO is the process of optimizing your website and content to rank higher in search engine results pages (SERPs), making it easier for potential customers to find you when they search for relevant keywords. In a world where Google processes over 3.5 billion searches daily, being visible in organic search results can significantly impact your brand's reach and credibility.

Key elements of SEO mastery:

1. **Keyword research:** The foundation of any SEO strategy is **keyword research**. This involves identifying the search terms your target audience uses when looking for products, services, or information related to your niche. Use tools like Ahrefs, SEMrush, Moz, or Google Keyword Planner to uncover high-volume, low-competition keywords that align with your business goals.

   o **Long-tail keywords:** Focus on long-tail keywords (e.g., "best organic skincare for sensitive skin") rather than broad terms (e.g., "skincare"). Long-tail keywords are more specific, less competitive, and indicate higher intent, which often leads to better conversion rates.

2. **On-page optimization:** On-page SEO involves optimizing individual pages on your website to rank higher in search results. This includes:

   o **Title tags:** Incorporate your target keyword into the title tag of each page. Keep it under 60 characters to ensure it displays fully in search results.

   o **Meta descriptions:** Write compelling meta descriptions (150-160 characters) that include relevant keywords and encourage users to click through to your page.

- o **Header tags (H1, H2, H3):** Use header tags to structure your content and signal its relevance to search engines. Include keywords naturally within these headers.

- o **URL structure:** Keep URLs short, descriptive, and keyword-rich. Avoid lengthy, complex URLs that may confuse both users and search engines.

3. **High-quality content:** Quality content is at the heart of SEO. Search engines prioritize content that provides value, answers user queries, and keeps visitors engaged. Focus on creating in-depth, informative content that addresses the needs and pain points of your audience. This not only helps you rank for relevant keywords but also builds trust and authority in your niche.

4. **Technical SEO:** Technical SEO refers to optimizing the backend of your website to improve its visibility in search engines. Key areas include:

- o **Site speed:** Ensure your website loads quickly. Slow-loading pages lead to higher bounce rates and lower search rankings.

- o **Mobile-friendliness:** With the majority of searches now happening on mobile devices, having a mobile-optimized website is crucial. Use responsive design to ensure your site looks great on all screen sizes.

- o **Sitemap and indexing:** Create an XML sitemap and submit it to search engines like Google to help them crawl and index your site effectively.

5. **Backlink building:** Backlinks (links from other websites to yours) are a critical ranking factor in SEO. They signal to search engines that your content is valuable and authoritative. Focus on building high-quality backlinks through tactics such as guest blogging, creating shareable content, and building relationships with industry influencers.

Content marketing: engaging and nurturing your audience

If SEO is about getting found, **content marketing** is about what happens when users arrive. It involves creating and distributing valuable, relevant content that attracts, engages, and nurtures your target audience, ultimately driving them toward conversion.

Key components of content marketing mastery:

1. **Understand your audience:** Effective content marketing starts with a deep understanding of your audience's needs, pain points, and interests. Develop detailed buyer personas that outline your ideal customers' demographics, behaviors, challenges, and goals. Use these personas to guide your content strategy, ensuring that every piece of content you create aligns with your audience's needs.

2. **Develop a content strategy:** A successful content marketing strategy is built on clear objectives and a content calendar. Define your goals (e.g., brand awareness, lead generation, customer education) and identify the types of content that will help you achieve them. Common content formats include:

   o **Blog posts:** In-depth articles that provide valuable insights, how-to guides, industry news, or thought leadership.

- o **Videos:** Engaging videos that demonstrate products, explain complex concepts, or showcase customer testimonials.

- o **Infographics:** Visual content that distills complex information into easy-to-understand graphics.

- o **Ebooks and whitepapers:** Comprehensive, downloadable resources that offer in-depth knowledge on a particular topic.

3. Plan your content calendar to cover a mix of topics that address various stages of the customer journey, from awareness to consideration to decision-making.

4. **Create high-value content:** Quality trumps quantity. Focus on creating high-value, well-researched content that answers your audience's questions, solves their problems, or provides new insights. Incorporate relevant keywords naturally, but avoid keyword stuffing, which can harm your SEO and user experience.

5. **Distribute and promote content:** Content marketing doesn't end with creation; distribution is equally important. Share your content across multiple channels, including your website, social media platforms, email newsletters, and industry forums. Repurpose content into different formats (e.g., turn a blog post into an infographic) to reach a broader audience.

6. **Measure performance:** Use analytics tools to measure the performance of your content marketing efforts. Track metrics such as website traffic, time on page, social shares, lead generation, and conversion rates. Analyze which types of content resonate most with your audience and optimize your strategy accordingly.

Social media mastery: building community and amplifying reach

Social media is a dynamic platform for brand building, community engagement, and amplifying your content's reach. Mastering social media involves not just posting regularly but creating meaningful interactions with your audience.

Key practices for social media mastery:

1. **Choose the right platforms:** Not all social media platforms are created equal. Choose platforms that align with your target audience and content style. For example:

    o **LinkedIn:** Ideal for B2B marketing, professional content, and thought leadership.

    o **Instagram:** Great for visually-driven content, lifestyle brands, and direct-to-consumer products.

    o **Twitter:** Best for real-time updates, news, and industry engagement.

    o **Facebook:** Offers a mix of community building, paid advertising, and diverse content sharing.

2. **Create a consistent brand voice:** Your social media presence should reflect your brand's personality and values. Develop a consistent brand voice that resonates with your audience, whether it's witty and casual or professional and informative. This consistency builds brand recognition and trust.

3. **Engage with your audience:** Social media is not just a broadcasting tool; it's a platform for conversation. Engage with your followers by responding to comments, participating in discussions, sharing user-generated content, and addressing customer inquiries. Building a

genuine connection with your audience fosters loyalty and encourages word-of-mouth promotion.

4. **Leverage storytelling:** People connect with stories, not just products. Use social media to tell your brand's story, share customer success stories, showcase behind-the-scenes content, and highlight your team's culture. Storytelling humanizes your brand and creates an emotional bond with your audience.

5. **Use social media for content promotion:** Social media is a powerful channel for distributing and promoting your content. Share blog posts, videos, infographics, and other content to reach a wider audience. Utilize hashtags, mentions, and tags to increase visibility and encourage engagement.

6. **Analyze and iterate:** Use social media analytics tools to track performance metrics such as engagement rates, follower growth, website clicks, and conversions. Identify which types of posts generate the most engagement and refine your strategy accordingly. Experiment with different formats (e.g., live videos, polls, stories) to keep your content fresh and engaging.

Integrating SEO, content marketing, and social media for maximum impact

While SEO, content marketing, and social media are powerful individually, they are even more effective when integrated into a cohesive strategy. Here's how to bring them together:

1. **SEO-driven content:** Use SEO insights to guide your content strategy. Identify high-value keywords and topics that align with your audience's search intent, then create in-depth, optimized content to rank for those terms. Share this content on social media to amplify its reach and drive traffic back to your website.

2. **Content repurposing:** Repurpose content into different formats to cater to various platforms. Turn a blog post into an infographic for Instagram or a short video for LinkedIn. This approach not only maximizes the value of your content but also extends its reach across multiple channels.

3. **Social media signals for SEO:** While social media shares and engagement are not direct ranking factors, they can influence SEO. High social engagement can drive traffic, increase brand awareness, and lead to more backlinks, all of which contribute to improved search rankings.

4. **Cross-promotion:** Use social media to promote your content and encourage backlinks from other websites. Share posts in relevant industry groups, tag influencers, and participate in online discussions to build relationships and drive organic backlinks to your content.

The bottom line: a holistic approach to organic growth

Mastering SEO, content marketing, and social media is essential for building a sustainable organic growth engine. Each component plays a unique role: SEO makes you discoverable, content marketing engages and nurtures your audience, and social media amplifies your reach and fosters community. Together, they create a comprehensive strategy that not only attracts new customers but also builds lasting relationships that drive long-term growth.

Paid advertising: PPC, display, and beyond

Paid advertising is a critical component of growth marketing, offering a fast and scalable way to drive traffic, generate leads, and boost sales. Unlike organic marketing, which can take months to build momentum, **paid advertising** provides immediate visibility and targeted reach. However, to make the most of your investment, it's essential to understand the different types of paid advertising channels and how to use them strategically.

Whether it's **Pay-Per-Click (PPC) ads**, **display advertising**, **social media ads**, or **native advertising**, each channel offers unique benefits and targeting options. The key is to align your paid advertising strategy with your growth goals, audience behavior, and the customer journey, ensuring that every dollar spent contributes to acquiring high-quality leads and driving conversions.

PPC advertising: capturing high-intent leads

Pay-Per-Click (PPC) advertising is one of the most popular forms of paid advertising. It involves paying for ad placements on platforms like Google Ads and Bing Ads, with costs determined by clicks on your ads. PPC campaigns are highly effective for capturing high-intent leads, as they target users who are actively searching for products, services, or information related to your business.

Key elements of PPC advertising:

1. **Keyword targeting:** The success of a PPC campaign starts with **keyword research**. Identify high-value keywords that your target audience is likely to use when searching for solutions in your niche. Focus on a mix of short-tail and long-tail keywords to cover various stages of the customer journey, from broad awareness to specific purchase intent.

   o **Broad match:** Targets a wide range of searches related to your keyword. Useful for building brand awareness but may result in less targeted traffic.

   o **Phrase match:** Shows ads for searches that include your keyword phrase. Provides more control over ad targeting while still capturing related search terms.

- o **Exact match:** Targets specific search queries that exactly match your keyword. Offers the highest precision and is ideal for high-intent, targeted campaigns.

2. **Ad copy and design:** Effective PPC ads require compelling copy and design that resonates with your target audience. Highlight your unique selling points (USPs), use strong calls-to-action (CTAs), and include relevant keywords to capture attention and drive clicks. Ad extensions (e.g., sitelinks, callouts) can also enhance your ads by providing additional information, increasing click-through rates (CTR).

3. **Landing pages:** Your PPC ads are only as effective as the landing pages they direct users to. Create dedicated landing pages that align with the ad's message and provide a clear path to conversion, whether it's signing up for a newsletter, downloading a guide, or making a purchase. Optimize landing pages for speed, mobile-friendliness, and user experience to maximize conversions.

4. **Bid management:** PPC platforms use bidding systems to determine ad placements. Set your bids based on factors like keyword competition, budget, and target cost-per-click (CPC). Use automated bidding strategies (e.g., target CPA, maximize conversions) to optimize for specific goals and reduce manual adjustments.

5. **Performance tracking:** Monitor key performance indicators (KPIs) such as CTR, CPC, conversion rate, and Quality Score. Analyze the data to identify high-performing keywords, optimize ad copy, and adjust bids to improve overall campaign performance.

When to use PPC advertising: PPC is ideal for driving immediate traffic and capturing high-intent leads. It's particularly effective for:

- Launching new products or promotions.

- Targeting users actively searching for specific solutions.

- Testing keywords, ad copy, and landing page variations.

Display advertising: building brand awareness and retargeting

Display advertising involves placing visual ads (banners, images, videos) on websites, apps, and social media platforms. Unlike PPC ads, which target specific search queries, display ads target users based on demographics, interests, behaviors, and browsing history. They are an excellent way to build brand awareness, reach a broader audience, and retarget users who have previously interacted with your brand.

Key components of display advertising:

1. **Targeting options:** Display advertising offers a variety of targeting options, allowing you to reach specific audience segments. Common targeting methods include:

   o **Demographic targeting:** Target users based on age, gender, location, language, and more.

   o **Interest targeting:** Show ads to users who have expressed interest in topics related to your business (e.g., fitness, travel, finance).

   o **Behavioral targeting:** Target users based on their online behavior, such as past website visits, app usage, or purchase history.

o **Retargeting:** Re-engage users who have previously visited your website, used your app, or interacted with your content but haven't converted. Retargeting ads serve as gentle reminders to bring users back to your site and complete the desired action.

2. **Ad creatives:** Display ads rely on eye-catching visuals and compelling messaging. Create visually appealing ads that align with your brand identity and convey a clear value proposition. Use different ad formats, such as static images, animated banners, and videos, to capture attention and increase engagement.

3. **Placement networks:** Display ads are delivered through ad networks like Google Display Network (GDN), Facebook Audience Network, and programmatic advertising platforms. Choose networks that align with your target audience and business objectives. For example, GDN allows you to display ads across millions of websites, apps, and YouTube, providing extensive reach.

4. **Performance measurement:** Track metrics such as impressions, CTR, cost-per-mille (CPM), and conversion rate to evaluate the effectiveness of your display campaigns. Use A/B testing to compare different ad variations and optimize performance based on data insights.

When to use display advertising: Display ads are best for:

- Building brand awareness among a broad audience.

- Retargeting users to re-engage them and drive conversions.

- Supporting upper-funnel marketing efforts, such as introducing new products or promoting brand messaging.

Social media advertising: targeting users where they spend their time

Social media advertising leverages platforms like Facebook, Instagram, LinkedIn, Twitter, TikTok, and Pinterest to reach users based on their social behavior, interests, demographics, and engagement. With billions of active users across these platforms, social media advertising offers unparalleled targeting capabilities and the opportunity to engage with your audience in a more personal way.

Key elements of social media advertising:

1. **Audience targeting:** Social media platforms provide advanced targeting options, including:

   o **Demographic targeting:** Narrow down your audience based on age, gender, location, education, job title, and more.

   o **Interest targeting:** Target users based on their interests, hobbies, and activities (e.g., travel enthusiasts, fitness lovers, business professionals).

   o **Custom audiences:** Create custom audiences from your existing customer lists, website visitors, or app users for highly personalized campaigns.

   o **Lookalike audiences:** Use data from your existing customer base to target new users who share similar characteristics and behaviors.

2. **Ad formats:** Social media platforms offer a variety of ad formats, from image and video ads to carousel, slideshow, story, and collection ads. Choose formats that align with your campaign objectives and engage users effectively. For example, Instagram Stories ads are great for creating immersive, full-screen experiences, while LinkedIn Sponsored Content is ideal for promoting B2B thought leadership.

3. **Ad creatives:** Craft visually appealing and engaging creatives that resonate with your target audience. Incorporate compelling copy, strong CTAs, and branded visuals to capture attention and drive action. For video ads, keep content short, dynamic, and optimized for sound-off viewing.

4. **Performance tracking:** Use social media analytics to monitor key metrics such as engagement rate, video views, click-through rate, and conversions. Continuously analyze performance data to optimize targeting, ad creatives, and budget allocation.

When to use social media advertising: Social media ads are ideal for:

- Engaging users based on interests, demographics, and behaviors.

- Promoting brand storytelling and lifestyle content.

- Building custom and lookalike audiences for highly targeted campaigns.

- Enhancing content distribution and amplifying reach.

Native advertising: blending in for a seamless experience

Native advertising involves placing ads that match the form and function of the platform on which they appear. Unlike traditional display ads, native ads blend seamlessly with the surrounding content, providing a non-disruptive user experience. Examples include sponsored content on news websites, in-feed ads on social media, and recommended articles.

Key advantages of native advertising:

1. **Non-intrusive:** Native ads appear as natural content, making them less disruptive and more engaging than traditional ads.

2. **High engagement:** Because native ads align with the user experience, they tend to generate higher engagement rates and drive better performance, particularly for content-based campaigns.

When to use native advertising: Native advertising is well-suited for:

- Promoting content marketing assets (e.g., blog posts, videos) in a natural, engaging way.

- Reaching users in a non-disruptive manner across content-focused platforms (e.g., news websites, content discovery networks).

The bottom line: choosing the right mix of paid channels

Paid advertising offers a range of channels and strategies to capture the right audience and drive conversions. The key to success lies in choosing the right mix of channels that align with your business goals, audience behavior, and marketing funnel. PPC is ideal for targeting high-intent leads, display ads build brand awareness, social media ads provide advanced targeting capabilities, and native ads offer a seamless, engaging experience.

By mastering these paid advertising tactics and continually testing and optimizing your campaigns, you can create a powerful acquisition engine that accelerates growth and maximizes ROI.

CHAPTER 4

Demand generation and marketing funnels

Creating demand in saturated markets

In today's business landscape, nearly every market feels crowded. From SaaS platforms to beauty products, consumers are bombarded with choices. Entering a saturated market can seem daunting, as you face established players, fierce competition, and customers who have likely seen it all. But, as a growth marketer, this is where you can shine. Creating demand in saturated markets is not about shouting louder than the competition; it's about **differentiation**, **customer insight**, and **innovation**.

Standing out in a sea of sameness requires more than just a great product. It demands a deep understanding of your audience, a unique value proposition, and a strategy to connect with customers in a way that your competitors can't. The good news? Saturated markets often indicate high demand and a robust customer base, making them ripe with potential for brands that know how to carve their niche.

Why saturated markets can be an opportunity

While saturated markets pose challenges, they also come with significant advantages:

1. **Proven demand:** The presence of many competitors typically signals a healthy demand. Customers are already interested in the products or services being offered, which means you don't have to educate the market from scratch.

2. **Customer awareness:** In saturated markets, customers are already familiar with the problem your product solves. This awareness can speed up the decision-making process, especially if you can differentiate your offering effectively.

3. **Learning from competitors:** Established players in a saturated market provide valuable insights. By analyzing their strengths, weaknesses, and strategies, you can identify gaps, avoid pitfalls, and innovate your approach to meet unmet customer needs.

Crafting a unique value proposition (UVP)

The first step in creating demand in a saturated market is to define what makes your product or service **unique**. Your **Unique Value Proposition (UVP)** is what sets you apart from the competition. It's not just about having more features; it's about addressing your audience's specific pain points in a way that others don't.

Key elements of a compelling UVP:

1. **Specificity:** Avoid vague statements like "the best solution" or "high quality." Instead, focus on specific benefits that resonate with your target audience. For example, Slack's UVP revolves around simplifying team communication, making it more efficient and enjoyable than email.

2. **Customer-centric:** Frame your UVP around the customer's problem. Highlight how your product solves their pain points or fulfills their desires in a way that competitors don't.

3. **Clarity:** Your UVP should be clear and easy to understand at a glance. Customers should immediately grasp why they should choose you over the competition.

Example: When Dollar Shave Club entered the highly saturated razor market dominated by giants like Gillette, they differentiated themselves with a UVP focused on affordability and convenience: "A great shave for a few bucks a month." This simple, direct message resonated with customers tired of overpaying for razors and visiting stores, creating demand in a market that seemed impenetrable.

Understanding and exploiting market gaps

Saturated markets may seem overcrowded, but they are rarely fully optimized. By identifying **market gaps**, you can find opportunities to attract customers that competitors may have overlooked.

Strategies for finding market gaps:

1. **Customer research:** Talk to potential customers to uncover pain points, frustrations, and unmet needs within the existing market. Surveys, interviews, and social listening can reveal insights into what customers wish they had but aren't getting from current offerings.

2. **Competitive analysis:** Study your competitors to identify their weaknesses and gaps in their product or marketing strategies. Are they neglecting a specific customer segment? Are their products too complex or overpriced? Use these gaps to position your product as the better alternative.

3. **Niche targeting:** Consider focusing on a niche segment within the larger market. By catering to a specific audience's unique needs, you can create demand where competition is less intense. For example, instead of targeting the entire fitness market, a brand could focus on "fitness gear for travelers," offering products designed specifically for portability and convenience.

Example: Notion, a productivity app, entered the saturated market of task management tools. Rather than competing directly with giants like Evernote and Trello, Notion positioned itself as an all-in-one workspace, offering flexibility and customization that traditional tools lacked. By targeting power users who wanted more control over their workflow, Notion created demand in an otherwise crowded space.

Leveraging storytelling to connect emotionally

In saturated markets, where products and features often look similar, **storytelling** becomes a powerful tool to differentiate your brand. Customers are drawn to brands that resonate with them on an emotional level. By telling a compelling story, you humanize your brand, make it memorable, and connect with customers beyond the transactional level.

Key components of effective storytelling:

1. **Brand narrative:** Share your brand's origin story, mission, and values. Explain why your company exists and how it aims to make a difference. Customers are more likely to support brands whose values align with their own.

2. **Customer stories:** Highlight customer success stories, testimonials, and case studies. Showcase how your product has positively impacted real people, illustrating the value it provides in a relatable way.

3. **Transparency:** In a crowded market, authenticity and transparency can set you apart. Share behind-the-scenes content, discuss challenges you've faced, and be open about your brand's journey. Customers appreciate honesty and are more likely to trust brands that are genuine.

Example: Warby Parker disrupted the eyewear market by telling a story about accessibility and social impact. Their narrative of offering stylish, affordable glasses while giving back to communities in need resonated with consumers tired of high-priced eyewear from traditional retailers. This storytelling approach created a loyal customer base and demand in a market previously dominated by a few players.

Creating scarcity and exclusivity

In a saturated market, scarcity and exclusivity can generate buzz and create a sense of urgency among potential customers. **Scarcity marketing** leverages the fear of missing out (FOMO) to drive demand, particularly in markets where customers have an abundance of choices.

Scarcity and exclusivity tactics:

1. **Limited-time offers:** Introduce time-limited promotions, sales, or product launches to create urgency. Highlight phrases like "limited-time only," "exclusive offer," or "while supplies last" to encourage immediate action.

2. **Exclusive access:** Offer exclusive access to new products, features, or events for early adopters, loyal customers, or members of your community. This tactic not only drives demand but also fosters a sense of belonging among your audience.

3. **Waitlists:** When launching a new product, create a waitlist to build anticipation and exclusivity. Use the

waitlist as an opportunity to engage with potential customers, provide updates, and build excitement.

Example: Glossier, a beauty brand, leveraged scarcity and exclusivity by launching limited-edition products and building hype through their community-driven marketing. This approach made their products highly sought after, creating demand even in the saturated beauty industry.

Innovating your marketing approach

In a crowded market, standard marketing tactics often blend into the noise. To create demand, think **outside the box** and innovate your marketing approach:

1. **Experiential marketing:** Host events, workshops, or virtual experiences that allow customers to engage with your brand in a memorable way. Experiences create emotional connections and leave a lasting impression.

2. **Influencer partnerships:** Collaborate with influencers who align with your brand values and target audience. Influencers provide authentic endorsements and reach customers in niche communities, adding credibility and visibility to your product.

3. **Content-driven demand:** Use content marketing to educate and inspire your audience. Create educational blogs, videos, guides, and webinars that address your audience's challenges and offer solutions. High-quality content positions your brand as a thought leader and builds trust, making customers more likely to choose you over competitors.

Example: When Spotify launched, it faced stiff competition in the music streaming market. Instead of relying solely on traditional advertising, Spotify created demand by offering personalized experiences, such as "Discover Weekly" playlists, and data-driven marketing campaigns like "Spotify Wrapped." These innovative approaches made Spotify stand out, creating buzz and attracting millions of users.

The bottom line: differentiation in a crowded marketplace

Creating demand in saturated markets is not about competing on features or shouting the loudest; it's about **differentiation**, understanding customer pain points, and telling a story that resonates. By crafting a unique value proposition, finding market gaps, leveraging storytelling, creating exclusivity, and innovating your marketing tactics, you can carve out your niche and attract customers even in the most crowded markets.

Building and optimizing marketing funnels

A **marketing funnel** is the path that potential customers take from their first interaction with your brand to becoming loyal advocates. Think of it as a journey, where each stage represents a step closer to conversion. In growth marketing, building an effective funnel is essential for guiding prospects, nurturing leads, and driving long-term growth. However, it's not just about getting people into the funnel; it's about optimizing each stage to ensure that your prospects move smoothly from one phase to the next.

A well-designed marketing funnel reflects the customer journey, addressing their needs, questions, and objections at every stage. By understanding and optimizing each part of the funnel, you can attract the right audience, nurture relationships, and ultimately convert prospects into loyal customers.

The marketing funnel: an overview

While the specific structure of a marketing funnel may vary depending on the business and industry, it generally consists of four main stages: **Awareness**, **Interest**, **Decision**, and **Action** (often abbreviated as AIDA). Here's a closer look at each stage and its role in the customer journey:

1. **Awareness (Top of the Funnel - TOFU):** The awareness stage is where potential customers first encounter your brand. At this point, they might be unaware of their problem or the solutions available. The goal at this stage is to capture their attention and build brand awareness through educational and engaging content.

   o   **Tactics:** Blog posts, social media content, SEO, PPC ads, infographics, and videos.

   o   **Key Metrics:** Website traffic, social media reach, ad impressions, and brand mentions.

2. **Interest (Middle of the Funnel - MOFU):** During the interest stage, prospects are aware of their problem and are actively researching solutions. Here, they are evaluating their options, comparing brands, and seeking more in-depth information. Your goal is to nurture their interest and showcase how your product or service can meet their needs.

   o   **Tactics:** Educational content (ebooks, whitepapers, guides), email newsletters, webinars, case studies, and product demos.

   o   **Key Metrics:** Content engagement (downloads, views), email open rates, webinar attendance, and website behavior (time on page, bounce rate).

3. **Decision (Bottom of the Funnel - BOFU):** At the decision stage, prospects are ready to make a purchase decision. They are weighing their options and may have some final objections or concerns. Your job is to provide the information and incentives that make choosing your product the obvious choice.

- **Tactics:** Free trials, product demos, discounts, testimonials, comparison guides, and sales consultations.

- **Key Metrics:** Free trial sign-ups, demo requests, cart abandonment rate, and lead-to-customer conversion rate.

4. **Action (Conversion and Beyond):** The action stage is where the prospect becomes a customer. However, the funnel doesn't end with the sale. Post-purchase engagement, customer support, and retention efforts are crucial for turning one-time buyers into loyal advocates.

   - **Tactics:** Onboarding emails, customer support, loyalty programs, upselling, and customer feedback surveys.

   - **Key Metrics:** Customer retention rate, Net Promoter Score (NPS), upsell and cross-sell rates, and customer lifetime value (CLV).

Building your marketing funnel

Constructing an effective marketing funnel involves creating targeted content, campaigns, and experiences that address the needs and behaviors of your audience at each stage. Here's how to build a funnel that guides prospects smoothly from awareness to conversion:

1. **Define your target audience:** Start by identifying your ideal customer personas. Understand their demographics, interests, pain points, and decision-making process. This knowledge will shape your messaging, content, and strategies at each funnel stage.

2. **Map the customer journey:** Outline the typical journey your customers take from discovering your brand to

making a purchase. Identify key touchpoints, potential obstacles, and decision triggers. This mapping helps you understand what information and support prospects need as they move through the funnel.

3. **Create TOFU content:** At the top of the funnel, focus on creating content that attracts attention and builds awareness. This content should be educational, informative, and geared toward solving common problems your audience faces. Examples include:

    o **Blog posts:** Publish articles that address your audience's pain points, answer their questions, and offer insights. Optimize these posts for SEO to attract organic traffic.

    o **Videos:** Create engaging videos that introduce your brand, showcase your expertise, or explain complex concepts in a digestible format.

    o **Social media:** Use social media channels to share valuable content, engage with your audience, and boost brand visibility.

4. **Develop MOFU content:** In the middle of the funnel, focus on nurturing leads and providing them with more detailed, solution-oriented information. Content at this stage should help prospects evaluate their options and understand how your product can meet their specific needs. Examples include:

    o **Ebooks and whitepapers:** Offer in-depth guides that provide actionable insights and highlight your product's value. Gated content, such as ebooks, can also help capture leads through sign-up forms.

o **Webinars:** Host webinars that dive deeper into industry topics, showcase your expertise, and demonstrate your product's capabilities.

o **Case studies:** Share stories of how your product or service has successfully solved real customer problems, providing social proof and credibility.

5. **Optimize BOFU content:** At the bottom of the funnel, focus on content that addresses final objections and encourages prospects to take action. This is where you showcase your product's unique value and provide clear calls to action (CTAs). Examples include:

o **Free trials and demos:** Offer free trials or product demos to allow prospects to experience your product firsthand, easing their decision-making process.

o **Customer testimonials:** Highlight testimonials, reviews, and success stories from satisfied customers to build trust and confidence.

o **Comparison guides:** Create detailed comparison guides that highlight how your product stands out against competitors, helping prospects make an informed decision.

6. **Plan post-conversion engagement:** Once a prospect converts, your job isn't over. Post-purchase engagement is crucial for customer retention, upselling, and turning customers into brand advocates. Implement a post-purchase plan that includes onboarding emails, customer support, loyalty programs, and regular communication to keep customers engaged and satisfied.

Optimizing your marketing funnel

Building a funnel is just the beginning. To maximize its effectiveness, you need to continuously monitor, analyze, and optimize each stage. Here's how to optimize your marketing funnel for better results:

1. **Track and analyze metrics:** Use analytics tools (e.g., Google Analytics, HubSpot, Mixpanel) to monitor key performance indicators (KPIs) at each funnel stage. Identify areas where prospects drop off or underperform, such as high bounce rates on landing pages or low conversion rates in free trials. This data-driven approach helps pinpoint bottlenecks and areas for improvement.

2. **A/B testing:** Regularly run A/B tests on your landing pages, CTAs, email campaigns, and content to identify what resonates best with your audience. For example, test different headline variations, images, CTA button colors, or offer formats to see which options drive higher engagement and conversions.

3. **Refine targeting:** Use data insights to refine your audience targeting. Segment your leads based on behavior, demographics, and interactions with your content. Tailor your messaging and content to match each segment's needs and interests, increasing the likelihood of moving them through the funnel.

4. **Personalize experiences:** Personalization can significantly improve funnel performance. Use customer data to deliver personalized content, recommendations, and offers based on their behavior, preferences, and stage in the journey. For example, send tailored follow-up emails to prospects who downloaded a specific guide, addressing their potential concerns and offering the next steps.

5. **Improve user experience:** A seamless user experience (UX) is vital for keeping prospects moving through the

funnel. Optimize your website and landing pages for speed, mobile-friendliness, and intuitive navigation. Simplify forms, remove unnecessary friction, and provide clear CTAs to guide prospects toward the desired action.

6. **Retargeting:** Use retargeting ads to re-engage prospects who interacted with your content or visited your website but didn't convert. Retargeting keeps your brand top-of-mind and encourages users to return and complete their journey.

Example: HubSpot's marketing funnel is a masterclass in optimization. The company uses SEO and content marketing to attract leads at the awareness stage, offering free resources like blog posts, ebooks, and webinars. Once prospects express interest, they enter the middle of the funnel, where they receive tailored emails, product demos, and case studies. At the bottom of the funnel, HubSpot provides free trials, personalized consultations, and customer testimonials to drive conversions. Post-purchase, they focus on onboarding, customer success, and upselling to maximize lifetime value.

The bottom line: guiding prospects through a seamless journey

Building and optimizing a marketing funnel is key to creating a seamless journey that guides prospects from awareness to conversion. By understanding the customer's needs at each stage and delivering targeted content and experiences, you nurture relationships, build trust, and drive sustainable growth.

However, the funnel is not static; it requires ongoing optimization based on data insights, testing, and customer feedback. The more you refine your funnel, the more effectively you can attract, engage, and convert your target audience, turning prospects into loyal customers and advocates.

From awareness to purchase: mapping the customer journey

The **customer journey** is the path that a potential customer takes from the moment they first encounter your brand to when they become a paying customer—and ideally, a loyal advocate. It's more than just a series of touchpoints; it's a dynamic process that involves emotions, perceptions, and decisions. In growth marketing, understanding and mapping out this journey is crucial to crafting personalized experiences that guide customers seamlessly from awareness to purchase.

Mapping the customer journey enables you to pinpoint what customers need at each stage, identify potential obstacles, and optimize your marketing strategies accordingly. When done right, it helps you connect with customers on a deeper level, providing the right content, at the right time, through the right channels, thereby improving engagement, conversions, and loyalty.

The stages of the customer journey

While the customer journey can vary across industries and business models, it typically follows a series of stages: **Awareness**, **Consideration**, **Decision**, and **Post-Purchase**. Here's a breakdown of each stage and what customers are experiencing:

1. **Awareness:** At the top of the funnel, potential customers become aware of your brand or realize they have a problem that needs solving. They might not know exactly what they need yet, but they're open to learning more about solutions available in the market.

    o   **Customer mindset:** "I have a problem, but I'm not sure what the solution is."

    o   **Key questions:** What is the problem? What options are available to address this problem?

o   **Brand's role:** Provide educational content that addresses the problem, builds trust, and introduces your brand as a credible source of information.

2.   **Consideration:** In the middle of the funnel, customers are actively researching their options. They're comparing different products, reading reviews, and evaluating features to find the best solution for their needs.

o   **Customer mindset:** "I know what I need, but which product or service is best for me?"

o   **Key questions:** How does this product/service work? How does it compare to other solutions? What are the benefits and drawbacks?

o   **Brand's role:** Offer in-depth information that showcases your product's value, addresses common objections, and positions your brand as the best fit for their needs/

3.   **Decision:** At the bottom of the funnel, customers are ready to make a purchase decision. They may have some final questions or concerns that need to be addressed before they commit.

o   **Customer mindset:** "I think this is the right solution, but is it worth the investment?"

o   **Key questions:** Is this product/service worth the price? What do other customers think? Are there any guarantees or support available?

o   **Brand's role:** Provide persuasive content, such as customer testimonials, case studies, free trials, discounts, or guarantees, to alleviate concerns and motivate the purchase.

4. **Post-Purchase:** The customer journey doesn't end with the purchase. The post-purchase stage is crucial for building loyalty, encouraging repeat business, and turning customers into advocates.

    o   **Customer mindset:** "Now that I've made the purchase, what's next?"

    o   **Key questions:** How do I get the most out of this product/service? What support is available if I have issues?

    o   **Brand's role:** Deliver a positive onboarding experience, provide support, request feedback, and nurture the customer relationship through engagement and loyalty programs.

Mapping the customer journey

Customer journey mapping is the process of visualizing the steps your customers take as they interact with your brand. This map helps you identify key touchpoints, customer pain points, and opportunities for improvement. Here's how to create an effective customer journey map:

1. **Define your customer personas:** Start by creating detailed personas that represent your ideal customers. Include demographic information, behaviors, preferences, pain points, goals, and typical decision-making processes. Understanding your personas will guide the mapping process and help you empathize with customers at each journey stage.

2. **Identify touchpoints:** List all potential touchpoints where customers interact with your brand, both online and offline. Common touchpoints include social media, website visits, ads, blog posts, emails, product pages,

customer support, reviews, and sales interactions. Consider touchpoints at every stage of the journey, from initial awareness to post-purchase.

3. **Understand customer goals and needs:** For each touchpoint, identify the customer's goals, needs, and emotions. What are they trying to achieve? What information are they seeking? What concerns or obstacles might they encounter? This step helps you tailor your messaging and content to address customer needs effectively.

4. **Create the journey map:** Visualize the journey by laying out the stages (Awareness, Consideration, Decision, Post-Purchase) and mapping the corresponding touchpoints, actions, thoughts, and emotions. This map provides a holistic view of how customers experience your brand, highlighting areas for improvement and optimization.

Example: A journey map for a fitness app might look like this:

- **Awareness:** The customer sees a targeted ad on Instagram promoting tips for staying fit at home (Touchpoint: Social media ad). They click through to a blog post offering free workout routines (Touchpoint: Blog).

- **Consideration:** After reading the blog, they sign up for the app's newsletter to receive more fitness tips (Touchpoint: Email). They receive a series of emails introducing the app's features, including guided workouts, meal plans, and community support (Touchpoint: Email campaign).

- **Decision:** They explore the app's website and find testimonials from users who achieved their fitness goals using the app (Touchpoint: Website). They sign up for a free trial to experience the app firsthand (Touchpoint: Free trial).

- **Post-Purchase:** After subscribing, they receive onboarding emails with tips on maximizing the app's features (Touchpoint: Onboarding email). They join the app's community forum for support and motivation (Touchpoint: Community).

Optimizing the customer journey

Mapping the customer journey is only the first step. To maximize its effectiveness, you need to continuously optimize each stage to improve the customer experience and drive conversions:

1. **Address pain points:** Use your journey map to identify pain points or friction that customers encounter at each stage. For example, if prospects drop off during the decision stage, they may need more social proof, such as testimonials or reviews. Address these obstacles by refining your content, touchpoints, and messaging.

2. **Personalize interactions:** Use customer data to personalize experiences at each stage of the journey. Personalization can include tailored product recommendations, customized emails based on user behavior, or targeted ads that reflect previous interactions. Personalization enhances relevance, builds trust, and increases the likelihood of conversion.

3. **Create seamless transitions:** Ensure that each touchpoint leads smoothly to the next, guiding customers through the journey. For example, if a prospect clicks on an ad for a free guide, take them directly to a dedicated landing page with the guide, followed by an email sequence that nurtures their interest. Avoid dead-ends in the journey, such as broken links or disconnected content.

4. **Monitor and analyze:** Use analytics tools to track customer behavior at each touchpoint. Analyze metrics

such as website traffic, bounce rate, email open rates, conversion rates, and customer support interactions. Identify patterns, bottlenecks, and opportunities for improvement based on data insights.

5. **Gather feedback:** Collect customer feedback through surveys, reviews, or direct interactions to gain insights into their experience. Use this feedback to refine your journey map, address pain points, and enhance the customer experience.

Creating a journey beyond purchase

A common mistake is to focus solely on getting customers to the point of purchase, neglecting the post-purchase experience. In reality, the **post-purchase journey** is critical for customer satisfaction, retention, and advocacy. Here's how to nurture customers beyond their first purchase:

1. **Onboarding:** Provide a seamless onboarding experience that helps new customers get the most out of your product. Use onboarding emails, tutorials, guides, and check-ins to welcome customers and guide them through key features.

2. **Customer support:** Make it easy for customers to access support if they have questions or issues. Offer multiple support channels (e.g., chat, email, phone) and provide helpful resources such as FAQs and knowledge bases.

3. **Engagement:** Keep customers engaged through regular communication, such as newsletters, product updates, and personalized recommendations. Encourage interaction by creating a community or loyalty program that rewards participation and repeat purchases.

4. **Gather and act on feedback:** Request customer feedback through surveys, reviews, and direct outreach. Use this

feedback to improve your product, address customer concerns, and demonstrate that you value their input.

Example: After a customer purchases a subscription to an online learning platform, they receive a series of onboarding emails guiding them through the platform's features. They also receive personalized course recommendations based on their interests and progress. To foster engagement, the platform invites them to join a community forum and participate in monthly webinars. This post-purchase journey not only enhances their experience but also encourages ongoing use and subscription renewal.

The bottom line: creating a seamless customer journey

Mapping and optimizing the customer journey is key to creating an experience that resonates with your audience and drives growth. By understanding the different stages and touchpoints, you can craft targeted content, remove friction, and nurture relationships that guide prospects smoothly from awareness to purchase and beyond. Remember, the journey doesn't end at conversion; a well-designed post-purchase experience is essential for customer retention and advocacy.

C H A P T E R 5

Account-based marketing for hyper-targeted growth

What is ABM and why it matters for B2B growth

Account-Based Marketing (ABM) has been making waves in the B2B marketing landscape as a strategy that turns the traditional marketing funnel on its head. Instead of casting a wide net to attract as many leads as possible, ABM focuses on identifying and targeting high-value accounts that are most likely to become valuable customers. It's a highly targeted, personalized approach that aligns marketing and sales efforts to win over specific accounts, making it a powerful strategy for driving B2B growth.

ABM's impact in B2B growth marketing is profound. Unlike traditional marketing, which often operates in silos, ABM brings marketing and sales together to work collaboratively on a shared list of target accounts. By focusing on quality over quantity, ABM allows companies to deliver highly personalized experiences that resonate with key decision-makers, leading to deeper relationships and higher conversion rates.

What is account-based marketing (ABM)?

ABM is a **strategic marketing approach** in which an organization treats individual high-value accounts as a market of one. Instead of marketing to a broad audience, you select a set of target accounts based on specific criteria (e.g., company size, industry, revenue potential) and create tailored campaigns for each account. The idea is to deliver relevant, personalized content and messaging that addresses the unique challenges, needs, and goals of each target account, building trust and fostering strong relationships.

Key characteristics of ABM:

1. **Targeted:** ABM is laser-focused on a specific list of high-value accounts, identified based on factors such as revenue potential, fit with your product, strategic importance, and likelihood of becoming a long-term customer.

2. **Personalized:** ABM campaigns are highly personalized to resonate with the unique needs of each target account. This can include customized content, tailored messaging, and individual outreach that speaks directly to the account's specific pain points and goals.

3. **Sales and marketing alignment:** ABM requires close collaboration between marketing and sales teams. Together, they identify target accounts, create account-specific strategies, and work cohesively throughout the customer journey to convert these accounts into loyal clients.

4. **Long-term relationships:** ABM isn't just about closing a sale; it's about building long-term relationships with key accounts. By nurturing these relationships, companies can drive repeat business, upsell opportunities, and customer advocacy.

Why ABM matters for B2B growth

ABM has become a cornerstone of B2B growth strategies, and for good reason. Here's why ABM is particularly valuable in the B2B context:

1. **Focus on high-value accounts:** In B2B, not all leads are created equal. Some accounts offer significantly higher revenue potential and strategic value than others. ABM allows you to focus your resources on these high-value accounts, ensuring that your marketing and sales efforts are directed toward opportunities that matter most.
    For example, a software company may identify a handful of Fortune 500 companies as target accounts for its enterprise solution. By concentrating its resources on these key accounts, the company can develop highly tailored campaigns that resonate with decision-makers, increasing the chances of landing large, lucrative contracts.

2. **Personalized experiences:** In B2B, purchasing decisions often involve multiple stakeholders, longer sales cycles, and more complex buying processes. ABM addresses these complexities by delivering personalized experiences tailored to the specific needs of each account. This level of customization builds trust and credibility, making it easier to engage with decision-makers and move them through the buying journey.

3. **Stronger sales and marketing alignment:** One of the biggest challenges in B2B marketing is the disconnect between marketing and sales. ABM bridges this gap by aligning both teams around a shared list of target accounts and objectives. This collaboration ensures a seamless handoff of leads, a unified approach to nurturing prospects, and consistent messaging throughout the customer journey.

4.   **Higher ROI:** ABM has been shown to deliver a higher return on investment (ROI) compared to traditional marketing tactics. According to a study by the Altera Group, 97% of marketers reported that ABM had a higher ROI than other marketing initiatives. By focusing on quality over quantity, ABM reduces wasted resources and maximizes the impact of your marketing and sales efforts.

5.   **Enhanced customer lifetime value:** ABM is not just about acquiring new customers; it's about cultivating long-term relationships with key accounts. By nurturing these relationships, companies can increase customer lifetime value through upselling, cross-selling, and renewal opportunities. This ongoing engagement also fosters brand loyalty and turns customers into advocates, further driving growth.

ABM vs. traditional marketing: what makes it different?

To understand the value of ABM, it's helpful to compare it with traditional marketing approaches:

Aspect	Traditional Marketing	Account Based Marketing
Audience	Broad, mass audience	Narrow, specific high-value accounts
Focus	Lead generation	Account engagement and relationship building
Approach	One-to-many (mass communication)	One-to-one or one-to-few (personalized)
Content	General, one-size-fits-all messaging	Customized, account-specific content
Sales Collaboration	Often siloed from sales	Close alignment with sales
Success Metrics	Lead volume, conversion rates	Account engagement, deal size, customer lifetime value

In traditional marketing, the focus is often on **lead generation**—capturing as many leads as possible and nurturing them through a funnel. ABM flips this approach by focusing on a specific set of **target accounts** from the outset. Instead of mass communication, ABM uses personalized, one-to-one engagement to build relationships and guide accounts through a tailored journey.

How ABM drives B2B growth

ABM's focus on personalization, strategic targeting, and long-term relationships makes it a powerful engine for B2B growth. Here's how ABM drives success:

1. **Higher quality leads:** By focusing on a curated list of high-value accounts, ABM ensures that your marketing and sales teams are investing time and resources in opportunities with the highest potential. This targeted approach leads to higher-quality leads, better engagement, and more meaningful conversations.

2. **Shortened sales cycles:** In B2B, sales cycles can be long and complex, often involving multiple stakeholders. ABM's personalized, account-specific approach helps address objections, answer questions, and provide tailored solutions that meet each account's unique needs. This process builds trust and accelerates decision-making, shortening the sales cycle.

3. **Deeper relationships:** ABM is about building relationships, not just transactions. By nurturing key accounts through personalized interactions, content, and support, you establish a deep connection with decision-makers. This relationship-driven approach not only increases the chances of closing deals but also fosters loyalty and customer advocacy.

4. **Cross-selling and upselling opportunities:** ABM doesn't end once a deal is closed. By continuing to nurture

relationships with existing accounts, you open the door to cross-selling and upselling opportunities. As you build trust and demonstrate value, accounts are more likely to invest in additional products or services, increasing customer lifetime value.

5. **Alignment with complex B2B buying processes:** In B2B markets, purchasing decisions often involve multiple stakeholders, such as executives, department heads, and procurement teams. ABM aligns marketing efforts with this reality by delivering tailored content and messaging that addresses the specific concerns of each stakeholder, making it easier to gain buy-in and move the deal forward.

Implementing ABM: the basics

Implementing an ABM strategy requires careful planning, collaboration, and a commitment to personalization. Here's a basic overview of how to get started with ABM:

1. **Identify target accounts:** Work with your sales team to identify high-value target accounts. Use criteria such as company size, industry, revenue potential, and fit with your product to curate a list of accounts that align with your growth goals.

2. **Research accounts:** Conduct in-depth research on each target account to understand their business, pain points, goals, and decision-making process. Identify key stakeholders and their roles to tailor your messaging and content effectively.

3. **Create personalized content:** Develop content and campaigns specifically tailored to each target account. This can include customized emails, targeted ads, account-specific landing pages, personalized videos, case studies, and product demos. The goal is to deliver relevant

information that speaks directly to the account's needs and challenges.

4. **Align marketing and sales:** Foster close collaboration between marketing and sales teams throughout the ABM process. Regularly communicate insights, share progress, and adjust strategies based on account engagement and feedback.

5. **Measure and optimize:** Track account engagement metrics, such as website visits, email interactions, content downloads, and sales meetings. Use this data to evaluate the effectiveness of your ABM campaigns and optimize your approach for better results.

The bottom line: ABM as a growth accelerator

Account-Based Marketing is more than just a marketing tactic; it's a **growth accelerator** for B2B companies. By focusing on high-value accounts, delivering personalized experiences, and aligning marketing and sales efforts, ABM drives deeper engagement, shorter sales cycles, and long-term customer relationships. In a world where B2B buyers expect tailored solutions and meaningful interactions, ABM stands out as a strategy that not only captures attention but also wins trust.

Developing personalized strategies for high-value accounts

The cornerstone of **Account-Based Marketing (ABM)** is personalization. While traditional marketing often employs a one-size-fits-all approach, ABM focuses on crafting strategies tailored to each high-value account. This level of personalization allows you to build deeper connections with key stakeholders, address specific pain points, and position your product or service as the ideal solution. Developing personalized strategies for each account involves understanding their unique needs, challenges, and objectives and then designing targeted content, campaigns, and interactions to engage them effectively.

Why personalization matters in ABM

In B2B markets, buying decisions are complex and involve multiple stakeholders, each with their own priorities and concerns. Generic marketing messages often fail to resonate in this environment because they don't address the specific challenges and goals of individual accounts. Personalization, on the other hand, demonstrates that you understand their unique situation and are committed to providing a solution tailored to their needs.

Benefits of personalization in ABM:

- **Builds trust:** Personalized messaging shows that you've done your homework and genuinely understand the account's business, industry, and challenges. This level of understanding builds trust and credibility with decision-makers.

- **Increases engagement:** Personalized content and campaigns are more likely to capture attention and drive engagement because they speak directly to the account's pain points and objectives

- **Accelerates the buying process:** When you address specific concerns and provide tailored solutions, stakeholders can more easily see the value in your offering, which helps to shorten the decision-making process.

Steps to developing personalized strategies for high-value accounts

Creating an effective personalized strategy for each account requires in-depth research, collaboration with sales, and a creative approach to content and engagement. Here's how to develop tailored ABM strategies that resonate with your high-value accounts:

1. Conduct in-depth account research

Before you can personalize your strategy, you need a deep understanding of each target account. Research is the foundation of any successful ABM campaign, providing the insights you need to tailor your messaging, content, and approach.

Key research areas:

- **Company overview:** Gather information about the account's industry, size, products or services, market position, and competitors.

- **Business goals and challenges:** Identify the company's key objectives, challenges, and pain points. For example, are they looking to expand into new markets, improve operational efficiency, or enhance customer satisfaction? Understanding their goals allows you to align your messaging with their strategic priorities.

- **Decision-makers and stakeholders:** Map out the key decision-makers and influencers within the account. What are their roles, responsibilities, and priorities? What pain points or challenges do they face in their daily operations? This information helps you create tailored messaging for each stakeholder.

- **Current solutions and gaps:** Investigate the solutions or products the account is currently using. Identify gaps or areas where your offering can provide a better alternative or complement their existing tools.

2.   Create account-specific value proposition.

Armed with insights from your research, develop a **unique value proposition** (UVP) for each target account. Unlike a general UVP, an account-specific UVP addresses the specific needs, pain points, and goals of the individual account.

Crafting an account-specific UVP:

- Highlight how your product or service solves the account's unique challenges.

- Emphasize the potential benefits, such as cost savings, increased efficiency, revenue growth, or improved customer experience.

- Tailor your UVP to resonate with the specific decision-makers you are targeting. For example, if you're addressing a CFO, focus on financial benefits like ROI and cost reduction. For a CTO, emphasize technical integrations, scalability, and innovation.

Example: If you're targeting a retail company looking to improve its e-commerce operations, your account-specific UVP might focus on how your product can enhance their online customer experience, increase website conversion rates, and provide detailed analytics for data-driven decision-making.

3.   Develop personalized content and campaigns

With your UVP in place, design **personalized content and campaigns** that speak directly to the account's needs and interests. The goal is to create a series of touchpoints that guide them through the customer journey, from awareness to decision, in a way that feels relevant and valuable.

Types of personalized content:

- **Custom emails:** Craft personalized email outreach for key stakeholders within the account. Reference specific pain points, industry challenges, or recent news related to their company to demonstrate that you've tailored your message.

- **Account-specific landing pages:** Create dedicated landing pages for each target account. These pages should highlight the benefits of your product in the context of their specific needs, include case studies from similar companies, and offer tailored CTAs, such as booking a demo or downloading a customized guide.

- **Tailored content assets:** Develop content assets designed specifically for the account, such as whitepapers, reports, or videos. For example, create a detailed case study showing how your product helped a similar company achieve its goals, or produce a video walkthrough that addresses the account's unique use case.

- **Direct mail and gifting:** In some cases, direct mail or gifting can be a powerful way to capture attention and build rapport. Send a customized gift or resource that aligns with the account's industry or challenges. For instance, a technology company might send a branded notebook along with a personalized letter discussing how your software can streamline their operations.

4.   Personalize outreach and engagement

Personalization extends beyond content; it also involves the way you **interact** with target accounts. Use multiple channels and personalized outreach tactics to engage with key decision-makers and influencers.

Personalized engagement tactics:

- **Social media engagement:** Follow and engage with key stakeholders on platforms like LinkedIn. Share relevant content, comment on their posts, and participate in industry discussions to build visibility and rapport.

- **Customized product demos:** Offer personalized product demos that focus on the account's specific needs. Highlight the features and capabilities most relevant to their business, showing how your product can solve their unique challenges.

- **Events and webinars:** Invite target accounts to exclusive events, webinars, or roundtable discussions. Tailor the event content to address their industry trends, pain points, and opportunities, positioning your brand as a thought leader in their space.

5.   Coordinate with sales for tailored follow-ups

ABM requires close collaboration between marketing and sales. After initiating personalized campaigns, work with your sales team to plan **tailored follow-ups** based on the account's engagement.

Key collaboration strategies:

- **Share insights:** Provide sales with detailed insights from marketing interactions, such as which content assets the account engaged with or what pain points they expressed interest in. This information allows sales to tailor their follow-up conversations effectively.

- **Joint strategy sessions:** Hold regular strategy sessions with the sales team to review the progress of each target account, adjust tactics, and identify new opportunities for engagement.

- **Custom proposals:** When the account reaches the decision stage, collaborate with sales to develop a custom proposal or presentation that addresses the account's specific needs, goals, and objections.

6. Measure and refine your personalized strategy

To maximize the effectiveness of your personalized strategies, track key metrics and analyze the performance of your ABM campaigns. Look at engagement metrics such as email open rates, landing page visits, content downloads, meeting requests, and the progression of accounts through the funnel. Use these insights to refine your approach, test new tactics, and continuously improve your ABM efforts.

Example of a personalized ABM strategy in action

Imagine you're marketing a cybersecurity software solution, and one of your target accounts is a large financial institution. Here's how you might develop a personalized strategy:

1. **Research:** You learn that the institution is expanding its digital banking services and is concerned about data security and compliance. The key stakeholders are the CISO (Chief Information Security Officer) and the Head of IT.

2. **Account-specific UVP:** You craft a UVP highlighting how your software provides advanced threat detection and compliance monitoring tailored to the banking sector's regulatory requirements.

3. **Personalized content:** Create a whitepaper on "Top Cybersecurity Challenges in Digital Banking" and feature it on a custom landing page with the bank's logo and messaging aligned with their industry challenges.

4.   **Outreach:** Send a personalized email to the CISO, referencing recent industry news on data breaches and inviting them to a webinar on "Enhancing Data Security in Financial Services." Follow up with a LinkedIn message to the Head of IT, sharing insights from the whitepaper.

5.   **Customized demo:** Offer a product demo tailored to the bank's specific concerns, showcasing how your software can integrate seamlessly with their existing systems and enhance data protection.

6.   **Measure and refine:** Track engagement metrics, such as webinar attendance, content downloads, and demo requests. Use these insights to inform your ongoing interactions and refine your approach based on what resonates most with the account.

The bottom line: personalization drives meaningful engagement

Developing personalized strategies for high-value accounts is the essence of ABM. By understanding each account's unique needs, crafting targeted content, and engaging through tailored interactions, you create meaningful connections that set the stage for successful, long-term relationships. Remember, the goal of ABM is not just to close deals but to build trust and demonstrate that your product is the best fit for solving their challenges.

Tools and techniques to implement ABM at scale

Account-Based Marketing (ABM) relies heavily on personalization, targeted messaging, and close collaboration between sales and marketing teams. While the approach can be incredibly effective, scaling ABM across numerous high-value accounts can be a daunting task. How do you maintain the level of personalization required for ABM without overwhelming your resources?

The key to implementing ABM at scale lies in leveraging **the right tools and techniques** to streamline processes, automate tasks, and gather insights. By combining advanced technology with thoughtful strategies, you can effectively scale your ABM efforts without sacrificing the personalized touch that makes them successful.

The essentials of ABM at scale

Scaling ABM means extending your reach to a broader set of high-value accounts while still delivering the tailored experiences that resonate with decision-makers. To do this, you need to:

1. **Segment target accounts:** Use a tiered approach to categorize target accounts based on their value, potential revenue, and strategic importance. This allows you to allocate resources and personalize interactions appropriately, focusing more effort on the highest-value accounts while employing broader strategies for others.

2. **Automate where possible:** Automation is crucial for handling repetitive tasks, managing data, and delivering personalized content at scale.

3. **Leverage data and analytics:** Data is at the core of ABM. Utilize analytics to track engagement, measure performance, and refine your strategies for each account.

Top ABM tools for scaling your efforts

Here's a breakdown of some of the top tools that can help you implement and scale your ABM strategy effectively:

1. **Customer Relationship Management (CRM) systems:** CRMs like **Salesforce**, **HubSpot**, and **Zoho CRM** serve

as the backbone of your ABM efforts. They house detailed information about your target accounts, including company size, industry, contact history, engagement levels, and more.

> o   **How to use CRMs for ABM:** Use your CRM to create detailed account profiles, segment your target accounts into tiers, and track every interaction with key decision-makers. Integrate your CRM with marketing automation tools to align marketing and sales efforts seamlessly, ensuring that all teams have access to up-to-date account insights.

2. **Marketing automation platforms:** Tools like **Marketo**, **HubSpot**, **Pardot**, and **ActiveCampaign** allow you to automate and personalize email campaigns, landing pages, and workflows for different account segments.

> o   **How to use marketing automation for ABM:** Set up personalized email drip campaigns that are triggered based on specific account behaviors, such as content downloads or website visits. Create dynamic content blocks in emails and landing pages that change based on account characteristics, such as industry or job role, to provide a tailored experience.

3. **Account targeting and engagement platforms:** Platforms like **Demandbase**, **6sense**, **Terminus**, and **RollWorks** specialize in account-based targeting and engagement. These tools use AI and data analytics to identify target accounts, track their online behavior, and deliver personalized advertising and messaging.

> o   **How to use targeting platforms for ABM:** Identify high-value accounts showing intent signals (e.g., researching relevant keywords,

visiting your website) and use this data to prioritize outreach. Serve targeted ads to decision-makers within these accounts across display, social media, and search channels. These platforms also provide insights into account engagement, allowing you to adjust your strategies in real time.

4. **Personalization and content creation tools:** ABM requires a high degree of content personalization. Tools like **Uberflip**, **PathFactory**, and **Outgrow** allow you to create personalized content hubs, interactive experiences, and account-specific landing pages that speak directly to your target accounts.

   o **How to use personalization tools for ABM:** Create content hubs that are dynamically tailored to each account's interests and behavior. For example, if an account interacts with content related to cybersecurity, serve them additional resources like whitepapers, case studies, and webinars that delve deeper into cybersecurity solutions. Personalization tools also help you track content consumption patterns to gain insights into account preferences.

5. **Sales enablement platforms:** Tools like **Outreach**, **SalesLoft**, and **Highspot** enable your sales team to engage with accounts more effectively. These platforms provide sales reps with insights, automated sequences, and content libraries tailored to specific account needs.

   o **How to use sales enablement for ABM:** Equip your sales team with tailored email templates, call scripts, and content recommendations based on account segmentation and engagement history. Automate follow-up sequences for outreach efforts to ensure timely and consistent communication.

6. **Analytics and reporting tools:** To measure the success of your ABM efforts, use analytics tools like **Google Analytics**, **Tableau**, **Power BI**, and the analytics features within your CRM or marketing automation platform. These tools help you track key metrics, analyze account engagement, and optimize your strategies.

    o   **How to use analytics for ABM:** Set up custom dashboards that track account-level metrics such as website visits, email engagement, content downloads, ad impressions, and sales interactions. Use this data to identify high-engagement accounts, refine your messaging, and adjust your tactics based on what resonates most with your target accounts.

Techniques to implement ABM at scale

Alongside the right tools, certain techniques are essential for effectively scaling your ABM efforts while maintaining a personalized touch:

1. **Tiered account segmentation:** Not all accounts require the same level of personalization. Use a tiered segmentation approach to categorize accounts into different levels of value and strategic importance:

    o   **Tier 1:** High-value accounts that receive full, one-to-one personalization. These accounts are the top priority for sales and marketing teams, receiving highly customized content, outreach, and engagement strategies.
    o   **Tier 2:** Mid-value accounts that receive one-to-few personalization. For these accounts, you create tailored campaigns for groups of accounts with similar characteristics, such as industry or company size.

o   **Tier 3:** Lower-value accounts that receive one-to-many personalization. Use automated, scalable tactics like targeted ads, dynamic emails, and content hubs to engage these accounts efficiently.

2. This tiered approach allows you to allocate resources wisely, focusing intensive efforts on your most valuable accounts while scaling engagement with a broader set.

3. **Dynamic content and personalization tokens:** Use dynamic content and personalization tokens within your marketing automation platform to scale personalized messaging. These tools automatically insert account-specific information (e.g., company name, industry) into emails, landing pages, and ads, creating a tailored experience for each account without manual effort.

4. **Intent data monitoring:** Use intent data platforms like **Bombora** and **G2** to monitor target accounts for signs of buying intent. These platforms track online behavior, such as searches for relevant keywords or engagement with industry content, to signal when an account is in the market for your solution.

    o   **How to leverage intent data:** Identify accounts displaying high intent signals and prioritize them for outreach. Use this data to tailor your messaging and timing, reaching out when the account is most likely to be receptive.

5. **Orchestrated multi-channel campaigns:** Implement multi-channel campaigns that coordinate messaging across email, social media, ads, and direct outreach. Use your marketing automation platform to create workflows that automatically deliver personalized content based on account engagement.

o **Example:** If a target account visits your website and downloads an industry report, trigger a sequence of personalized follow-up emails, targeted LinkedIn ads, and sales outreach tailored to the account's interests. By orchestrating your efforts across multiple channels, you create a cohesive and consistent experience for the account.

6. **Account scoring and prioritization:** Use an account scoring model to rank target accounts based on criteria such as engagement level, firmographic data, and intent signals. This scoring helps your team prioritize high-potential accounts for more personalized efforts while automating engagement for lower-priority accounts.

Measuring the success of ABM at scale

Scaling ABM requires ongoing measurement and optimization. Key metrics to track include:

- **Account engagement:** Measure engagement metrics such as website visits, email opens, content downloads, and event participation for each target account.

- **Pipeline influence:** Assess how your ABM efforts contribute to pipeline creation, deal progression, and closing rates. Track which accounts move through the funnel and how ABM activities impact their journey.

- **Deal size and velocity:** Analyze whether ABM leads to larger deal sizes and shorter sales cycles compared to traditional marketing tactics.

- **Customer lifetime value (CLV):** Monitor the lifetime value of accounts acquired through ABM to evaluate the long-term impact of your strategy.

The bottom line: scaling ABM with technology and strategy

Scaling ABM doesn't mean sacrificing the personalization that makes it effective. By using a combination of tools—like CRM systems, marketing automation platforms, account targeting solutions, and analytics software—and employing techniques such as tiered segmentation and dynamic content, you can extend your ABM strategy to a broader set of high-value accounts. This blend of technology and thoughtful strategy allows you to maintain the tailored experiences that resonate with decision-makers while achieving the scalability needed for sustained growth.

C H A P T E R   6

Customer-centric growth: putting the customer at the heart of your strategy

The importance of customer centricity in growth marketing

In today's competitive business landscape, customers are no longer simply purchasing products or services; they are seeking meaningful experiences and relationships with the brands they choose. As a result, **customer-centric growth marketing** has emerged as a critical strategy for companies looking to build long-term, sustainable growth. Customer centricity is about putting the customer at the heart of every decision, interaction, and strategy, ensuring that your marketing efforts align with their needs, preferences, and desires.

Unlike traditional marketing strategies that often prioritize sales targets and product features, a customer-centric approach focuses on delivering value to customers at every stage of their journey. This shift in perspective transforms how companies engage with their audience, driving stronger customer loyalty, higher retention rates, and increased advocacy. In essence, customer-centric growth is not just about acquiring new customers; it's about creating exceptional experiences that turn customers into lifelong advocates for your brand.

What does it mean to be customer-centric?

Customer centricity is more than just a marketing buzzword; it's a mindset that permeates every aspect of a company's operations. Being customer-centric means understanding your customers' needs, challenges, and goals, and using this insight to shape your product development, marketing strategies, and customer interactions.

Key characteristics of a customer-centric approach:

1. **Empathy:** A deep understanding of your customers' pain points, motivations, and aspirations is at the core of customer centricity. This empathy drives the creation of products, services, and marketing campaigns that resonate with customers on a personal level.

2. **Proactive engagement:** Customer-centric companies don't wait for customers to come to them with problems. They actively seek feedback, listen to customer concerns, and anticipate needs before they arise, offering solutions that enhance the overall experience.

3. **Personalization:** Delivering personalized experiences is a hallmark of customer-centric growth. By leveraging customer data and insights, companies tailor their interactions, content, and product offerings to meet the unique preferences of each customer.

4. **Customer feedback integration:** Customer-centric organizations use customer feedback as a valuable input for decision-making. They incorporate feedback into product development, marketing strategies, and customer support processes to continually improve and align with customer expectations.

5. **Long-term relationships:** Rather than focusing solely on one-time sales, customer-centric companies prioritize building long-term relationships. They understand that loyal customers not only drive repeat business but also become brand advocates, referring new customers and contributing to sustainable growth.

Why customer centricity is essential for growth marketing

A customer-centric approach is crucial for growth marketing because it transforms the way you attract, engage, and retain customers. Here's why customer centricity matters for growth:

1. **Higher customer retention:** Acquiring new customers is often more expensive than retaining existing ones. By putting the customer at the center of your strategy and providing exceptional experiences, you foster loyalty and increase retention rates. Retained customers are more likely to make repeat purchases, upgrade their services, and contribute to your revenue over time.

2. **Positive word-of-mouth and referrals:** Satisfied customers are more likely to become advocates for your brand, sharing their positive experiences with friends, family, and colleagues. In the digital age, word-of-mouth has become even more powerful, as customers share reviews, testimonials, and social media posts that can significantly influence potential buyers.

3. **Increased customer lifetime value (CLV):** When you focus on delivering value to customers throughout their journey, you increase their lifetime value. Loyal customers are more likely to engage with upsells, cross-sells, and premium offerings, contributing to a higher CLV and driving sustainable growth.

4. **Improved customer experience (CX):** Customer-centric growth marketing emphasizes the importance of creating a

seamless, positive experience at every touchpoint. By optimizing the customer experience, you reduce friction, increase satisfaction, and encourage customers to stay engaged with your brand.

5.   **Better product-market fit:** Customer feedback and insights play a vital role in refining your product offerings. By listening to customers and understanding their evolving needs, you can continuously improve your products and services to achieve a better product-market fit, leading to higher adoption rates and customer satisfaction.

Building a customer-centric growth strategy

Transitioning to a customer-centric growth strategy requires a shift in mindset, processes, and metrics. Here's how to build a strategy that puts the customer at the center of your growth efforts:

1.   Understand your customer journey

The first step in building a customer-centric strategy is to map out the **customer journey**. This journey includes all the touchpoints and interactions that customers have with your brand, from the initial awareness stage to post-purchase and advocacy.

Key actions:

- **Identify key touchpoints:** Determine where and how customers interact with your brand across various channels, such as your website, social media, email, customer support, and in-store visits.

- **Gather customer insights:** Use customer data, surveys, interviews, and analytics to gain a deep understanding of customer behavior, preferences, and pain points at each stage of the journey.

- **Pinpoint opportunities for improvement:** Analyze the customer journey to identify friction points, gaps, and areas where you can enhance the experience. Use these insights to inform your marketing strategies, content creation, and product development.

2. Leverage customer data for personalization

Personalization is a key aspect of customer-centric growth. By leveraging customer data, such as purchase history, browsing behavior, and preferences, you can tailor your marketing efforts to meet each customer's unique needs.

How to personalize customer interactions:

- **Segment your audience:** Use customer data to segment your audience based on characteristics such as demographics, behavior, purchase history, and engagement level. This segmentation allows you to create targeted campaigns that resonate with specific customer groups.

- **Customize content:** Deliver personalized content, offers, and recommendations based on customer behavior and preferences. For example, send tailored product suggestions in follow-up emails, offer personalized discounts, or create content that addresses individual pain points.

- **Automate personalized communication:** Use marketing automation tools to send personalized emails, notifications, and messages at the right time, based on customer actions and engagement signals. Automated workflows ensure that customers receive relevant information throughout their journey.

3. Proactively seek and act on customer feedback

Customer feedback is a valuable source of insights that can drive product improvements, marketing strategies, and customer experience enhancements. Proactively gathering and acting on feedback demonstrates that you value your customers' opinions and are committed to meeting their needs.

Best practices for gathering customer feedback:

- **Surveys and questionnaires:** Use surveys to collect feedback on customer satisfaction, product features, support experiences, and overall brand perception. Tools like SurveyMonkey, Typeform, and Google Forms make it easy to gather and analyze feedback.

- **Customer reviews and testimonials:** Encourage customers to leave reviews and share their experiences on your website, social media, or review platforms. Use this feedback to identify strengths, address concerns, and build social proof.

- **Direct outreach:** Reach out to customers directly, especially after key interactions, such as product purchases or customer support interactions. Personal follow-ups show that you care about their experience and are open to feedback.

4. Enhance the customer experience (CX) at every touchpoint

Customer experience is a critical factor in customer-centric growth. A positive, seamless experience at every touchpoint increases satisfaction, builds trust, and fosters loyalty.

How to optimize CX:

- **Simplify interactions:** Make it easy for customers to interact with your brand, whether they are browsing your website, making a purchase, or reaching out for support. Ensure that your website is user-friendly, mobile-responsive, and easy to navigate.

- **Offer omnichannel support:** Provide multiple support channels, such as live chat, email, phone, and social media, to meet customers where they are. Ensure that your support team is responsive, knowledgeable, and empowered to resolve issues promptly.

- **Deliver value through content:** Create content that provides real value to your customers, whether it's educational resources, how-to guides, product updates, or industry insights. Valuable content reinforces your brand's authority and builds trust with your audience.

5. **Prioritize long-term relationships over short-term sales**

A customer-centric approach prioritizes building **long-term relationships** rather than focusing solely on one-time sales. Loyal customers are more likely to become repeat buyers, refer others, and provide valuable feedback that can drive ongoing improvements.

Tactics for building long-term relationships:

- **Onboarding:** Provide an excellent onboarding experience for new customers, guiding them through product features, tips, and best practices to help them get the most out of their purchase.

- **Loyalty programs:** Create a customer loyalty program that rewards repeat purchases, referrals, and engagement. Loyalty programs not only incentivize ongoing interactions but also make customers feel valued and appreciated.

- **Regular communication:** Maintain regular communication with customers through newsletters, product updates, and personalized offers. Keeping customers informed and engaged strengthens the relationship and encourages loyalty.

Examples of customer-centric brands

Amazon is a prime example of a customer-centric brand. From personalized product recommendations to a seamless checkout process and reliable customer support, Amazon prioritizes the customer experience at every stage. Their commitment to fast, convenient shipping and hassle-free returns further solidifies their reputation as a customer-focused company.

Spotify is another brand that excels in customer centricity. By using customer data to create personalized playlists, music recommendations, and year-end wrap-ups, Spotify delivers a unique, engaging experience tailored to each user's preferences. This level of personalization not only enhances user satisfaction but also fosters loyalty and advocacy.

The bottom line: putting the customer first drives growth

Customer-centric growth marketing is about more than just meeting sales targets; it's about building lasting relationships and delivering value to your customers at every stage of their journey. By putting the customer at the heart of your strategy—understanding their needs, personalizing interactions, seeking feedback, and enhancing their experience—you create a loyal customer base that drives sustainable growth through repeat business and advocacy.

Building strategies around customer feedback, needs, and desires

One of the most powerful assets a company can have in its growth marketing toolkit is a deep understanding of its customers' needs, desires, and feedback. In a customer-centric approach, growth strategies are not based solely on assumptions or internal ideas but are shaped and refined by actively listening to customers. By collecting and analyzing customer feedback, you gain valuable insights into their pain points, preferences, and expectations. These insights then become the foundation for strategies that deliver real value, build loyalty, and drive sustainable growth.

Why customer feedback is the cornerstone of growth

Customer feedback is more than just opinions; it's a direct line to understanding how your product or service fits into the lives of your customers. By tapping into this resource, you uncover:

- **Pain points:** Identifying common customer frustrations or challenges allows you to develop solutions that directly address these issues.

- **Unmet needs:** Feedback can reveal gaps in your offerings or areas where customers feel something is lacking, guiding product improvements or new feature development.

- **Preferences and desires:** Understanding what customers value most helps you tailor your marketing messages, product features, and customer experiences to align with their desires.

- **Customer sentiment:** Feedback provides insights into how customers perceive your brand, allowing you to adjust strategies to strengthen positive sentiment and address negative perceptions.

Collecting customer feedback: channels and techniques

To build strategies around customer feedback, you first need to collect it systematically. There are various channels and methods to gather feedback, each providing different types of insights:

1. **Surveys and questionnaires:** Use surveys to gather structured feedback from a broad audience. Surveys can cover various topics, such as product satisfaction, customer experience, feature requests, and brand perception. Tools like **SurveyMonkey**, **Typeform**, and **Google Forms** make it easy to create and distribute surveys.
   Best practices for surveys:

   - Keep surveys concise to encourage participation.
   - Use a mix of quantitative (e.g., rating scales, multiple-choice) and qualitative (e.g., open-ended questions) questions to capture both measurable data and in-depth insights.
   - Segment respondents based on criteria such as customer journey stage, purchase history, or demographics to analyze feedback from different customer segments.

2. **Customer interviews and focus groups:** Direct conversations with customers provide rich, qualitative insights into their experiences, needs, and perceptions. Customer interviews and focus groups allow you to delve deeper into specific topics, exploring emotions, motivations, and attitudes that surveys may not capture.
   How to conduct effective interviews:

   - Prepare a list of open-ended questions that encourage customers to share detailed feedback.
   - Use follow-up questions to explore topics further and uncover underlying issues or desires.

o   Listen actively and avoid leading questions that might bias responses.

3. **Feedback forms and widgets:** Integrate feedback forms or widgets on your website or within your app to collect real-time feedback from users as they interact with your product. These tools enable customers to provide input quickly and easily, offering valuable insights into the user experience.

4. **Social listening:** Monitor social media platforms, forums, review sites, and community discussions to gauge customer sentiment and identify common themes in customer feedback. Tools like **Hootsuite**, **Sprout Social**, and **Brandwatch** help you track brand mentions, customer comments, and industry conversations.
Social listening insights: Social media is a valuable source of unfiltered feedback, where customers often share candid opinions, frustrations, and desires. By listening to these conversations, you gain a deeper understanding of customer attitudes and preferences.

5. **Customer support interactions:** Customer support teams are on the front lines of customer interactions and often have valuable insights into common questions, issues, and feedback. Regularly review support tickets, chat transcripts, and call logs to identify recurring themes and areas for improvement.

6. **Net Promoter Score (NPS):** Use NPS surveys to measure customer satisfaction and loyalty. NPS asks customers how likely they are to recommend your product or service to others, providing a quick snapshot of customer sentiment. Follow up with open-ended questions to gather more detailed feedback.

Analyzing feedback to uncover actionable insights

Collecting feedback is just the beginning. To build effective strategies around customer feedback, you need to analyze the data and extract actionable insights that guide your decisions.

Steps for analyzing customer feedback:

1. **Organize feedback:** Categorize feedback into themes or topics, such as product features, customer service, pricing, user experience, or marketing messages. This categorization makes it easier to identify patterns and prioritize areas for action.

2. **Identify common pain points and desires:** Look for recurring issues, requests, or desires mentioned by customers. Are there specific features they consistently ask for? Are there aspects of the customer experience that regularly receive complaints? Identifying these patterns helps you focus on the most impactful improvements.

3. **Segment insights by customer type:** Analyze feedback based on customer segments, such as new customers, long-term customers, or high-value accounts. This segmentation reveals unique needs and preferences within different groups, enabling you to tailor strategies for each segment.

4. **Prioritize actions:** Use the insights gathered to prioritize the most critical actions that will address customer pain points, fulfill unmet needs, or enhance the customer experience. Prioritization can be based on factors like impact, feasibility, and alignment with your growth goals.

Building customer-centric strategies based on feedback

Once you have a clear understanding of your customers' needs and desires, use these insights to shape your growth strategies across various aspects of your business:

1. Product development and innovation

Customer feedback is a goldmine of information for refining your product and developing new features that address unmet needs. Incorporating customer input into your product roadmap ensures that your offerings align with market demands and provide real value.

Examples of feedback-driven product strategies:

- **Feature prioritization:** If customers frequently request a specific feature, prioritize its development to enhance the product's value proposition. For example, a SaaS company might add an integration with a popular CRM system if multiple customers express the need for seamless data transfer.

- **Product improvements:** Use feedback to identify pain points in the user experience, such as complex navigation or slow loading times. Implementing improvements based on these insights can significantly enhance customer satisfaction and retention.

2. Personalized marketing campaigns

Feedback insights help you understand your customers' preferences, interests, and pain points, allowing you to create highly targeted and personalized marketing campaigns.

How to use feedback for marketing:

- **Content creation:** Develop content that addresses common questions, challenges, or misconceptions identified through customer feedback. For example, if customers express confusion about a specific feature, create a blog post or video tutorial that explains its benefits and use cases.

- **Segmentation:** Use feedback to segment your audience based on interests, behavior, or stage in the customer journey. Tailor your messaging and offers to resonate with each segment, improving engagement and conversion rates.

3. Enhanced customer experience (CX)

Improving the customer experience is a key driver of customer satisfaction and loyalty. Use feedback to identify areas of friction in the customer journey and implement changes that create a smoother, more enjoyable experience.

CX enhancements based on feedback:

- **Streamline processes:** If customers indicate that the checkout process is cumbersome, simplify it by reducing the number of steps, offering more payment options, or improving mobile responsiveness.

- **Proactive support:** If feedback reveals common issues or questions, update your support resources, such as FAQs, knowledge bases, and onboarding guides, to address these topics proactively.

4. Retention and loyalty programs

Customer feedback can inform strategies for retaining existing customers and fostering brand loyalty. By understanding what customers value and enjoy, you can design loyalty programs, rewards, and engagement tactics that keep them coming back.

Loyalty-building strategies:

- **Reward feedback participation:** Show customers that their input is valued by offering incentives, such as discounts or exclusive access to new features, for providing feedback.
- **Personalized loyalty offers:** Use insights from feedback to create loyalty offers that align with customer preferences. For example, if a segment of your customer base prefers eco-friendly products, offer them early access to a new sustainable product line.

Examples of feedback-driven companies

Slack is a prime example of a company that actively listens to its customers and incorporates their feedback into its product strategy. By engaging with users through direct feedback, surveys, and community forums, Slack continuously refines its platform, adding features like custom integrations, new messaging options, and workflow automation to meet users' evolving needs.

Airbnb also excels in leveraging customer feedback. The company uses reviews, surveys, and support interactions to gain insights into guest and host experiences. This feedback shapes Airbnb's platform updates, such as implementing new security features, improving the booking process, and creating educational resources for hosts.

The bottom line: feedback as a growth driver

Building strategies around customer feedback, needs, and desires is a powerful way to create products, services, and experiences that resonate with your audience. By actively listening to your customers, analyzing their input, and incorporating it into your growth strategies, you foster deeper connections, enhance customer satisfaction, and drive sustainable growth. In a customer-centric world, feedback is not just a tool for improvement—it's a roadmap to success.

Creating emotional connections and building brand loyalty

In a marketplace where products and services are often indistinguishable in terms of features and pricing, **emotional connections** have become a key differentiator. Customers are not just looking for transactions; they seek brands that align with their values, understand their needs, and foster genuine relationships. Creating an emotional connection with customers goes beyond the functional aspects of your product or service—it's about building trust, offering memorable experiences, and demonstrating that your brand cares about their well-being.

Emotional connections drive **brand loyalty**, turning one-time buyers into repeat customers and advocates. Loyal customers are more forgiving of mistakes, less sensitive to price changes, and more likely to refer others to your brand. In growth marketing, focusing on creating these deep, emotional connections can transform your customer base into a powerful engine for sustained growth.

Why emotional connections matter

Emotional connections are rooted in the psychological and emotional experiences customers have with your brand. When customers feel emotionally connected, they are more likely to choose your brand over competitors, even when there are similar options available. Here's why emotional connections are essential for building loyalty:

1. **Increased customer retention:** Emotionally connected customers are more loyal and less likely to switch to

competitors. They have a strong attachment to your brand and feel that it meets their needs on a deeper level.

2. **Higher customer lifetime value (CLV):** Loyal customers tend to spend more over time, whether through repeat purchases, upsells, or cross-sells. They are also more likely to explore new products and services offered by your brand, increasing their lifetime value.

3. **Positive word-of-mouth:** Customers who feel an emotional connection with your brand become advocates, spreading positive word-of-mouth and referrals. Their genuine enthusiasm and trust in your brand influence others' purchasing decisions, helping you acquire new customers.

4. **Reduced price sensitivity:** Emotionally connected customers are less likely to be swayed by competitors' discounts or lower prices. They perceive the value of your brand as more than just the sum of its products, making them willing to pay a premium for the relationship and experience you provide.

How to create emotional connections with your customers

Building emotional connections requires a deliberate focus on the **customer experience**, **brand values**, and meaningful interactions that resonate with your audience. Here are strategies to help you create these connections and foster brand loyalty:

1. **Define and communicate your brand values**

Your **brand values** serve as the foundation for creating emotional connections. They represent what your brand stands for, how it operates, and what it aims to achieve beyond profit. Customers are increasingly seeking brands that align with their values, whether it's sustainability, inclusivity, innovation, or community support.

How to leverage brand values:

- **Identify your values:** Define the core values that represent your brand's identity and mission. Consider what matters most to your customers and how your brand can make a positive impact in their lives and the world.

- **Communicate your values:** Clearly communicate your brand values through your messaging, content, and actions. Highlight your values on your website, social media, and marketing campaigns to showcase what you stand for.

- **Live your values:** It's not enough to state your values; you must live them in your business practices. For example, if sustainability is a core value, take tangible steps to implement eco-friendly practices in your operations, products, and packaging.

Example: Patagonia, the outdoor apparel brand, is known for its commitment to environmental sustainability. The company's "Worn Wear" program encourages customers to buy used gear and repair their existing clothing rather than buying new. By aligning their brand values with their actions, Patagonia builds strong emotional connections with environmentally conscious customers who share their values.

2. Create personalized experiences

Personalization is a powerful way to show customers that you understand and value their unique preferences, needs, and desires. When customers feel that your brand knows them on a personal level, it strengthens their emotional connection.

How to personalize customer experiences:

- **Use customer data:** Leverage customer data, such as purchase history, browsing behavior, and interactions, to tailor recommendations, offers, and content. For example, send personalized product suggestions based on a customer's previous purchases or create email campaigns that address their specific interests.

- **Customize interactions:** Make every interaction with your brand feel personalized, whether it's through targeted emails, tailored website experiences, or one-on-one customer support. Address customers by their names, acknowledge their preferences, and provide support that's relevant to their individual needs.

Example: Spotify's annual "Wrapped" campaign is a prime example of personalized experiences. By showing users their most-listened-to songs, artists, and genres, Spotify creates a unique, personal recap that resonates with each user's musical journey. This personalized touch strengthens emotional bonds and encourages users to share their experiences, further promoting brand loyalty.

3.   Engage with customers authentically

Authentic engagement is about creating genuine, meaningful interactions with your customers. Whether it's responding to comments on social media, sharing behind-the-scenes content, or simply listening to customer feedback, authentic engagement humanizes your brand and builds trust.

Ways to engage authentically:

- **Show your brand's human side:** Use storytelling to showcase your brand's journey, culture, and team members. Share behind-the-scenes looks at your company, highlight the people behind your products, and celebrate milestones. This transparency helps customers connect with your brand on a personal level.

- **Listen and respond:** Actively listen to customer feedback, both positive and negative, and respond thoughtfully. Acknowledge customer concerns, show empathy, and take steps to address issues. When customers see that you care about their opinions and are willing to take action, it fosters trust and loyalty.

Example: Zappos, the online shoe retailer, is renowned for its exceptional customer service and authentic engagement. Their customer support team goes above and beyond to assist customers, often engaging in friendly, meaningful conversations rather than simply following scripted responses. This commitment to authenticity has earned Zappos a loyal customer base that appreciates the brand's customer-first approach.

4.   Deliver memorable experiences

A memorable customer experience leaves a lasting impression and strengthens the emotional connection customers have with your brand. This involves not only meeting their expectations but exceeding them in ways that surprise and delight.

How to create memorable experiences:

- **Offer exceptional support:** Provide fast, friendly, and proactive customer support across all channels. Offer solutions before customers encounter problems, provide useful resources, and go the extra mile to resolve their concerns.

- **Surprise and delight:** Introduce unexpected moments of delight in the customer journey, such as sending a personalized thank-you note, offering a surprise discount, or including a small gift with their order. These gestures show that you value your customers and appreciate their loyalty.

Example: Chewy, the pet supply retailer, excels in delivering memorable experiences. When customers contact their support team with issues, Chewy often responds with more than just a solution—they may send a handwritten card, flowers, or even a custom pet portrait. These thoughtful gestures create emotional connections that turn customers into loyal advocates.

5.   Build a community around your brand

Creating a sense of **community** around your brand allows customers to feel that they are part of something bigger than just a transaction. A strong community fosters belonging, loyalty, and advocacy.

How to build a brand community:

- **Create engagement platforms:** Use social media groups, online forums, or branded events to bring customers together and encourage discussions. For example, create a Facebook group where customers can share experiences, ask questions, and connect with others who share their interests.

- **Involve customers:** Involve your community in your brand's journey. Seek their input on product development, invite them to participate in challenges, or highlight customer stories and testimonials. Making customers feel included strengthens their emotional connection with your brand.

Example: Glossier, the beauty brand, has built a passionate community of customers who actively engage with the brand and each other on social media. Glossier frequently features user-generated content, involves its community in product development, and hosts events that bring its customers together. This community-driven approach has created a loyal fan base that advocates for the brand.

Cultivating brand loyalty: turning customers into advocates

Once you have established an emotional connection with your customers, the next step is to **cultivate loyalty** that turns them into brand advocates. Here's how to foster and reward loyalty:

1. **Implement a loyalty program:** Create a customer loyalty program that rewards repeat purchases, referrals, and engagement. Offer points, discounts, exclusive access, or special gifts to incentivize ongoing interactions.

2. **Engage with customers post-purchase:** Continue engaging with customers after the sale. Send personalized follow-up emails, request feedback, and offer tips or guides to help them get the most out of their purchase. Ongoing engagement reinforces the relationship and encourages future interactions.

3. **Acknowledge and celebrate loyalty:** Recognize your most loyal customers and show appreciation for their support. Highlight their stories on your website or social media, send them exclusive gifts, or provide VIP access to new products or events. Acknowledging loyalty makes customers feel valued and deepens their connection to your brand.

The bottom line: emotional connections drive loyalty and growth

Creating emotional connections is at the heart of building brand loyalty. By understanding your customers' needs, aligning with their values, and delivering memorable experiences, you forge relationships that go beyond transactions. These emotional bonds not only encourage repeat business but also turn customers into enthusiastic advocates who help drive your brand's growth through word-of-mouth and referrals.

CHAPTER 7

Customer experience (CX) and user experience (UX) as growth drivers

The role of CX in customer retention and advocacy

In the current market landscape, where customers have more choices than ever before, **Customer Experience (CX)** has become a crucial differentiator. While product quality, pricing, and features are important, the experience customers have with your brand often determines whether they stay loyal or switch to a competitor. CX is more than just customer service; it encompasses every interaction a customer has with your brand, from the initial touchpoint to post-purchase engagement.

A positive customer experience fosters **retention** by building trust, satisfaction, and emotional connection. It also fuels **advocacy** by inspiring loyal customers to share their experiences and promote your brand to others. In essence, CX is a driving force behind sustainable growth, enabling companies to retain customers longer, increase lifetime value, and acquire new customers through word-of-mouth.

What is customer experience (CX)?

Customer Experience (CX) refers to the overall impression that customers have of your brand throughout their journey. It includes every interaction, whether it's browsing your website, engaging with your content, speaking with customer support, or using your product. A seamless, positive CX not only meets customer expectations but also delights them at every touchpoint.

Key components of CX:

1. **Ease of use:** How easy is it for customers to navigate your website, use your product, or find the information they need? Simplicity and intuitiveness are essential for creating a smooth customer journey.

2. **Consistency:** Consistency across channels—be it your website, mobile app, social media, or customer support—ensures that customers receive the same high-quality experience regardless of where they interact with your brand.

3. **Personalization:** Personalized interactions, such as tailored product recommendations, targeted messaging, and custom offers, enhance CX by showing customers that you understand and value their unique preferences.

4. **Emotional connection:** CX goes beyond functionality; it also involves creating an emotional bond with customers. Engaging content, empathetic support, and brand storytelling contribute to building a deeper connection.

The impact of CX on customer retention

A positive customer experience plays a pivotal role in customer retention. When customers feel valued and satisfied with their interactions, they are more likely to stay loyal to your brand, resulting in repeat purchases and long-term engagement. Here's how CX drives retention:

1. **Building trust and loyalty:** Consistently delivering a great experience fosters trust. Customers who trust your brand are more likely to return, as they feel confident that you will continue to meet or exceed their expectations. Over time, this trust develops into loyalty, turning casual buyers into repeat customers.
   Example: Apple has built a loyal customer base not only through innovative products but also by offering a seamless and intuitive customer experience. From the simplicity of its online store to the knowledgeable in-store support at the Genius Bar, Apple provides a consistent, high-quality experience that keeps customers coming back.

2. **Reducing churn:** A poor customer experience is a common reason for customer churn. Issues such as complicated checkout processes, slow customer support, and confusing product interfaces can lead to frustration and drive customers to seek alternatives. By optimizing CX to minimize friction, you reduce the risk of losing customers to competitors.
   Example: Amazon's emphasis on convenience—such as one-click ordering, fast shipping, and a hassle-free return policy—has made it a preferred choice for online shoppers. By addressing potential pain points, Amazon reduces customer churn and encourages ongoing engagement.

3. **Increasing customer lifetime value (CLV):** Satisfied customers are more likely to explore other products or services you offer, leading to increased cross-sell and upsell opportunities. The better the experience you provide, the more value customers see in continuing to engage with your brand, resulting in a higher CLV.
   Example: Starbucks leverages its mobile app to enhance

the customer experience, offering features like order-ahead, loyalty rewards, and personalized offers. This seamless experience not only drives repeat visits but also encourages customers to try new menu items, increasing their lifetime value.

CX as a driver of customer advocacy

Customer advocacy is a powerful growth driver. Advocates are customers who have had such positive experiences with your brand that they actively recommend it to others, becoming unpaid marketers. A well-crafted CX is the catalyst that turns satisfied customers into passionate advocates. Here's how CX fuels advocacy:

1. **Encouraging word-of-mouth referrals:** When customers have an exceptional experience with your brand, they naturally want to share it with friends, family, and colleagues. This word-of-mouth marketing is invaluable, as potential customers are more likely to trust recommendations from people they know.
    Example: Spotify's "Wrapped" campaign, which provides users with a personalized summary of their music listening habits for the year, creates a shareable and enjoyable experience. By allowing users to easily share their "Wrapped" results on social media, Spotify turns a positive user experience into a viral advocacy moment.

2. **Boosting social proof:** A positive customer experience often leads to glowing reviews, testimonials, and user-generated content. This social proof builds credibility and trust for your brand, influencing the decision-making of potential customers.
    Example: Glossier, the beauty brand, encourages customers to share their product experiences on social media. By featuring user-generated content on its website and social platforms, Glossier leverages authentic

customer stories to create social proof and attract new customers.

3. **Creating brand ambassadors:** Exceptional CX inspires customers to become brand ambassadors who actively promote your brand. These ambassadors don't just recommend products; they share your brand's values, mission, and story, deepening the emotional connection with others in their network.
    Example: Lululemon cultivates brand ambassadors by building a community around health, fitness, and mindfulness. Through events, collaborations, and social media engagement, Lululemon creates a sense of belonging that motivates customers to advocate for the brand both online and offline.

Strategies for enhancing CX to drive retention and advocacy

1. **Map the customer journey:** Start by mapping out the customer journey to understand the different touchpoints where customers interact with your brand. Identify areas where friction or confusion may occur, and prioritize improvements that create a smoother, more enjoyable experience.

2. **Listen to customer feedback:** Gather customer feedback through surveys, reviews, support interactions, and social media. Use this feedback to identify pain points, understand customer expectations, and make data-driven improvements to the customer experience.
    Example: Netflix continually gathers feedback on its interface and content recommendations. By analyzing viewing patterns and customer input, Netflix optimizes its platform to enhance the user experience, making it easier for customers to find content they love.

3. **Deliver omnichannel support:** Provide seamless customer support across various channels, including

email, chat, social media, and phone. Ensure that customers receive consistent, helpful, and timely responses, regardless of the channel they choose. **Example:** Zendesk's customer support platform enables companies to offer integrated support across multiple channels, providing a unified experience. When customers can switch between channels without repeating information, it enhances satisfaction and loyalty.

4. **Personalize interactions:** Use customer data to personalize interactions, recommendations, and offers. Tailoring the experience to individual preferences makes customers feel valued and understood, deepening their emotional connection to your brand.

5. **Reward advocacy:** Encourage and reward customer advocacy through referral programs, loyalty points, or recognition on social media. By acknowledging your advocates, you strengthen their bond with your brand and motivate them to continue spreading the word. **Example:** Dropbox's referral program rewards customers who refer friends with additional storage space. This simple incentive not only increases customer engagement but also turns satisfied customers into active brand promoters.

Measuring the impact of CX on retention and advocacy

To understand the effectiveness of your CX initiatives, track key metrics that indicate customer satisfaction, loyalty, and advocacy:

1. **Net Promoter Score (NPS):** NPS measures how likely customers are to recommend your brand to others. A high NPS indicates strong advocacy, while a low score suggests areas for improvement in the customer experience.

2. **Customer Satisfaction (CSAT) score:** CSAT surveys capture customer satisfaction at specific touchpoints, such

as after a support interaction or product purchase. Monitoring CSAT scores helps you identify areas of the customer journey that may need enhancement.

3. **Customer retention rate:** Track the percentage of customers who continue to engage with your brand over time. A high retention rate is a sign that your CX efforts are effective in keeping customers loyal.

4. **Churn rate:** Measure the rate at which customers stop using your product or service. A decreasing churn rate often indicates that improvements in CX are successfully addressing customer needs and reducing dissatisfaction.

The bottom line: CX as a growth multiplier

Customer experience is a powerful growth multiplier that influences customer retention, satisfaction, and advocacy. By prioritizing CX, you build trust, foster loyalty, and create advocates who help your brand grow through word-of-mouth. In today's competitive market, delivering a seamless, personalized, and delightful customer experience is not just a nice-to-have — it's a strategic imperative for sustainable growth.

Optimizing the digital experience: from websites to apps

In today's digital era, a brand's website and mobile app are often the first points of interaction for customers. The **digital experience** encompasses every touchpoint within these platforms, from the initial landing page to the checkout process and customer support. A well-optimized digital experience is critical for keeping customers engaged, meeting their needs efficiently, and providing the seamless interactions that modern consumers expect.

When executed effectively, an optimized digital experience not only enhances customer satisfaction but also influences key growth metrics, including customer retention, conversion rates, and lifetime value. Whether it's a website that effortlessly guides visitors to relevant content or an app that offers a personalized, intuitive interface, the digital experience can be the driving force behind customer loyalty and advocacy.

Why the digital experience matters for growth

A smooth, enjoyable digital experience directly impacts how customers perceive your brand. Here's why optimizing this experience is crucial for growth:

1. **First impressions:** Your website or app is often the first touchpoint customers have with your brand. A well-designed, user-friendly interface creates a positive first impression, building trust and encouraging users to explore further.

2. **Engagement:** An optimized digital experience keeps users engaged by providing relevant, personalized content, smooth navigation, and easy access to information or products. High engagement increases the likelihood of conversions and repeat visits.

3. **Retention:** A frustrating or confusing digital experience can lead to high bounce rates and customer churn. By offering a seamless, enjoyable digital journey, you encourage users to return and stay loyal to your brand.

4. **Competitive advantage:** In crowded markets, the quality of your digital experience can set you apart from competitors. Brands that prioritize UX often see higher customer satisfaction, stronger loyalty, and better growth outcomes.

Key elements of an optimized digital experience

To optimize your website and app experience, focus on key elements that drive user satisfaction, engagement, and conversion:

1.   Responsive and mobile-friendly design

In an age where users access digital platforms on various devices, a **responsive design** is essential. A mobile-friendly website or app adapts to different screen sizes, ensuring a consistent and user-friendly experience on smartphones, tablets, and desktops.

Best practices for responsive design:

- **Use flexible layouts:** Implement responsive design techniques, such as fluid grids and flexible images, to ensure that your website adjusts seamlessly to different screen sizes.

- **Optimize for touch:** On mobile devices, prioritize touch-friendly elements, such as larger buttons and easy-to-tap links. Avoid small or tightly spaced clickable areas that can frustrate users.

- **Simplify navigation:** Streamline your mobile navigation by using a collapsible menu (e.g., a "hamburger" menu) and limiting the number of menu items. Make it easy for users to find what they're looking for without excessive scrolling or clicking.

Example: Airbnb's website and mobile app offer a consistent, responsive experience. The platform's minimalist design, clear navigation, and mobile-friendly interface make it easy for users to browse listings, book accommodations, and manage reservations, whether they're using a smartphone, tablet, or desktop.

2.   Fast loading speed

Speed is a crucial factor in digital experience. Users expect websites and apps to load quickly, and even a few seconds of delay can result in higher bounce rates and lost conversions. Research shows that a one-second delay in page load time can lead to a significant drop in customer satisfaction.

How to improve loading speed:

- **Compress images:** Use image compression tools to reduce file sizes without sacrificing quality, ensuring that your website or app loads quickly on all devices.

- **Minimize code:** Reduce unnecessary code, scripts, and CSS files to streamline page rendering. Use minification tools to remove whitespace, comments, and redundant code.

- **Leverage caching:** Implement browser caching to store frequently accessed elements, such as images and stylesheets, locally on users' devices, reducing load times for returning visitors.

Example: Google's focus on speed is evident in its search engine and suite of products. With its minimalist design and optimized code, Google Search delivers instant results, setting a high standard for fast, efficient digital experiences.

3.   Intuitive navigation

Navigation is at the core of user experience. An intuitive navigation system guides users effortlessly through your website or app, helping them find the information, products, or features they need. When navigation is clear and logical, users are more likely to engage with your content and move through the conversion funnel.

Best practices for intuitive navigation:

- **Use a simple menu structure:** Keep your navigation menu simple and concise, grouping related content under clear, descriptive headings. Avoid overwhelming users with too many options.

- **Implement search functionality:** Include a prominent search bar on your website or app, enabling users to quickly find specific content, products, or information.

- **Provide breadcrumbs:** Use breadcrumb navigation to show users their current location within the website's structure, allowing them to easily retrace their steps.

Example: Shopify's website offers straightforward navigation with a clear menu structure, featuring categories like "Features," "Pricing," and "Resources." The search bar allows users to find relevant content quickly, while the use of clear calls-to-action guides visitors through the journey of building an online store.

4.   Personalization and dynamic content

Personalization is key to creating a digital experience that resonates with users. By delivering content, product recommendations, and offers tailored to each user's behavior, preferences, and history, you enhance engagement and satisfaction.

How to implement personalization:

- **Use data-driven recommendations:** Leverage customer data, such as browsing history and past purchases, to provide personalized product recommendations, content, or offers.

- **Dynamic content blocks:** Incorporate dynamic content blocks on your website or app that change based on user behavior. For example, show returning users recently viewed products or suggest related blog posts based on their interests.

- **Location-based customization:** Use geolocation data to tailor the experience, such as displaying local events, relevant shipping options, or region-specific promotions.

Example: Amazon's website and app are known for their highly personalized user experiences. Through data-driven algorithms, Amazon provides customized product recommendations, "Buy It Again" options, and tailored promotions based on each user's browsing and purchasing history.

5. **Clear calls-to-action (CTAs)**

Effective **CTAs** guide users toward desired actions, such as signing up for a newsletter, downloading a resource, or making a purchase. Clear, compelling CTAs help users understand what to do next and make it easy for them to take action.

CTA optimization tips:

- **Be specific:** Use action-oriented language that clearly conveys the benefit, such as "Get Your Free Guide" or "Start Your Free Trial." Avoid vague phrases like "Submit" or "Click Here."

- **Create visual contrast:** Design CTAs that stand out from the surrounding content by using contrasting colors, bold text, and sufficient whitespace.

- **Test placement:** Experiment with different CTA placements to find the most effective spots, whether it's above the fold, at the end of a blog post, or within the shopping cart page.

Example: Dropbox's website features prominent CTAs like "Sign up for free" and "Get started with Dropbox," paired with a simple, uncluttered design. The CTAs use contrasting colors and concise wording to guide users toward account creation and product exploration.

6.   Seamless checkout process

For e-commerce websites and apps, the **checkout process** is a critical part of the digital experience. A smooth, streamlined checkout minimizes friction and reduces cart abandonment rates, increasing the likelihood of conversion.

Checkout optimization strategies:

- **Enable guest checkout:** Allow users to make purchases without requiring them to create an account, reducing barriers to conversion for first-time customers.

- **Minimize form fields:** Keep the checkout form simple by asking for only essential information. Break the process into manageable steps if necessary, and use autofill options to speed up form completion.

- **Offer multiple payment options:** Provide a range of payment methods, including credit cards, digital wallets (e.g., PayPal, Apple Pay), and buy-now-pay-later services, to accommodate different user preferences.

Example: Shopify-powered stores often use a streamlined checkout process that offers autofill options, guest checkout, and multiple payment methods. This seamless approach reduces friction and makes it easy for customers to complete their purchases quickly.

Testing and optimizing the digital experience

Optimization is an ongoing process that requires regular testing, feedback gathering, and data analysis. Here's how to ensure your digital experience continues to meet customer expectations:

1. **A/B testing:** Conduct A/B tests on key elements, such as CTAs, landing pages, navigation menus, and forms, to determine which variations yield the best user engagement and conversion rates.

2. **Monitor analytics:** Use analytics tools like Google Analytics, Hotjar, and Mixpanel to track user behavior, identify pain points, and measure the effectiveness of changes.

3. **Collect user feedback:** Incorporate feedback mechanisms, such as surveys, feedback forms, or in-app messaging, to gather insights directly from users about their experience and areas for improvement.

The bottom line: seamless digital experiences drive growth

Optimizing the digital experience across websites and apps is essential for meeting customer expectations, enhancing engagement, and driving growth. By focusing on responsive design, fast loading speeds, intuitive navigation, personalization, effective CTAs, and a streamlined checkout process, you create a seamless journey that keeps users coming back and fosters brand loyalty. Remember, the digital experience is a reflection of your brand; investing in its optimization not only boosts satisfaction but also strengthens your competitive edge in the market.

User experience principles that drive conversions

User experience (UX) is more than just aesthetics; it's about creating an interface that is intuitive, efficient, and enjoyable for users. At its core, great UX is centered around understanding user needs, behaviors, and motivations, and then designing digital interactions that align with these insights. When done well, UX design leads users seamlessly through the customer journey, making it easier for them to take desired actions, such as signing up for a service, making a purchase, or completing a form.

For growth marketing, **driving conversions** is often a top priority. By applying UX principles that prioritize clarity, simplicity, and user-centricity, you can significantly improve conversion rates. Whether you're designing a website, landing page, or mobile app, these UX principles will help you create a path that guides users toward conversion while delivering a satisfying experience.

Why UX is key to conversions

A positive user experience directly impacts a user's willingness to engage with your brand and complete desired actions. Here's how UX drives conversions:

1. **Reduces friction:** Clear, intuitive design reduces obstacles that might otherwise prevent users from converting. By streamlining navigation, forms, and calls-to-action (CTAs), UX minimizes frustration and creates a smoother path to conversion.

2. **Builds trust:** A well-designed interface with a professional, consistent look and feel instills confidence in users. When customers trust your website or app, they are

more likely to provide personal information, make a purchase, or engage further.

3. **Enhances engagement:** UX that prioritizes relevance and interactivity keeps users engaged. Engaged users spend more time exploring your platform, increasing the chances of them taking the next step in the conversion funnel.

UX principles that drive conversions

1. Simplicity: less is more

One of the most effective ways to drive conversions is to **keep it simple**. A cluttered, overly complex interface can overwhelm users and lead to decision paralysis. By simplifying your design and focusing on the essentials, you create a clear path for users to follow.

How to apply simplicity in UX:

- **Limit distractions:** Minimize visual clutter by removing unnecessary elements, such as excessive graphics, ads, or links that may distract users from the primary conversion goal.

- **Use whitespace:** Incorporate sufficient whitespace around content, buttons, and forms to make them more prominent and easier to interact with. Whitespace guides users' attention and prevents the interface from feeling cramped.

- **Focus on one primary CTA:** For each page, identify the main action you want users to take (e.g., "Sign Up," "Add to Cart") and highlight it as the primary CTA. Avoid presenting multiple CTAs that compete for attention, which can confuse users.

Example: Google's homepage is the epitome of simplicity. With a clean design centered around a single search bar and a clear

"Google Search" button, it offers users a straightforward path to the action they want to take, resulting in a seamless, high-conversion experience.

2.   Clarity: guide users with clear messaging and design

Clarity is crucial in UX design, especially when it comes to driving conversions. Users should instantly understand what your website or app offers, what they can do next, and how to complete the desired actions.

Best practices for clarity in UX:

- **Use clear, concise language:** Write straightforward copy that clearly communicates the value proposition and instructions. For example, instead of using "Submit," opt for specific CTAs like "Get Your Free Guide" or "Start Your Free Trial" to inform users about the result of their actions.

- **Highlight key information:** Emphasize important details, such as pricing, features, or benefits, using bold text, headings, or contrasting colors. Ensure that the most relevant information is visible above the fold to capture attention immediately.

- **Use familiar design patterns:** Employ common design patterns, such as a three-line "hamburger" menu for navigation or a shopping cart icon for the checkout process. Familiar patterns reduce the learning curve, helping users understand how to interact with your platform intuitively.

Example: Dropbox's homepage conveys its value proposition — "Everything you need for work, all in one place" — in a simple, clear headline. The primary CTA, "Sign up for free," is prominently displayed, using direct language to guide users toward the desired action.

3.　Visual hierarchy: direct user attention

Visual hierarchy refers to the arrangement and presentation of elements in a way that naturally guides users' attention to the most important parts of the page. By strategically using size, color, contrast, and placement, you can direct users toward the CTA or key information.

How to create an effective visual hierarchy:

- **Use size and contrast:** Make your primary CTA larger and more contrasting than other elements to draw the user's eye. For example, a bold, brightly colored "Buy Now" button stands out against a minimalist background, signaling its importance.
- **Prioritize content:** Place the most critical content, such as headlines, benefits, and CTAs, above the fold, where it's visible without scrolling. Supporting information, like testimonials or additional details, can be placed lower on the page.

- **Apply the F-pattern:** Design content layouts to follow the natural eye movement of users, which often follows an "F" or "Z" pattern. Position key information along these paths to ensure that it captures attention.

Example: Shopify's landing page features a headline that clearly explains the value of its platform, followed by a prominent CTA button. The use of contrasting colors and ample whitespace creates a visual hierarchy that guides users toward starting their free trial.

4.　Accessibility: design for everyone

A user-friendly experience is an **accessible experience**. Designing with accessibility in mind ensures that your website or app is usable by people of all abilities, including those with visual, auditory, motor, or cognitive impairments. Prioritizing accessibility not only creates an inclusive experience but also broadens your potential customer base.

Accessibility best practices:

- **Use readable fonts and colors:** Choose fonts that are easy to read and maintain sufficient contrast between text and background colors. Avoid using color alone to convey information; instead, use labels, icons, or text to enhance comprehension.

- **Incorporate keyboard navigation:** Ensure that all interactive elements, such as buttons, links, and forms, are accessible via keyboard navigation for users who cannot use a mouse.

- **Provide alt text for images:** Include descriptive alt text for images to aid screen readers in conveying information to visually impaired users.

Example: Microsoft's website incorporates accessibility features, such as high-contrast text, keyboard-friendly navigation, and clear, descriptive alt text for images. This commitment to accessibility makes the website usable for a wider audience, enhancing the overall user experience.

5.   Speed: optimize for quick interactions

Speed is a critical component of UX. Users expect fast-loading pages and quick interactions, especially on mobile devices. Slow performance can lead to frustration, causing users to abandon the site before converting.

Ways to optimize speed:

- **Compress media files:** Use image compression tools and appropriate file formats to reduce image and video sizes without compromising quality.

- **Enable browser caching:** Store frequently accessed elements, like images and stylesheets, locally on the user's device to speed up subsequent visits.

- **Minimize scripts:** Reduce the number of HTTP requests and optimize CSS, JavaScript, and HTML files to streamline page rendering.

Example: LinkedIn continuously optimizes its platform for speed, ensuring that profile pages, job listings, and messaging load quickly. This fast performance keeps users engaged, reducing the likelihood of drop-offs and increasing conversion opportunities.

6.   Trustworthiness: build credibility through design

Users are more likely to convert if they trust your website or app. Incorporating elements that convey **trustworthiness**into your design helps build credibility and reduces hesitation.

Building trust through UX:

- **Use trust signals:** Include trust badges, security icons (e.g., SSL certification), customer testimonials, and reviews to provide social proof and assurance.

- **Provide transparent information:** Clearly state pricing, terms, and privacy policies. Avoid using hidden fees or fine print that could erode trust.

- **Offer easy access to support:** Display contact information, live chat, or support resources prominently. Knowing they can easily reach you if needed makes users feel more secure in taking action.

Example: Squarespace's website uses customer testimonials, transparent pricing, and a visible support link to instill confidence.

The clean, professional design further enhances trust, signaling to users that they are engaging with a reputable brand.

Testing and refining UX for optimal conversions

Improving UX is an ongoing process that requires testing, gathering user feedback, and analyzing performance data:

1. **A/B testing:** Test different variations of key elements, such as headlines, CTAs, form fields, and button placements, to determine which designs lead to higher conversion rates.

2. **Heatmaps and analytics:** Use heatmaps and analytics tools like Hotjar, Crazy Egg, and Google Analytics to monitor user interactions. Identify areas where users may be dropping off or struggling to engage, and refine your design accordingly.

3. **User feedback:** Collect feedback through surveys, usability tests, and in-app messages to understand user frustrations, preferences, and suggestions for improvement.

The bottom line: UX as a conversion driver

User experience is at the heart of driving conversions. By applying UX principles like simplicity, clarity, visual hierarchy, accessibility, speed, and trustworthiness, you create an environment that guides users effortlessly toward desired actions. A well-crafted UX not only boosts conversion rates but also enhances overall customer satisfaction, fostering loyalty and long-term growth.

C H A P T E R   8

Retention is the new acquisition

The power of customer retention in sustainable growth

In the world of growth marketing, the spotlight often shines on customer acquisition. While attracting new customers is undeniably important, focusing on **customer retention** can yield even greater returns. Retained customers are not only more valuable over time but also become advocates who help bring in new customers through positive word-of-mouth and referrals. In many ways, retention is the backbone of sustainable growth.

Studies show that acquiring a new customer can cost **five to seven times more** than retaining an existing one. Additionally, the probability of selling to an existing customer is significantly higher than converting a new prospect. This underscores the strategic importance of investing in customer retention to drive profitability and long-term business success.

Why customer retention is critical for growth

Retention isn't just about keeping customers on board; it's about maximizing the value of each customer relationship over time.

Here's why customer retention is a key driver of sustainable growth:

1. **Increased customer lifetime value (CLV):** Retained customers contribute to a higher **customer lifetime value (CLV).** They are more likely to make repeat purchases, explore new products or services, and engage with upsell and cross-sell opportunities. The longer a customer stays with your brand, the more revenue they generate, making retention a powerful multiplier of growth.

2. **Reduced acquisition costs:** High customer retention rates reduce the need for constant spending on acquisition campaigns. By maintaining a solid base of loyal customers, you can allocate more resources toward enhancing products, improving customer experiences, and expanding into new markets.

3. **Positive word-of-mouth:** Satisfied, loyal customers are more likely to recommend your brand to friends, family, and colleagues. This **word-of-mouth marketing** is highly effective, as people tend to trust recommendations from others in their network. Happy customers essentially become brand advocates, driving new customer acquisition organically.

4. **Stability and predictability:** A loyal customer base provides a **steady revenue stream**, making financial forecasting more predictable. With a reliable cohort of returning customers, you can better anticipate revenue fluctuations, seasonality, and long-term growth trends.

5. **Competitive advantage:** In markets where products and services are increasingly similar, **customer loyalty**becomes a key differentiator. Brands that prioritize customer retention build strong relationships, fostering trust and creating a sense of community that competitors struggle to replicate.

Understanding customer retention metrics

To effectively measure and improve customer retention, it's essential to track key metrics that provide insight into customer behavior, loyalty, and engagement:

1. **Customer retention rate (CRR):** This metric measures the percentage of customers who continue to do business with you over a specific period. A high retention rate indicates strong customer loyalty and satisfaction.

CRR formula: $CRR = \left(\dfrac{\text{Customers at end of period} - \text{New customers acquired during period}}{\text{Customers at start of period}} \right) \times 100$

2. **Churn rate:** The churn rate is the percentage of customers who stop doing business with you during a given period. A low churn rate suggests that your retention strategies are effective.

Churn rate formula: $\text{Churn Rate} = \left(\dfrac{\text{Customers lost during period}}{\text{Customers at start of period}} \right) \times 100$

3. **Customer lifetime value (CLV):** CLV estimates the total revenue a business can expect from a customer over the entire span of their relationship. A higher CLV indicates that customers are staying longer and spending more, reflecting successful retention efforts.

4. **Repeat purchase rate:** This metric measures the percentage of customers who make more than one purchase. A high repeat purchase rate is a strong indicator of customer loyalty and satisfaction.

Strategies for boosting customer retention

1. Deliver exceptional customer service

Outstanding **customer service** is at the heart of customer retention. When customers feel valued and supported, they are more likely to remain loyal to your brand. Addressing issues promptly and exceeding customer expectations can turn potentially negative experiences into positive ones, reinforcing loyalty.

Best practices for customer service:

- **Be responsive:** Provide quick and helpful responses to customer inquiries through multiple channels, such as live chat, social media, email, and phone support.

- **Offer self-service options:** Create a comprehensive knowledge base, FAQs, and how-to guides that allow customers to find answers and resolve issues on their own.

- **Personalize support:** Use customer data to tailor support interactions. For example, greet returning customers by name and reference their previous interactions or purchases.

Example: Zappos has built its brand reputation on customer service excellence. By offering free shipping, hassle-free returns, and 24/7 support, Zappos creates an experience that encourages customers to return and become loyal advocates.

2. Implement a customer loyalty program

A **customer loyalty program** incentivizes repeat purchases and ongoing engagement by rewarding customers for their loyalty. By offering points, discounts, or exclusive perks, you create a sense of appreciation and encourage customers to choose your brand over competitors.

Loyalty program ideas:

- **Point-based rewards:** Allow customers to earn points for every purchase or action (e.g., signing up for a newsletter, writing a review). Customers can redeem points for discounts, free products, or special gifts.

- **Tiered membership:** Introduce a tiered loyalty program with different levels of rewards based on customer spending or engagement. Higher-tier members receive more exclusive benefits, incentivizing customers to reach higher tiers.

- **Referral bonuses:** Encourage existing customers to refer new customers by offering both parties a reward, such as a discount or bonus points.

Example: Starbucks Rewards is a successful loyalty program that allows customers to earn stars for each purchase. Customers can redeem stars for free drinks, food items, or merchandise, incentivizing repeat visits and fostering brand loyalty.

3.   Personalize the customer experience

Personalization is a powerful way to deepen customer relationships and show that you value each customer as an individual. By tailoring experiences, recommendations, and communications to each customer's preferences and behaviors, you create a more engaging and relevant experience that enhances loyalty.

How to personalize for retention:

- **Use data-driven recommendations:** Utilize customer data, such as past purchases and browsing behavior, to offer personalized product recommendations and targeted promotions.

- **Segment communications:** Segment your customer base and send tailored emails or messages based on customer interests, purchase history, and engagement levels.

- **Celebrate milestones:** Recognize and celebrate customer milestones, such as birthdays, anniversaries of their first purchase, or loyalty program achievements, with special offers or personalized messages.

Example: Amazon excels in personalization by offering "Recommended for You" product suggestions based on each user's browsing and purchase history. This personalized approach keeps customers engaged and encourages repeat purchases.

4.   Engage customers with valuable content

Providing valuable, engaging content keeps customers connected to your brand and reinforces the relationship. Content marketing not only educates and entertains but also demonstrates your ongoing commitment to delivering value beyond the initial sale.

Content strategies for retention:

- **Create educational resources:** Develop how-to guides, tutorials, webinars, or blog posts that help customers get the most out of your products or services.

- **Offer exclusive content:** Share members-only content, such as early access to new product launches, behind-the-scenes insights, or VIP-only newsletters, to make customers feel valued and special.

- **Send follow-up communications:** Reach out to customers post-purchase with helpful content, tips for using their new product, or suggestions for complementary products.

Example: Notion, the productivity app, engages customers by offering a robust library of templates, guides, and community-generated content. This valuable resource helps users maximize the app's potential, increasing their satisfaction and encouraging continued use.

5.   Seek and act on customer feedback

Actively seeking **customer feedback** and acting on it demonstrates that you listen to your customers and are committed to improving their experience. By addressing concerns, implementing suggestions, and closing the feedback loop, you show customers that their input matters, which strengthens loyalty.

How to use feedback for retention:

- **Conduct surveys:** Use surveys to gather feedback on customer satisfaction, product usage, and areas for improvement. Analyze the results to identify trends and prioritize changes that will enhance the customer experience.

- **Implement a feedback loop:** Inform customers when their feedback has led to specific changes or updates. Closing the feedback loop reinforces the value you place on their input and builds trust.

- **Address pain points:** Use feedback to identify and address common pain points, such as website navigation issues, slow support response times, or product shortcomings. Improving these areas can significantly impact customer satisfaction and retention.

Example: Slack frequently solicits user feedback and releases product updates based on user suggestions. By continually refining its platform in response to customer input, Slack enhances user satisfaction and cultivates a loyal customer base.

The bottom line: retention as a growth engine

Customer retention is a powerful growth engine that offers long-term benefits. By delivering exceptional experiences, personalizing interactions, rewarding loyalty, and listening to customer feedback, you create a foundation of satisfied, loyal customers. This loyalty not only drives repeat business but also fuels word-of-mouth advocacy, bringing in new customers and multiplying your growth potential.

Creating loyalty programs and customer engagement loops

Customer loyalty isn't just about repeat purchases; it's about building a long-term relationship with your customers that goes beyond transactions. One of the most effective ways to foster loyalty and engagement is through **loyalty programs**and **customer engagement loops**. These strategies are designed to reward customers for their continued support, deepen their connection to your brand, and create a cycle of engagement that sustains customer retention over time.

Loyalty programs incentivize customers to engage with your brand by offering rewards, discounts, or exclusive perks. Meanwhile, **customer engagement loops** involve ongoing interactions that encourage customers to continually use your product, explore new features, or participate in community activities. When thoughtfully implemented, these tactics help turn one-time buyers into lifelong advocates.

Why loyalty programs matter for retention

Loyalty programs are powerful tools for driving customer retention because they provide tangible benefits for staying engaged with your brand. Customers who feel valued and rewarded for their loyalty are more likely to:

- **Make repeat purchases:** Rewards and incentives motivate customers to choose your brand over competitors, increasing their repeat purchase rate and lifetime value.

- **Advocate for your brand:** Satisfied, loyal customers are more inclined to recommend your brand to others, boosting word-of-mouth marketing and attracting new customers.

- **Engage with your brand:** Regular rewards and recognition encourage ongoing interactions, deepening the customer relationship and making your brand a part of their routine.

Designing an effective loyalty program

To create a loyalty program that resonates with your customers and drives retention, consider the following key elements:

1. Define clear goals and objectives

Before designing a loyalty program, define its primary goals. Are you aiming to increase repeat purchases, encourage higher spending, boost customer engagement, or promote advocacy? Clear objectives will guide your program's structure, rewards, and marketing strategies.

Example: Sephora's Beauty Insider program focuses on driving repeat purchases and brand engagement. By offering rewards at different tiers (Insider, VIB, Rouge) based on annual spending,

Sephora encourages customers to increase their purchases to unlock more exclusive perks.

2. Offer valuable rewards

A loyalty program's success hinges on the value of its rewards. The more relevant and valuable the rewards are to your customers, the more motivated they will be to participate. Consider offering a mix of tangible benefits (e.g., discounts, freebies) and experiential perks (e.g., early access, exclusive events).

Reward ideas:

- **Points-based rewards:** Allow customers to earn points for every dollar spent, which they can redeem for discounts, free products, or gift cards.

- **Tiered rewards:** Implement tier levels (e.g., Silver, Gold, Platinum) that offer progressively better rewards as customers spend more or engage more frequently. Higher tiers create a sense of achievement and incentivize customers to climb the ranks.

- **Experiential rewards:** Offer non-monetary perks, such as early access to new products, members-only events, personalized recommendations, or free samples. These experiences make customers feel special and deepen their emotional connection to your brand.

Example: Starbucks Rewards allows customers to earn "Stars" for every purchase. Customers can redeem stars for free drinks, food items, or merchandise. The program also offers personalized promotions, birthday rewards, and the ability to order ahead, enhancing the overall customer experience.

3. Keep it simple and easy to understand

A loyalty program should be straightforward and easy to use. If the rules, point system, or redemption process are too complicated, customers may lose interest. Clarity is key: ensure that customers understand how to earn points, what rewards are available, and how they can redeem their benefits.

Best practices for simplicity:

- **Provide clear instructions:** Use simple language to explain how the program works, including earning, tracking, and redeeming rewards.

- **Offer easy access:** Allow customers to view their points balance, rewards status, and available offers through your website, app, or emails.

- **Automate the process:** Use technology to automatically track points, notify customers of their status, and streamline redemption. Avoid manual processes that could cause delays or confusion.

Example: The North Face's XPLR Pass program is simple and transparent. Members earn 1 point for every dollar spent, and points can be redeemed for discounts on future purchases. The program also provides members with early access to new collections, further encouraging engagement.

4.   Incorporate personalized experiences
Personalization enhances loyalty programs by making customers feel seen and valued. Use customer data to tailor rewards, offers, and communications based on individual preferences and behaviors.

How to personalize loyalty programs:

- **Customized rewards:** Offer rewards that align with customers' past purchases, interests, or activity. For example, a beauty brand might send skincare enthusiasts a free sample of a new moisturizer as part of their loyalty benefits.

- **Targeted offers:** Use customer segmentation to send personalized offers, such as birthday discounts, anniversary bonuses, or product recommendations based on previous purchases.
- **Engagement-based rewards:** Recognize non-purchase actions, such as writing reviews, sharing on social media, or referring friends. Rewarding these behaviors fosters a sense of community and deepens brand engagement.

Example: Amazon Prime delivers a highly personalized loyalty experience. By paying an annual fee, members gain access to benefits like free shipping, exclusive deals, and tailored recommendations based on their browsing and purchasing history. This creates a VIP experience that drives retention and engagement.

Building customer engagement loops

Customer engagement loops involve creating ongoing interactions that keep customers actively engaged with your brand. These loops are not one-time events but continuous cycles that encourage customers to return, explore, and participate, ultimately leading to stronger loyalty and retention.

Components of an effective engagement loop:

1. **Regular touchpoints**

Engagement loops rely on regular touchpoints that keep your brand top-of-mind. Use a mix of communication channels to deliver value, provide updates, and invite customers to take action.

Touchpoint ideas:

- **Email newsletters:** Send monthly or weekly newsletters featuring exclusive content, product announcements, tips, and special offers.

- **Push notifications:** For mobile app users, send timely push notifications about promotions, rewards, or product restocks to prompt interaction.
- **In-app messages:** Use in-app messaging to share updates, recommend new features, or offer personalized suggestions based on user behavior.

Example: Duolingo uses push notifications to encourage users to complete their daily language lessons. By regularly prompting users to engage with the app, Duolingo creates a habit-forming loop that sustains user activity and progress.

2.   Gamification and challenges

Gamification adds an element of fun and achievement to customer engagement. By incorporating elements like points, badges, progress tracking, and challenges, you create a rewarding experience that motivates customers to continue interacting with your brand.

How to gamify engagement:

- **Points and badges:** Award points for various actions, such as completing a purchase, writing a review, or participating in a community event. Display badges or progress indicators to show customers their achievements.
- **Challenges and contests:** Create time-limited challenges, such as a "7-day fitness challenge" for a fitness app or a "Product Review Week" for an e-commerce store. Offer rewards or recognition for customers who participate.
- **Progress tracking:** Use visual progress bars or levels to show customers how close they are to reaching the next reward or tier, adding an element of anticipation and goal-setting.

Example: Nike Run Club app gamifies fitness by tracking users' runs, awarding badges for achievements, and offering guided challenges. This approach keeps users engaged, motivated, and connected to the Nike brand.

3. Encourage community involvement

Building a **community** around your brand fosters a sense of belonging and encourages ongoing engagement. When customers connect with like-minded individuals and participate in brand-related activities, they develop a deeper attachment to your brand.

Ways to build community engagement:

- **Social media groups:** Create branded social media groups where customers can share experiences, ask questions, and participate in discussions. Engage with the community by sharing content, hosting live events, or spotlighting customer stories.
- **User-generated content:** Encourage customers to share their own content, such as photos, videos, or reviews, featuring your products. Recognize their contributions by featuring their content on your website, social media, or newsletters.
- **Exclusive events:** Host members-only events, such as webinars, product launch previews, or virtual meetups, to provide unique experiences and strengthen community bonds.

Example: Lululemon cultivates a fitness-focused community by hosting local workout events, featuring user-generated content on social media, and fostering conversations within its brand app. This sense of community encourages customers to engage with the brand beyond just shopping.

The bottom line: fostering loyalty and engagement for long-term growth

Creating loyalty programs and customer engagement loops is a powerful way to build lasting relationships, deepen customer engagement, and drive sustainable growth. By offering valuable rewards, personalized experiences, and ongoing touchpoints, you nurture a loyal customer base that not only returns but also advocates for your brand. In a market where retention is the new acquisition, investing in loyalty and engagement is key to staying ahead and achieving long-term success.

Using email and in-app notifications to keep users engaged

In today's digital world, customers are bombarded with messages and advertisements from countless brands. To stand out, businesses need to use **email** and **in-app notifications** effectively to create meaningful connections and provide ongoing value. When done right, these tools can serve as personalized touchpoints that keep your brand top-of-mind, nurture the customer relationship, and encourage engagement with your products or services.

Emails offer a versatile way to communicate with customers, providing opportunities to share updates, promotions, personalized recommendations, and educational content. **In-app notifications**, on the other hand, are real-time messages sent directly within your app, providing timely and context-specific information that can enhance the user experience. Together, these communication channels create a multi-faceted engagement strategy that drives retention and loyalty.

Why email and in-app notifications are essential for engagement

Effective use of email and in-app notifications can significantly impact customer engagement and retention by:

1. **Maintaining consistent communication:** Regular communication through emails and notifications keeps your brand in front of customers, reminding them of your offerings and value.

2.   **Providing personalized content:** These channels allow for tailored messaging based on user behavior, preferences, and past interactions, creating a more relevant and engaging experience.

3.   **Prompting timely actions:** In-app notifications can guide users to explore new features, complete actions, or take advantage of limited-time offers, driving them to engage with your product more frequently.

Crafting an effective email engagement strategy

1.   Segment your audience

Segmentation is key to ensuring that your emails are relevant and tailored to the needs of different customer groups. By dividing your audience based on factors such as purchase history, behavior, demographics, and engagement levels, you can create targeted messages that resonate with each segment.

Segmentation strategies:

- **Behavioral:** Segment customers based on their actions, such as previous purchases, website visits, or email engagement. For instance, send special offers to customers who recently made a purchase or re-engage inactive users with a "We Miss You" campaign.

- **Lifecycle stage:** Tailor your messaging based on the customer's journey stage. New customers might receive onboarding emails, while long-term customers get loyalty-focused content or exclusive previews.

- **Personal preferences:** Use customer data to create segments based on interests, preferences, or product categories they frequently explore.

Example: Netflix sends personalized emails based on users' viewing history, recommending shows and movies that align with their interests. This targeted approach keeps subscribers engaged and encourages them to explore more content on the platform.

2.   Create valuable and relevant content

The content of your emails should provide genuine value to your customers, whether it's through helpful information, special promotions, or personalized recommendations. Valuable content fosters trust, encourages interaction, and makes customers look forward to receiving your emails.

Content ideas:

- **Personalized recommendations:** Send tailored product or content recommendations based on a customer's previous behavior, such as "Recommended for You" suggestions or "You might also like" items.

- **Exclusive promotions:** Offer special discounts, early access to sales, or members-only deals to reward loyalty and incentivize repeat purchases.

- **Educational content:** Share how-to guides, tips, product updates, or industry insights that help customers get the most out of your offerings.

Example: Sephora's email campaigns often include product recommendations based on a customer's past purchases, exclusive offers for loyalty program members, and beauty tips. By combining valuable content with personalization, Sephora maintains a strong connection with its customer base.

3.   Automate email workflows

Automated email workflows enable you to deliver timely, relevant messages at critical points in the customer journey.

Automation not only streamlines your engagement strategy but also ensures consistent communication with minimal manual intervention.

Workflow examples:

- **Welcome series:** Greet new subscribers or customers with a series of onboarding emails that introduce your brand, highlight key features, and offer a special welcome discount.

- **Abandoned cart reminders:** Send automated emails to customers who added items to their cart but didn't complete the purchase, prompting them to return and check out.

- **Re-engagement campaigns:** Reach out to inactive customers with a "We Miss You" email, offering a special incentive to encourage them to revisit your website or app.

Example: HubSpot's marketing automation tools enable businesses to create customized email workflows, such as sending a follow-up email to customers who viewed a specific product or offering content tailored to a customer's engagement history.

4. Optimize for mobile devices

A significant portion of emails is opened on mobile devices, so it's crucial to ensure that your emails are **mobile-friendly**. This means using a responsive design that adjusts to different screen sizes, keeping content concise, and including clear CTAs that are easy to tap.

Tips for mobile optimization:

- **Use a single-column layout:** Simplify your design to a single-column layout that adapts well to small screens.

- **Keep text concise:** Use short, clear sentences and headings to convey your message quickly and effectively.

- **Include prominent CTAs:** Use large, tappable buttons for CTAs, ensuring they stand out and are easy to interact with on mobile devices.

Example: Apple's marketing emails are known for their sleek, minimalist design that's optimized for mobile viewing. With clear visuals, concise copy, and bold CTAs, Apple makes it easy for customers to engage directly from their devices.

Leveraging in-app notifications for real-time engagement

In-app notifications are highly effective for real-time engagement, as they reach users directly while they are actively using your app. These notifications can guide users through key actions, introduce new features, or encourage continued use, all within the app environment.

1. **Use contextual messaging**

Context is key when using in-app notifications. Your messages should be relevant to the user's current activity, preferences, or progress within the app. Contextual notifications enhance the user experience by providing timely, helpful prompts that align with their behavior.

Examples of contextual messaging:

- **Feature discovery:** When a user first signs up, guide them through the app's features with helpful prompts, such as "Tap here to customize your profile" or "Try adding your first task to get started."

- **Progress nudges:** For apps that involve progress tracking (e.g., fitness, learning), send notifications that encourage users to continue their journey, like "You're just 2 steps away from completing this week's challenge!"

- **Personalized recommendations:** Use data on user activity to suggest relevant actions, such as "We noticed you enjoyed [Product X]. Check out similar items!"

Example: Duolingo uses in-app notifications to encourage users to continue their language learning streaks, prompting them to complete their daily lesson. By using contextual messaging based on the user's progress, Duolingo keeps learners motivated and engaged.

2.   Timing is everything

The effectiveness of in-app notifications often depends on when they are delivered. Sending notifications at the right time ensures that they are seen as helpful rather than intrusive, increasing the likelihood of positive engagement.

Timing strategies:

- **Action-based triggers:** Set notifications to trigger based on specific user actions or milestones, such as completing a purchase, finishing a tutorial, or reaching a new level in a game.

- **Behavior-based triggers:** Send notifications based on user behavior patterns, such as inactivity (e.g., "We miss you! Come back and explore new features") or frequent engagement (e.g., "You're on a roll! Keep exploring for more rewards").

- **Time-based triggers:** Schedule notifications to align with user preferences or app usage patterns. For example, a fitness app might send morning workout reminders or a food delivery app might offer lunch deals around midday.

Example: Spotify uses in-app notifications to suggest new music releases based on the user's listening habits, often delivering these suggestions when users open the app for their daily playlist.

3.   Provide clear and actionable message

In-app notifications should be **concise** and **actionable**, providing a clear benefit or prompt for the user. Avoid overwhelming users with too much information; instead, focus on one key message with a simple call-to-action (CTA).

How to create actionable notifications:

- **Use straightforward language:** Clearly state the action you want the user to take, such as "Complete your profile to unlock personalized recommendations" or "Claim your discount before it expires!"

- **Incorporate a CTA:** Include a direct CTA button, like "Start Now," "Explore More," or "Claim Offer," that guides the user toward the next step.

- **Personalize the message:** Use the user's name, preferences, or activity to tailor the notification, making it more relevant and compelling.

Example: Headspace, the meditation app, uses in-app notifications to gently nudge users toward their next meditation session, with messages like, "Take a moment for yourself. Your next session is ready." A simple CTA, like "Start Now," makes it easy for users to jump back into their practice.

4. Monitor and optimize

To maximize the impact of email and in-app notifications, monitor key performance indicators (KPIs) such as open rates, click-through rates, conversion rates, and user retention. Use this data to understand what types of messages resonate most with your audience and adjust your strategy accordingly.

Optimization tips:

- **A/B test messages:** Test different subject lines, content, CTAs, and timing for both emails and notifications to identify the most effective variations.

- **Analyze user behavior:** Use analytics tools to track user interactions with your notifications and emails, helping you refine messaging, timing, and personalization tactics.

- **Gather user feedback:** Solicit feedback on your communication strategy, asking customers if they find your messages helpful or if they have suggestions for improvement.

The bottom line: staying engaged for retention

Email and in-app notifications are invaluable tools for keeping customers engaged, guiding them through the customer journey, and fostering loyalty. By crafting relevant, personalized messages, using timely and contextual notifications, and continuously optimizing your strategy, you create a communication loop that maintains customer interest and drives long-term retention.

CHAPTER 9
Revenue and monetization strategies

Identifying growth levers that drive revenue

In growth marketing, **revenue generation** is the ultimate goal. While acquisition strategies and customer engagement play vital roles in building a strong customer base, identifying the specific **growth levers** that drive revenue is essential for scaling your business effectively. These levers are the high-impact factors that, when optimized, can accelerate revenue growth, maximize customer lifetime value (CLV), and enhance overall profitability.

Understanding and focusing on these growth levers enables you to make data-driven decisions and prioritize strategies that directly contribute to your bottom line. Whether it's optimizing pricing, enhancing product features, or improving customer retention, the right growth levers will vary depending on your business model, target market, and product offerings.

What are growth levers?

Growth levers are the specific elements or actions within your business that have the potential to significantly impact revenue and growth. Unlike general strategies, growth levers are highly focused areas where small adjustments can yield substantial results. They include a variety of factors, such as customer acquisition, pricing models, product optimizations, customer retention tactics, and upselling opportunities.

By identifying and activating the right growth levers, you can create a **multiplier effect** on revenue, driving sustained growth with strategic investments of time, resources, and marketing efforts.

Common growth levers that drive revenue

Here are some of the key growth levers that can have a direct impact on revenue growth, along with ways to leverage them effectively:

1.   **Customer acquisition channels**

Acquiring new customers is a foundational growth lever for driving revenue. However, not all acquisition channels offer the same return on investment (ROI). Identifying and focusing on high-ROI channels allows you to optimize your marketing spend and attract quality customers who are more likely to convert and generate long-term value.

How to optimize customer acquisition channels:

- **Identify high-performing channels:** Analyze the performance of various acquisition channels, such as social media, SEO, content marketing, paid advertising, email campaigns, and partnerships. Use metrics like customer acquisition cost (CAC), conversion rates, and customer lifetime value (CLV) to assess each channel's effectiveness.

- **Double down on best channels:** Allocate more resources to the channels that deliver the highest ROI. For example, if content marketing consistently attracts high-quality leads and conversions, invest in creating more targeted content, SEO optimization, and distribution strategies.

- **Experiment and iterate:** Continuously test new channels and tactics, such as influencer marketing or affiliate programs, to identify additional opportunities for customer acquisition. Use data-driven insights to refine your approach and scale the channels that show promise.

Example: Dollar Shave Club's viral video campaign on social media was a high-impact acquisition lever that helped them rapidly grow their customer base. By focusing on humorous, relatable content, they generated significant brand awareness and attracted subscribers at a low acquisition cost.

2. Pricing strategy

Pricing is one of the most critical levers affecting revenue. A well-designed pricing strategy can directly influence customer acquisition, retention, and CLV. By finding the optimal price points, you can attract more customers, encourage repeat purchases, and increase overall profitability.

Tips for optimizing pricing strategy:

- **Analyze market positioning:** Study competitors' pricing and market positioning to identify where your product fits within the market landscape. Determine whether a premium, mid-tier, or budget pricing model aligns with your target audience and brand value.

- **Offer tiered pricing:** Implement tiered pricing plans (e.g., basic, standard, premium) that cater to different customer segments. This allows customers to choose a plan that fits their needs and budget while providing opportunities to upsell to higher-priced tiers.

- **Test and adjust:** Use A/B testing and data analysis to experiment with different pricing models, such as subscription plans, discounts, or bundled offerings. Monitor customer behavior, churn rates, and revenue impact to identify the most effective pricing approach.

Example: SaaS companies like Spotify use tiered pricing to cater to different customer segments, offering a free version with ads, a standard premium subscription, and family or student plans. This flexibility maximizes revenue by appealing to a broad range of users.

3.   Customer retention and upselling

Retaining existing customers is more cost-effective than acquiring new ones. By focusing on retention strategies, you can increase CLV and create upselling and cross-selling opportunities that drive additional revenue from your current customer base.

How to leverage customer retention and upselling:

- **Create loyalty programs:** Implement a customer loyalty program that rewards repeat purchases, engagement, and referrals. Providing incentives, such as discounts, exclusive access, or points-based rewards, encourages customers to stay engaged and continue buying from your brand.

- **Upsell and cross-sell:** Use customer data to identify relevant upsell and cross-sell opportunities based on previous purchases, preferences, and behaviors. For example, recommend higher-priced plans, premium features, or complementary products that enhance the customer's experience.

- **Personalize post-purchase communication:** Engage customers with personalized follow-up emails, product recommendations, and tips for maximizing the use of their purchase. Tailored communication deepens customer relationships and encourages ongoing interaction with your brand.

Example: Amazon effectively uses upselling and cross-selling by showing customers related products, "Frequently Bought Together" suggestions, and "Customers Who Bought This Also Bought" recommendations on product pages. This strategy significantly boosts their average order value and overall revenue.

4.   Product-led growth (PLG)

Product-led growth is a strategy where the product itself serves as the primary driver of customer acquisition, retention, and expansion. By offering a product that delivers exceptional value and promotes user engagement, you can create a natural growth loop that generates revenue.

Key tactics for product-led growth:

- **Offer a freemium model:** Provide a free version of your product with limited features to attract users and showcase its value. As users experience the product's benefits, they are more likely to upgrade to paid plans for access to premium features.

- **Leverage in-product onboarding:** Implement an intuitive onboarding process that guides users through key features and helps them quickly realize the product's value. Engaged users are more likely to convert to paying customers and explore additional offerings.

- **Encourage virality:** Incorporate features that encourage users to invite others or share their experiences. For example, collaboration tools, social sharing options, or referral incentives can turn satisfied users into brand advocates who drive organic growth.

Example: Slack's freemium model allows teams to use the basic version for free, experiencing its collaboration benefits firsthand. As usage grows and teams require more features, many naturally upgrade to paid plans, driving revenue through product-led growth.

5.   Expansion into new markets

Entering new markets is a powerful way to expand your customer base and drive revenue growth. This lever involves identifying new geographic regions, customer segments, or industry verticals that can benefit from your products or services.

Strategies for market expansion:

- **Research market demand:** Conduct market research to identify regions or segments with high demand for your product. Analyze factors such as market size, competition, cultural preferences, and regulatory considerations.

- **Localize your offering:** Tailor your product, messaging, and marketing strategies to align with the cultural norms, language, and preferences of the new market. Localization enhances relevance and appeal to the target audience.

- **Partner with local influencers:** Collaborate with local influencers, affiliates, or distribution partners to increase brand visibility and build credibility within the new market.

Example: Airbnb's global expansion involved localizing its platform for different countries, offering support in multiple languages, and incorporating region-specific payment methods. By adapting its services to meet the needs of various markets, Airbnb successfully grew its international customer base.

6. Monetization of data and insights

If your business collects valuable data through customer interactions, consider **monetizing insights** as an additional revenue stream. This growth lever involves analyzing customer data to offer targeted advertising, market research, or insights-driven services to other businesses.

Monetization approaches:

- **Offer data-driven advertising:** If you operate a platform with high user engagement, consider offering targeted advertising options to other businesses based on user behavior and demographics.

- **Provide market insights:** Use aggregated data to generate market research reports, consumer behavior insights, or industry trends that can be sold to interested parties, such as marketers, researchers, or product developers.

Example: LinkedIn monetizes its platform through LinkedIn Marketing Solutions, which allows businesses to target ads based on user profiles and activity data. LinkedIn's access to a professional user base creates a valuable advertising opportunity, contributing to its revenue growth.

Prioritizing growth levers for maximum impact

With multiple growth levers available, it's important to prioritize the ones that align with your business model, goals, and market conditions. Here's how to identify and focus on the most impactful growth levers:

1. **Analyze data:** Use data analytics to assess the current performance of each potential growth lever. Identify which areas—such as customer acquisition, pricing, or product features—offer the greatest opportunity for optimization and revenue impact.

2. **Set measurable goals:** Define clear, measurable objectives for each growth lever you plan to activate. For example, aim to increase average order value by 20% through cross-selling or reduce churn by 15% through a revamped loyalty program.

3. **Experiment and iterate:** Implement small-scale experiments to test the effectiveness of different growth levers. Measure the results, learn from successes and failures, and refine your strategies for maximum impact.

The bottom line: driving revenue through targeted growth levers

Identifying and activating the right growth levers is key to driving sustainable revenue growth. By focusing on areas like customer acquisition channels, pricing strategy, customer retention, product-led growth, market expansion, and data monetization, you can create a strategic roadmap for scaling your business. Remember, the most successful growth strategies are dynamic, data-driven, and tailored to your unique business context.

Pricing strategies: when and how to optimize for growth

Pricing is one of the most critical decisions a business can make. The right pricing strategy can significantly impact your revenue, profit margins, and market positioning. Conversely, ineffective pricing can lead to missed revenue opportunities, reduced customer acquisition, and even churn. Optimizing your pricing involves not just setting an initial price but continually refining your strategy based on market conditions, customer behavior, and your overall business goals.

An effective pricing strategy aligns with your product's perceived value, your target audience's willingness to pay, and the competitive landscape. By understanding different pricing models and knowing when to adjust your prices, you can position your product to maximize revenue and growth.

The importance of pricing optimization

Optimizing your pricing strategy is vital for several reasons:

1. **Maximizes revenue:** Well-calibrated pricing can increase your average order value, boost conversions, and ultimately drive higher revenue.

2. **Increases customer lifetime value (CLV):** Pricing that reflects the value of your product encourages customer loyalty, leading to repeat purchases and higher CLV.

3. **Enhances market positioning:** Strategic pricing helps position your brand within the market, whether you're aiming for a premium or budget-conscious audience. A well-defined price point communicates your brand's value proposition and differentiates you from competitors.

Different pricing models and strategies

When considering how to price your products or services, explore various models and strategies to find what best suits your business and customer base:

1. Cost-plus pricing

Cost-plus pricing is a straightforward approach where you add a markup to the cost of producing your product or service to determine its price. This method ensures you cover production costs while achieving a desired profit margin.

When to use cost-plus pricing:

- In markets where pricing transparency is common, such as retail or manufacturing.

- When you have clear production costs and a desired profit margin.

- When competitors use similar pricing strategies, making cost-based pricing a standard approach.

Example: A retailer that sources products from manufacturers may apply a consistent markup percentage to cover costs, overhead, and profit, resulting in a final retail price for customers.

Advantages: Simple to implement, ensures cost recovery, provides predictable profit margins.

Disadvantages: Ignores market demand and customer willingness to pay, may not maximize revenue potential in dynamic markets.

2. Value-based pricing

Value-based pricing involves setting your price based on the perceived value of your product or service to the customer. This model focuses on what customers are willing to pay based on the benefits and unique value your offering provides.

When to use value-based pricing:

- When your product offers unique features or benefits that differentiate it from competitors.

- In markets where customers are willing to pay a premium for high-quality, innovative, or exclusive products.

- When you have a strong understanding of customer needs, preferences, and perceived value.

Example: Apple uses value-based pricing for its products, such as the iPhone, by positioning them as premium, innovative devices. Customers are willing to pay higher prices because they perceive value in Apple's design, quality, and ecosystem integration.

Advantages: Maximizes revenue by capturing the customer's willingness to pay, aligns pricing with perceived value, supports premium positioning.

Disadvantages: Requires in-depth market research, complex to implement, may limit market reach if prices are set too high.

3. Tiered pricing and subscription models

Tiered pricing offers different packages or plans at varying price points, each with a different set of features or benefits. This model is commonly used in **subscription-based businesses** such as SaaS (Software as a Service), media streaming, and online learning platforms.

When to use tiered pricing:

- When you serve multiple customer segments with different needs and budget levels.

- When you want to encourage customers to upgrade to higher-priced plans over time.

- For products or services that can be bundled into different feature sets or usage levels.

Example: Netflix offers tiered subscription plans (Basic, Standard, Premium) with varying levels of streaming quality and simultaneous viewing screens. This approach allows them to cater to different customer needs and willingness to pay.

Advantages: Increases revenue potential by appealing to diverse customer segments, facilitates upselling to higher tiers, encourages customer growth within your product ecosystem.

Disadvantages: Can be complex to structure and manage, requires clear differentiation between tiers to justify price differences.

4. Dynamic pricing

Dynamic pricing involves adjusting prices based on market demand, customer behavior, time, or other external factors. This model is often used in industries such as travel, hospitality, and e-commerce to maximize revenue by responding to real-time market conditions.

When to use dynamic pricing:

- In markets with fluctuating demand, such as airline tickets, hotel bookings, or event ticketing.

- When you have access to real-time data and analytics to monitor market conditions and customer behavior.

- For products with limited availability, seasonal demand, or high variability in customer willingness to pay.

Example: Uber uses dynamic pricing (surge pricing) during peak times when demand for rides is high. Prices increase to balance supply and demand, incentivizing more drivers to offer rides while maximizing revenue.

Advantages: Maximizes revenue by capturing the highest possible price based on market conditions, responsive to changes in supply and demand, creates a sense of urgency for customers.

Disadvantages: May lead to customer dissatisfaction if perceived as unfair, requires sophisticated data analytics and pricing algorithms.

5. Freemium and pay-as-you-go models

The **freemium model** provides a basic version of your product for free, while charging for advanced features or premium versions. **Pay-as-you-go** pricing charges customers based on their usage, making it flexible and appealing for those who prefer not to commit to long-term subscriptions.

When to use freemium or pay-as-you-go models:

- When your product benefits from a large user base that can be converted to paying customers over time.

- In markets where customers want to try before they buy or where usage varies significantly across users.

- For digital products, software, or services that can easily offer tiered features or usage-based billing.

Example: Dropbox offers a freemium model, providing free storage with limited features. Users who need more storage or advanced features can upgrade to paid plans, allowing Dropbox to monetize its large user base.

Advantages: Attracts a wide range of users, builds brand awareness, provides an opportunity to demonstrate product value before asking for payment.

Disadvantages: Requires a clear value proposition to convert free users to paid customers, risks customers remaining on the free tier if the premium offering isn't compelling.

When and how to optimize your pricing

Optimizing your pricing is an ongoing process that involves assessing market conditions, customer behavior, and your business goals. Here's how to know when to revisit your pricing strategy and the steps to take:

1.   **Monitor market changes and competition**
Regularly monitor market trends, competitor pricing, and industry standards to stay informed about shifts that may impact your pricing strategy. If you notice changes, such as new competitors entering the market or shifts in customer preferences, it may be time to reevaluate your pricing.

How to adapt: If competitors are lowering prices, consider whether you can justify maintaining your current price based on added value or unique features. Alternatively, if your product offers superior value, explore opportunities to raise prices while communicating the enhanced benefits to customers.

2.   **Assess customer feedback and behavior**

Collect customer feedback and analyze purchase behavior to understand how your pricing affects customer satisfaction, conversion rates, and retention. If customers frequently mention price as a barrier to purchasing or if you observe high churn rates, it may indicate that your pricing is misaligned with customer expectations.

How to adapt: Use customer feedback to adjust your pricing model, such as introducing a more affordable tier, offering flexible payment options, or providing discounts for long-term commitments.

3. Conduct pricing experiments

Testing different pricing strategies can provide valuable insights into customer willingness to pay and the impact on revenue. **A/B testing** different price points, discount offers, or tier structures allows you to gather data on customer response and refine your approach.

How to implement: Run experiments on a subset of your audience, such as offering a limited-time discount or introducing a new tier. Monitor metrics like conversion rates, average order value, and customer lifetime value to assess the impact.

4. Leverage psychological pricing

Psychological pricing tactics, such as charm pricing (e.g., $9.99 instead of $10) or offering "decoy" options, can influence customer perceptions and purchasing decisions. Small adjustments in how prices are presented can have a significant impact on conversions.

How to apply: Experiment with pricing formats, such as offering a premium plan alongside a lower-priced option to make the latter appear more valuable. Use rounded prices for high-end products to convey luxury or precise pricing for value-focused offerings.

5. Revisit pricing periodically

Regularly review your pricing strategy, ideally on a semi-annual or annual basis, to ensure it aligns with your product's evolving value, market conditions, and business objectives. Adjust your pricing as necessary to reflect new features, costs, and customer demand.

Example: Adobe transitioned its software suite to a subscription-based model (Adobe Creative Cloud) to adapt to changing market preferences. By offering flexible monthly and annual pricing, Adobe increased accessibility and revenue stability.

The bottom line: pricing as a dynamic growth lever

Pricing optimization is not a one-time decision but an ongoing process of experimentation, analysis, and adjustment. By selecting the right pricing model, understanding market dynamics, and listening to your customers, you can set prices that maximize revenue, enhance market positioning, and support sustainable growth. Remember, the goal is to find a balance between capturing customer value and maintaining competitiveness in the market.

Subscription models, upselling, and cross-selling

In today's digital economy, businesses are increasingly adopting **subscription models** to generate recurring revenue and build long-term customer relationships. Subscription models create a reliable revenue stream, offering predictable cash flow and the opportunity to nurture customer loyalty over time. When combined with **upselling** and **cross-selling**strategies, you can maximize customer lifetime value (CLV), enhance customer experiences, and unlock additional revenue potential.

Upselling involves encouraging customers to purchase a higher-priced product, service, or plan, while **cross-selling** focuses on offering complementary products or services that enhance the customer's primary purchase. Both techniques can significantly increase the average order value and create a richer, more personalized customer journey.

The power of subscription models

Subscription-based business models provide customers with ongoing access to products or services for a recurring fee, whether it's monthly, quarterly, or annually. This model has become popular across various industries, from software (SaaS) to media streaming, fitness, and consumer goods.

Benefits of subscription models:

1. **Predictable revenue:** Subscriptions create a consistent and predictable revenue stream, enabling better financial planning and resource allocation.

2. **Increased customer lifetime value (CLV):** By retaining customers over the long term, subscription models increase CLV. Customers are more likely to remain loyal and continue purchasing additional products or services.

3. **Stronger customer relationships:** Subscription models facilitate ongoing customer engagement, providing opportunities to build relationships, collect feedback, and tailor offerings to meet evolving needs.

Implementing a successful subscription model

To implement a subscription model that drives growth and revenue, consider the following key strategies:

1. **Offer flexible subscription tiers**

Creating **tiered subscription plans** allows you to cater to a wide range of customers with different needs and budgets. This approach can attract more customers at entry-level tiers while providing pathways for them to upgrade to higher-priced plans as they experience the value of your product.

How to design tiered plans:

- **Basic tier:** Provide a low-cost or free entry-level plan with limited features, allowing customers to try your product and experience its core benefits. This plan serves as a gateway to higher-tier subscriptions.

- **Standard tier:** Include additional features, enhanced functionality, or higher usage limits in the mid-tier plan to cater to the majority of your target audience.

- **Premium tier:** Offer a high-end plan with advanced features, priority support, or exclusive access to cater to power users or customers seeking the most comprehensive experience.

Example: Spotify offers a variety of subscription tiers, including a free ad-supported plan, an individual premium plan, family and student plans, and a high-quality "HiFi" audio tier. This variety appeals to different customer segments and provides opportunities for users to upgrade as their needs evolve.

2. Incentivize longer commitments

Encourage customers to commit to longer subscription periods, such as annual plans, by offering discounts or added benefits. This approach not only boosts customer retention but also increases upfront revenue, providing a more stable cash flow.

How to incentivize longer commitments:

- **Discounts for annual plans:** Offer a discounted rate for customers who commit to a yearly subscription compared to a monthly payment plan. For example, "Save 20% when you subscribe annually!"

- **Bonus perks:** Provide additional perks, such as free access to premium features, exclusive content, or complimentary gifts, to customers who choose a long-term commitment.

Example: Adobe Creative Cloud offers a monthly payment option and a discounted annual commitment. Customers who opt for the annual plan enjoy a lower price per month, incentivizing them to commit for the long term and increasing Adobe's customer retention.

3.   Provide a seamless upgrade path

Make it easy for customers to **upgrade** their subscription plan as they experience the value of your product. A seamless upgrade process encourages customers to move to higher tiers that offer more features or benefits, driving revenue growth.

Upgrade strategies:

- **In-app prompts:** Use in-app notifications or emails to highlight the benefits of upgrading. For example, "Unlock premium features like unlimited storage and priority support by upgrading to our Pro plan."

- **Freemium to premium:** For products with a freemium model, use automated prompts that showcase premium features and their added value. Encourage free users to upgrade when they reach usage limits or express interest in premium functionality.

Example: Zoom offers a freemium plan with a time limit on group meetings. Users often encounter prompts to upgrade to a Pro plan for unlimited group meeting durations, encouraging them to move to a higher subscription tier as their needs grow.

Upselling and cross-selling strategies

Upselling and **cross-selling** are powerful techniques for maximizing revenue from your existing customer base. When implemented thoughtfully, these strategies not only increase average order value but also enhance the customer experience by offering products or services that align with their needs and preferences.

1.   Upselling: encourage higher-value purchases

Upselling involves persuading customers to purchase a more expensive version of a product, add premium features, or switch to a higher subscription tier. This approach works best when you clearly communicate the added value of the upgrade and how it enhances the customer's experience.

Upselling tactics:

- **Highlight premium features:** Showcase the benefits of the upgraded product or plan, such as enhanced performance, additional support, or access to exclusive content. For example, "Upgrade to our Pro plan for unlimited storage and advanced analytics."

- **Use time-limited offers:** Create a sense of urgency by offering discounts or promotions for a limited time. For instance, "Upgrade to the Premium plan and save 15% for the first three months."

- **Provide a trial period:** Offer a free trial of premium features or higher-tier plans. This allows customers to experience the value firsthand and increases the likelihood of them choosing to pay for the upgrade afterward.

Example: Amazon Prime offers an upsell by allowing users to upgrade from a monthly payment to an annual payment at a discounted rate. Additionally, within the Prime membership,

Amazon promotes add-ons like Amazon Music Unlimited and Kindle Unlimited, further increasing the potential revenue per customer.

2.   Cross-selling: recommend complementary products

Cross-selling involves suggesting complementary products or services that enhance or align with the customer's initial purchase. This strategy can introduce customers to new offerings, encourage additional purchases, and increase overall satisfaction by providing a complete solution.

Cross-selling tactics:

- **Bundle related products:** Create product bundles that include complementary items, offering them at a discounted rate. For example, "Buy the complete skincare set and save 20%."

- **Suggest related items:** Use personalized recommendations to suggest products that complement the customer's existing purchase. For example, "Customers who bought this laptop also purchased a laptop sleeve and a wireless mouse."

- **Leverage post-purchase communication:** After a customer completes a purchase, follow up with emails recommending related products, accessories, or services that enhance their experience.

Example: Apple cross-sells by recommending accessories like cases, chargers, and headphones during the checkout process for customers purchasing an iPhone. This not only increases the average order value but also provides customers with a comprehensive product experience.

3.   Use customer data to personalize offers

Leverage customer data to **personalize upselling and cross-selling** offers, ensuring they align with the customer's preferences, past purchases, and behavior. Personalized recommendations are more likely to resonate with customers and result in successful conversions.

How to personalize offers:

- **Behavioral analysis:** Analyze customer behavior, such as browsing history, purchase patterns, and engagement with your product, to identify upsell or cross-sell opportunities. For example, a customer frequently viewing premium features in your app might be a prime candidate for an upgrade.

- **Segmented messaging:** Create targeted campaigns that tailor upsell and cross-sell offers based on customer segments. For example, new customers might receive introductory offers for add-ons, while long-term customers receive loyalty discounts for premium upgrades.

- **Dynamic product recommendations:** Use AI-powered algorithms to generate real-time, dynamic recommendations that adapt to each customer's interactions on your platform.

Example: Amazon's recommendation engine is highly personalized, offering cross-sell suggestions like "Frequently Bought Together" and "Customers Who Viewed This Item Also Viewed" based on individual browsing and purchase history. This approach drives incremental sales and enhances the shopping experience.

The bottom line: maximizing revenue through subscriptions, upselling, and cross-selling

Subscription models, when coupled with effective upselling and cross-selling strategies, provide a solid foundation for generating recurring revenue and maximizing customer lifetime value. By offering flexible subscription tiers, encouraging upgrades, and recommending complementary products, you can create a customer journey that both satisfies and drives additional revenue. Remember, the goal is to deliver value at each step, ensuring that customers feel they are gaining more from their purchases and ongoing relationship with your brand.

C H A P T E R   1 0

Marketing automation: scaling without burnout

Introduction to marketing automation and its importance

In today's fast-paced digital world, managing multiple marketing channels and customer interactions can be overwhelming, especially as your business grows. This is where **marketing automation** comes into play. Marketing automation involves using software platforms and technologies to automate repetitive marketing tasks, streamline processes, and enhance customer engagement.

By leveraging automation, businesses can effectively manage email campaigns, social media posts, lead nurturing, customer segmentation, and more—all with minimal manual effort. This not only boosts marketing efficiency but also allows teams to focus on higher-level strategic activities, ultimately driving revenue growth.

What is marketing automation?

Marketing automation refers to the use of software tools to automate and manage marketing activities across various channels. The primary goal is to nurture prospects, engage customers, and drive conversions at scale while delivering a personalized experience.

Automation can be applied to a wide range of marketing tasks, including:

- **Email marketing:** Sending targeted, personalized emails to different segments of your audience based on their behaviors and interactions.

- **Lead scoring:** Tracking and evaluating leads based on their engagement with your marketing materials to identify those most likely to convert.

- **Customer segmentation:** Automatically categorizing customers into segments based on demographics, behaviors, purchase history, and engagement levels.

- **Social media management:** Scheduling and publishing posts across multiple social media platforms, responding to comments, and tracking performance.

- **Campaign tracking:** Monitoring the performance of marketing campaigns in real time, allowing for data-driven adjustments and optimizations.

Why marketing automation is essential for growth

Marketing automation is more than just a time-saving tool—it's a strategic necessity for businesses aiming to scale. Here's why it's so crucial:

1. **Increased efficiency:** Automation streamlines repetitive marketing tasks, freeing up valuable time for your marketing team to focus on strategic activities like content creation, data analysis, and campaign optimization. This efficiency is particularly important as your business grows

and the number of campaigns and customer interactions increases.

2. **Improved personalization:** Marketing automation allows you to deliver highly personalized content and messages to different audience segments based on their behavior, preferences, and interactions. Personalization enhances customer engagement, boosts conversion rates, and strengthens customer relationships.

3. **Consistent communication:** Automation ensures that communication with prospects and customers is timely and consistent. From welcome emails to follow-up messages and nurturing sequences, automation maintains an ongoing dialogue that keeps your brand top-of-mind throughout the customer journey.

4. **Data-driven insights:** Marketing automation tools provide valuable data and analytics that help you track the performance of your campaigns, understand customer behavior, and make data-driven decisions. This insight is crucial for optimizing marketing strategies and maximizing ROI.

5. **Scalable marketing efforts:** As your customer base grows, manually managing every interaction becomes impractical. Automation enables you to scale your marketing efforts seamlessly, reaching more customers with tailored messages without compromising quality or accuracy.

Key components of marketing automation

A successful marketing automation strategy involves several core components that work together to enhance your marketing processes:

1.   Automated email marketing

Email marketing remains one of the most effective channels for nurturing leads, engaging customers, and driving conversions. Marketing automation platforms allow you to set up automated email workflows that send targeted messages based on customer actions, preferences, and lifecycle stages.

Key features of automated email marketing:

- **Triggered emails:** Automatically send emails based on user behavior, such as signing up for a newsletter, abandoning a cart, or downloading a resource. For example, send a welcome email series to new subscribers or a reminder email to customers who left items in their cart.

- **Drip campaigns:** Create a sequence of emails that nurture leads over time, gradually guiding them through the sales funnel with valuable content, product information, and special offers.

- **Personalization:** Use customer data to personalize emails with the recipient's name, product recommendations, and tailored content that resonates with their interests and needs.

Example: An e-commerce store can use marketing automation to send a series of onboarding emails to new customers, highlighting product features, offering discounts, and encouraging reviews — all triggered automatically based on customer interactions.

2.   Lead nurturing and scoring

Lead nurturing involves building relationships with potential customers by providing them with relevant information and content at various stages of their buying journey. Automation tools enable you to nurture leads effectively by delivering the right message at the right time.

How automation supports lead nurturing:

- **Lead scoring:** Automatically assign scores to leads based on their behavior, such as website visits, email opens, or content downloads. Higher scores indicate a higher likelihood of conversion, allowing your sales team to focus on the most promising leads.

- **Automated workflows:** Set up workflows that send targeted content to leads based on their score, engagement level, and position in the sales funnel. For example, send educational content to early-stage leads and product demos to those showing high intent.

Example: A SaaS company uses lead scoring to identify high-intent leads who have visited the pricing page multiple times. These leads are automatically enrolled in a workflow that sends personalized product demos and free trial offers, increasing the chances of conversion.

3.   Customer segmentation and targeting

Segmentation is critical for delivering personalized marketing messages that resonate with different customer groups. **Marketing automation** tools can automatically categorize customers into segments based on demographics, purchase history, behavior, and engagement levels.

How to use automated segmentation:

- **Dynamic segmentation:** Create dynamic segments that automatically update as customers' behavior changes. For example, a customer who makes a purchase moves from the "prospect" segment to the "customer" segment and receives a tailored post-purchase follow-up sequence.

- **Targeted campaigns:** Use segmentation to send targeted campaigns that align with each group's needs and preferences. For example, send VIP customers early access to new product launches or offer discounts to customers who haven't purchased in a while.

Example: An online clothing retailer segments its customers based on purchase history, browsing behavior, and preferred product categories. Using automation, the retailer sends personalized emails featuring new arrivals and promotions tailored to each customer's interests, boosting engagement and sales.

4.   Social media automation

Managing social media accounts manually can be time-consuming, especially when posting regularly across multiple platforms. **Social media automation** tools help schedule posts, track engagement, and even respond to comments or messages, maintaining a consistent brand presence without the need for constant manual intervention.

Benefits of social media automation:

- **Scheduled posts:** Plan and schedule social media content in advance, ensuring a steady stream of posts without daily oversight.

- **Performance tracking:** Monitor metrics such as likes, shares, comments, and clicks to gauge the performance of your social media campaigns. Use these insights to adjust your strategy and optimize content for better engagement.

- **Automated responses:** Set up automated responses for common questions or inquiries received through social media, providing quick support to customers and prospects.

Example: A fitness brand uses a social media automation tool to schedule daily motivational posts, workout tips, and product promotions across Instagram, Facebook, and Twitter. Automated analytics track which posts receive the most engagement, informing future content strategies.

5.   Campaign tracking and analytics

Campaign tracking and **analytics** are essential for understanding the effectiveness of your marketing efforts. Automation tools provide detailed insights into customer interactions, campaign performance, and ROI, enabling you to refine your strategies based on data.

Key analytics features:

- **Real-time tracking:** Monitor campaign performance in real-time, including metrics such as open rates, click-through rates, conversions, and customer engagement.

- **A/B testing:** Conduct A/B tests on different marketing elements (e.g., subject lines, CTAs, landing pages) to identify what resonates best with your audience and optimize campaigns for maximum impact.

- **Custom reports:** Generate reports that highlight key performance indicators (KPIs) and trends, allowing you to make data-driven decisions and demonstrate the ROI of your marketing efforts.

Example: A B2B software company uses marketing automation to track the performance of its email campaigns and content downloads. The data reveals which types of content drive the most engagement, informing future content creation and distribution strategies.

Getting started with marketing automation

To effectively implement marketing automation, follow these steps:

1. **Choose the right platform:** Select a marketing automation platform that suits your business size, industry, and specific needs. Popular options include **HubSpot**, **ActiveCampaign**, **Mailchimp**, and **Marketo**. Look for features such as email marketing, CRM integration, segmentation, analytics, and social media management.

2. **Map out your customer journey:** Define the key stages of your customer journey and identify touchpoints where automation can enhance the experience. Consider how automation can support lead nurturing, customer engagement, and post-purchase follow-up.

3. **Set up workflows:** Create automated workflows for different marketing activities, such as welcome emails, abandoned cart reminders, lead nurturing sequences, and re-engagement campaigns. Use triggers based on customer behavior to deliver timely and relevant messages.

4. **Monitor and optimize:** Continuously monitor the performance of your automated campaigns and workflows. Use analytics to identify areas for improvement, experiment with different approaches, and refine your strategy over time.

The bottom line: scaling marketing with automation

Marketing automation is an indispensable tool for businesses looking to scale their marketing efforts without burning out their teams. By automating repetitive tasks, personalizing customer interactions, and leveraging data-driven insights, you can enhance efficiency, increase engagement, and drive revenue growth. The key to successful automation lies in striking a balance between technology and human touch, ensuring that your marketing remains both efficient and customer-centric.

Exploring tools like Make, Zapier, HubSpot, and ActiveCampaign

Marketing automation tools have revolutionized the way businesses operate, enabling them to streamline marketing processes, manage customer interactions, and drive growth without overwhelming their teams. Choosing the right tools is crucial for effectively implementing marketing automation and achieving your business goals.

In this section, we'll explore several popular marketing automation tools—**Make**, **Zapier**, **HubSpot**, and **ActiveCampaign**—discussing their features, use cases, and how they can enhance your marketing strategy.

1. Make (formerly Integromat)

Make is a powerful automation tool that allows you to connect various apps and services, creating custom workflows to automate repetitive tasks. Previously known as Integromat, Make excels in integrating different tools and automating complex processes across marketing, sales, customer service, and other business functions.

Key features of Make:

- **Visual workflow builder:** Make offers an intuitive, drag-and-drop interface for creating automation workflows. Its visual builder lets you map out processes, set conditions, and customize data flows between apps without the need for coding.

- **Multi-step automation:** Unlike some basic automation tools, Make allows you to create complex, multi-step automation workflows that involve multiple apps and conditions. For example, you can set up a workflow to capture form submissions, add contacts to your CRM, send a follow-up email, and update a spreadsheet.

- **Data manipulation:** With Make, you can manipulate data within your workflows, such as filtering information, transforming text, and performing calculations, providing flexibility and control over your automation processes.

Use cases for Make:

- **Lead management:** Automatically capture leads from web forms and add them to your CRM, send personalized follow-up emails, and assign tasks to your sales team for lead nurturing.

- **Content distribution:** Create workflows that automatically post new blog content to your social media channels, schedule posts, and track engagement metrics.

- **E-commerce automation:** Set up workflows to process new orders, update inventory, generate invoices, and send order confirmation emails to customers.

Example: An e-commerce business can use Make to automate the entire order fulfillment process. When a customer places an order, Make captures the order details, updates the inventory database, sends a confirmation email to the customer, and notifies the warehouse for shipping—all seamlessly integrated in one workflow.

2. Zapier

Zapier is one of the most widely used automation platforms, known for its ease of use and extensive integration capabilities.

Zapier allows you to create **"Zaps,"** which are automated workflows that connect different apps and services, helping you automate tasks and reduce manual work.

Key features of Zapier:

- **Extensive app integrations:** Zapier integrates with over 3,000 apps, including CRM systems, email marketing tools, project management software, e-commerce platforms, and more. This broad range of integrations makes it a versatile tool for automating virtually any marketing process.

- **No-code automation:** Zapier is designed for non-technical users, offering a simple, step-by-step process for setting up Zaps without requiring coding knowledge. You can create workflows based on triggers (e.g., "New email received") and specify actions (e.g., "Add contact to CRM").

- **Conditional logic:** With **Zapier's Paths** feature, you can introduce conditional logic into your workflows, allowing you to create different outcomes based on specific conditions. This enables more tailored and dynamic automation sequences.

Use cases for Zapier:

- **Lead capture:** Automatically capture leads from Facebook Lead Ads, add them to a Google Sheet, and send them an introductory email via Mailchimp.

- **Social media automation:** When a new blog post is published on your website, create a Zap to automatically share it on LinkedIn, Twitter, and Facebook.

- **E-commerce notifications:** Send automated SMS or email notifications to customers when their order status changes, such as "Order Shipped" or "Out for Delivery."

Example: A digital marketing agency can use Zapier to streamline client onboarding. When a new client signs a contract (triggered through an e-signature tool like DocuSign), Zapier can automatically add their information to the agency's CRM, create a new project in the project management tool, and send a welcome email to the client.

3. HubSpot

HubSpot is a comprehensive inbound marketing, sales, and service platform that offers a wide range of automation tools. With its built-in CRM, marketing automation, and sales tools, HubSpot provides an all-in-one solution for managing the entire customer journey—from lead generation to customer support.

Key features of HubSpot:

- **Email marketing automation:** HubSpot allows you to create automated email workflows based on customer behavior, such as website visits, form submissions, or email interactions. You can send targeted emails, schedule follow-ups, and nurture leads throughout the sales funnel.

- **Lead scoring and segmentation:** Automatically score leads based on their activity, engagement, and interactions with your content. HubSpot's segmentation tools allow you to categorize contacts into lists for more targeted marketing campaigns.

- **CRM integration:** HubSpot's CRM is integrated into its marketing platform, allowing you to automate data entry, track customer interactions, and manage the sales pipeline. Automated workflows can update contact records, assign leads to sales reps, and set follow-up reminders.

- **Analytics and reporting:** HubSpot provides detailed analytics on campaign performance, website traffic, lead generation, and customer behavior. These insights help you refine your marketing strategies and measure ROI.

Use cases for HubSpot:

- **Lead nurturing:** Set up email workflows to nurture leads based on their interactions with your website, such as downloading an e-book or attending a webinar. HubSpot can send tailored content and track lead progress, notifying the sales team when a lead is ready for follow-up.

- **Customer onboarding:** Automate the onboarding process for new customers by sending them a series of welcome emails, tutorials, and resources, ensuring they have a smooth experience with your product or service.

- **Campaign analytics:** Track the performance of marketing campaigns in real-time, including email open rates, click-through rates, and conversion metrics. Use these insights to optimize future campaigns and improve customer engagement.

Example: A SaaS company uses HubSpot to automate lead scoring based on website interactions, such as visiting the pricing page or starting a free trial. When a lead reaches a certain score, HubSpot automatically assigns it to a sales representative for personalized outreach, increasing the chances of conversion.

4. ActiveCampaign

ActiveCampaign is a versatile marketing automation platform known for its powerful email marketing, CRM, and customer experience automation tools. It provides a range of features designed to help businesses nurture leads, segment audiences, and deliver personalized customer experiences.

Key features of ActiveCampaign:

- **Advanced email automation:** ActiveCampaign enables you to create complex email automation workflows using a visual builder. You can set up triggers, actions, conditions, and delays to deliver highly targeted and personalized email sequences.

- **Customer segmentation:** Segment your audience based on various criteria, such as demographics, purchase behavior, website activity, and engagement. Dynamic segmentation automatically updates lists based on changes in customer data.

- **CRM and sales automation:** ActiveCampaign's built-in CRM automates lead management, task assignments, and sales follow-ups. The CRM is integrated with email and automation tools, providing a unified platform for managing customer relationships.

- **Behavioral tracking:** Track customer interactions, such as email opens, link clicks, website visits, and form submissions, to trigger automated workflows that respond to customer behavior in real-time.

Use cases for ActiveCampaign:

- **Welcome series:** Automatically send a series of welcome emails to new subscribers, introducing them to your brand, products, and services. Follow up with tailored content based on their interactions with the emails.

- **Cart abandonment:** For e-commerce businesses, set up an automated cart abandonment workflow to remind customers of the items they left in their cart, offering incentives like discounts to encourage them to complete the purchase.

- **Sales follow-up:** Automate sales follow-ups by setting up workflows that notify sales reps when a lead reaches a certain stage in the sales pipeline or requests a demo, ensuring timely and personalized outreach.

Example: An online course provider uses ActiveCampaign to segment students based on their course progress and engagement. Automated emails are sent to encourage students to complete modules, recommend additional courses, and offer discounts on new enrollments.

Choosing the right tool for your business

When selecting a marketing automation tool, consider factors such as your business size, marketing goals, budget, and technical expertise. Each tool has unique features and strengths that cater to different needs:

- **Make:** Ideal for businesses looking for customizable, multi-step automation workflows across various apps and services.

- **Zapier:** Best suited for small to medium-sized businesses that want a simple, no-code solution to automate routine tasks and integrate multiple apps.

- **HubSpot:** An all-in-one solution for inbound marketing, CRM, and sales automation, perfect for businesses seeking a comprehensive platform to manage the entire customer journey.

- **ActiveCampaign:** A robust option for those focused on advanced email marketing, customer segmentation, and sales automation.

The bottom line: leveraging tools to streamline marketing automation

Marketing automation tools like Make, Zapier, HubSpot, and ActiveCampaign empower businesses to automate complex marketing processes, enhance customer experiences, and scale their efforts without burnout. By selecting the right tools and leveraging their capabilities, you can optimize your marketing strategy, nurture customer relationships, and drive sustainable growth.

Automating repetitive tasks: email campaigns, lead nurturing, CRM updates

In the realm of marketing, many tasks are repetitive yet crucial for driving engagement, nurturing leads, and maintaining customer relationships. These tasks, while time-consuming, can be automated to streamline workflows, enhance efficiency, and deliver consistent, personalized experiences. **Automating repetitive marketing tasks** such as email campaigns, lead nurturing, and CRM updates can significantly free up time for your team to focus on strategy, creativity, and growth initiatives.

1. Automating email campaigns

Email marketing is a powerful tool for engaging with customers, nurturing leads, and driving conversions. However, manually managing email campaigns can be a logistical challenge, particularly as your contact list grows. Automating email campaigns enables you to send targeted messages at the right time based on customer behavior, engagement, and lifecycle stage.

Key ways to automate email campaigns:

1.   **Drip campaigns:** A **drip campaign** is a series of automated emails sent over a set period to guide leads

through the sales funnel or keep customers engaged. You can use drip campaigns to onboard new customers, nurture prospects, or encourage repeat purchases.

- o **Example:** A SaaS company can create an onboarding drip campaign for new users. The series might start with a welcome email, followed by tutorials, tips, and feature highlights spaced out over the first few weeks of the user's journey.

2. **Triggered emails:** Set up **triggered emails** based on specific user actions or milestones. Triggered emails are personalized and sent at the most relevant moments, increasing the likelihood of engagement and conversions.

- o **Example:** An e-commerce store can automatically send an abandoned cart email when a customer adds items to their cart but doesn't complete the purchase. The email can include a reminder of the products left behind, along with an incentive like a discount to encourage the customer to finalize the purchase.

3. **Behavior-based targeting:** Marketing automation tools allow you to track customer interactions, such as website visits, email opens, and link clicks. You can then use this data to automatically segment contacts and send behavior-specific emails.

- o **Example:** A content platform can track which articles a user reads and send automated recommendations for related content or products, enhancing the user's experience and keeping them engaged.

4. **A/B testing:** Automate **A/B testing** within your email campaigns to test different subject lines, content, or CTAs. Automation tools like HubSpot and ActiveCampaign can

send different versions of an email to segments of your list and analyze the performance, allowing you to optimize future campaigns.

Benefits of automating email campaigns:

- **Consistency:** Ensures timely and consistent communication with your audience, maintaining brand presence and engagement.

- **Personalization:** Delivers tailored messages that resonate with individual customers based on their behavior, preferences, and lifecycle stage.

- **Scalability:** Allows you to manage large-scale campaigns without manual intervention, freeing up time for strategic planning and creativity.

2. Automating lead nurturing

Lead nurturing is the process of building relationships with prospects and guiding them through the buyer's journey. Nurturing requires ongoing communication and the delivery of relevant content, which can be resource-intensive if handled manually. **Automation** makes lead nurturing scalable and effective, ensuring that leads receive the right messages at the right time.

Automating lead nurturing involves:

1. **Lead scoring:** Lead scoring assigns values to leads based on their interactions, engagement level, and fit with your target customer profile. Automation tools track these interactions and automatically update lead scores, helping you identify which leads are most likely to convert.

   o **Example:** An automation system can assign points to a lead every time they visit a product page, download a resource, or open an email. When the lead reaches a predefined score threshold, the system automatically notifies the sales team to initiate a personalized outreach.

2. **Nurture sequences:** Set up **nurture sequences**—automated email workflows that deliver targeted content based on lead behavior and interests. These sequences guide leads through the buyer's journey, providing educational content, case studies, and product information that align with their needs.

   o **Example:** A marketing automation tool like HubSpot can automatically enroll new leads in a content-driven nurture sequence. The workflow might start with an introductory email, followed by educational articles, whitepapers, and success stories sent at intervals over several weeks.

3. **Dynamic content delivery:** Personalize your nurture efforts by using **dynamic content** in your emails, landing pages, and website. Automation tools can customize content based on a lead's profile, industry, or previous interactions, creating a tailored experience that resonates with them.

   o **Example:** An e-learning platform can use automation to display course recommendations on its website based on a visitor's browsing history and previous interactions, improving the chances of enrollment.

4. **Automatic follow-up:** Automation ensures timely follow-ups based on lead behavior. For example, if a lead clicks a link to download a product brochure, the system can automatically send a follow-up email offering a free consultation or demo.

    ○   **Example:** A real estate agency can use automated follow-ups to engage leads who have shown interest in a property. If a lead visits the property listing page multiple times, the system can trigger an email offering a virtual tour or requesting feedback on their interest level.

Benefits of automating lead nurturing:

- **Higher conversion rates:** Personalized, relevant content delivered at the right time increases the likelihood of converting leads into customers.

- **Efficient lead management:** Automated lead scoring and nurturing reduce the need for manual tracking, ensuring no lead falls through the cracks.

- **Enhanced customer relationships:** Automation supports consistent communication, keeping leads engaged and building trust over time.

3. Automating CRM updates

A **customer relationship management (CRM) system** is the central hub for managing customer interactions and tracking sales activities. Keeping your CRM up-to-date is essential for effective lead management, sales forecasting, and customer retention. However, manual data entry can be error-prone and time-consuming. **Automation** streamlines CRM updates, ensuring accurate and timely data while freeing your team to focus on high-value activities.

Ways to automate CRM updates:

1. **Lead capture:** Use automation tools like Zapier or Make to automatically capture new leads from various sources—such as web forms, social media, and email sign-ups—and add them to your CRM.

    o   **Example:** When a visitor fills out a contact form on your website, an automation tool can create a new lead record in your CRM, including the visitor's contact information and details from the form submission.

2. **Data enrichment:** Automate data enrichment processes to enhance lead and customer profiles with additional information. For example, use an integration with a data enrichment service to automatically update records with social media profiles, company details, or job titles.

    o   **Example:** A B2B company can use an automation tool to append LinkedIn profiles to new leads in the CRM, providing the sales team with more context for personalized outreach.

3. **Lead assignment:** Automatically assign leads to sales reps based on criteria such as territory, product interest, or lead score. This ensures leads are promptly followed up and routed to the most appropriate team member.

    o   **Example:** When a lead reaches a certain score in your lead scoring model, the system can automatically assign it to a sales rep and send a notification, prompting immediate action.

4. **Activity logging:** Track customer interactions and log them in the CRM automatically. For instance, you can automate the logging of email opens, link clicks, website visits, and form submissions, providing a complete history of the customer journey.

    o   **Example:** A marketing automation platform like HubSpot can automatically log every interaction a lead has with your content (e.g., emails opened, links clicked) in the CRM, giving the sales team a comprehensive view of the lead's engagement level.

5. **Pipeline updates:** Set up automated triggers to update pipeline stages based on lead activities. For example, when a lead schedules a product demo, the CRM can automatically move them to the "Demo Scheduled" stage in the sales pipeline.

   ○ **Example:** When a sales rep marks a deal as "Won" in the CRM, the automation system can trigger follow-up actions, such as sending a thank-you email to the customer and notifying the finance team for invoicing.

Benefits of automating CRM updates:

- **Data accuracy:** Automation reduces human error and ensures that customer records are accurate, complete, and up-to-date.

- **Time savings:** Eliminates manual data entry, freeing up sales and marketing teams to focus on high-impact activities, such as closing deals and building customer relationships.

- **Improved collaboration:** Real-time updates and centralized data in the CRM facilitate better collaboration between marketing, sales, and customer support teams.

The bottom line: enhancing efficiency with automation

Automating repetitive tasks like email campaigns, lead nurturing, and CRM updates is essential for scaling your marketing efforts efficiently and maintaining high-quality customer interactions. By leveraging marketing automation tools, you can ensure consistent communication, optimize lead management, and keep your CRM data accurate and actionable. This automation not only streamlines workflows but also provides a personalized customer experience that drives engagement, conversions, and long-term loyalty.

Case studies: companies that mastered automation

Marketing automation has become a game-changer for businesses of all sizes, enabling them to efficiently manage customer interactions, nurture leads, and scale their marketing efforts. Let's explore some case studies of companies that have mastered automation, highlighting their strategies and the results they achieved.

1. Airbnb: automating customer engagement

Company Overview: Airbnb is an online marketplace that connects people looking for lodging with those who have accommodations to rent. With millions of users and listings worldwide, Airbnb needed a way to manage customer communications efficiently while providing personalized experiences.

Automation strategies used:

- **Personalized email campaigns:** Airbnb uses marketing automation to send personalized emails to guests and hosts based on their behavior, preferences, and past interactions. For example, guests receive tailored recommendations for accommodations based on their previous searches, while hosts receive tips on optimizing their listings.

- **Automated notifications:** Airbnb leverages in-app notifications and SMS to provide timely updates, such as booking confirmations, check-in instructions, and reminders for hosts to review their guests. These automated messages keep users informed and engaged without the need for manual intervention.

- **A/B testing and optimization:** Airbnb conducts automated A/B tests on email content, subject lines, and notifications to optimize engagement rates. Automation tools track user interactions and provide data-driven insights that guide future communication strategies.

Results: By implementing automation, Airbnb has been able to manage millions of customer interactions seamlessly, delivering highly relevant content and improving user experience. The personalized, automated approach has helped increase booking rates and enhance customer satisfaction, contributing to Airbnb's continued growth.

2. HubSpot: scaling inbound marketing with automation

Company Overview: HubSpot is a leading provider of marketing, sales, and customer service software. As a company that offers marketing automation solutions, HubSpot has effectively implemented its own tools to scale its inbound marketing strategy.

Automation strategies used:

- **Lead nurturing workflows:** HubSpot uses its automation platform to create lead nurturing workflows that deliver tailored content to prospects based on their interactions with the website, emails, and other marketing materials. Leads are automatically enrolled in workflows that align with their lifecycle stage, such as new visitor, marketing-qualified lead, or sales-qualified lead.
- **Dynamic segmentation:** HubSpot's CRM automation allows for dynamic segmentation of contacts based on various criteria, such as behavior, demographics, and engagement level. Segments are automatically updated as

new data comes in, ensuring that contacts receive targeted content that matches their current needs and interests.

- **Automated sales alerts:** When a lead reaches a certain score or performs a high-intent action (e.g., requesting a product demo), HubSpot's automation system triggers an alert to the appropriate sales representative. This ensures timely and personalized follow-ups, increasing the chances of conversion.

Results: By utilizing marketing automation, HubSpot has been able to manage and nurture a vast number of leads effectively. The company's automated workflows have contributed to a streamlined sales process, improved lead qualification, and higher conversion rates. Additionally, HubSpot's use of dynamic segmentation has enhanced its ability to deliver personalized content, leading to increased customer engagement and retention.

3. Netflix: personalized content recommendations

Company Overview: Netflix is a global streaming service that offers a vast library of TV shows, movies, and original content. With a diverse user base, Netflix needed a way to personalize content recommendations and keep users engaged over the long term.

Automation strategies used:

- **Behavior-based content recommendations:** Netflix uses an advanced algorithm that analyzes user behavior, such as viewing history, ratings, and searches, to automatically generate personalized content recommendations. The system dynamically adjusts these recommendations in real-time, providing a unique browsing experience for each user.

- **Automated notifications:** Netflix sends automated notifications to users, such as new content alerts,

"Continue Watching" reminders, and suggestions for titles similar to those they've watched. These notifications are tailored to individual preferences, keeping users engaged with the platform.

- **A/B testing:** Netflix automates A/B testing to optimize various aspects of its platform, including content recommendations, user interface design, and promotional messaging. By analyzing user interactions, Netflix identifies the most effective elements and continuously refines the user experience.

Results: Netflix's use of automation has been instrumental in maintaining high user engagement and satisfaction. Personalized recommendations have led to longer viewing times, reduced churn rates, and increased subscription renewals. The company's ability to automatically adapt to user preferences has been a key factor in its success in the competitive streaming market.

4. Amazon: optimizing customer experience through automation

Company Overview: Amazon is a global e-commerce giant known for its vast product selection, competitive pricing, and customer-centric approach. To manage its extensive customer base and complex supply chain, Amazon heavily relies on automation.

Automation strategies used:

- **Personalized product recommendations:** Amazon's recommendation engine uses automation and machine learning to analyze customer behavior, including browsing history, past purchases, and items added to the cart. This data is used to automatically generate personalized product recommendations, such as "Customers Who Bought This Also Bought" and "Frequently Bought Together."

- **Automated email campaigns:** Amazon sends automated email campaigns based on customer behavior, such as abandoned cart reminders, order confirmation emails, and follow-up requests for product reviews. These targeted messages enhance the customer experience and encourage repeat purchases.

- **Dynamic pricing:** Amazon uses automated pricing algorithms to adjust product prices in real-time based on factors such as demand, competition, and inventory levels. This dynamic pricing strategy enables Amazon to remain competitive and maximize sales.

Results: Automation has allowed Amazon to deliver a seamless, personalized shopping experience that drives customer loyalty and repeat business. The automated recommendation engine alone has been responsible for a significant portion of Amazon's sales, as it effectively upsells and cross-sells products. Additionally, dynamic pricing automation has helped Amazon optimize revenue and maintain its market leadership.

5. Spotify: tailored user experiences with automation

Company Overview: Spotify is a leading music streaming platform known for its personalized playlists, music discovery features, and user-friendly interface. With millions of songs and a global user base, Spotify leverages automation to create tailored listening experiences.

Automation strategies used:

- **Personalized playlists:** Spotify's automation system uses algorithms and data analytics to analyze user listening habits, preferences, and activity. This information is used to create personalized playlists like "Discover Weekly" and "Release Radar," offering users tailored music recommendations.

- **Automated notifications:** Spotify sends automated notifications to users, such as new music alerts from their favorite artists, playlist updates, and concert announcements. These notifications keep users engaged with the app and encourage continued use.

- **Behavior tracking:** Spotify tracks user interactions, including song skips, favorites, and playlist additions. This data feeds into automated algorithms that continuously refine the recommendations, enhancing the personalization of each user's music experience.

-

Results: Spotify's use of automation has significantly contributed to its user engagement and retention. By providing highly personalized music recommendations, Spotify keeps users returning to the platform, driving subscription renewals and encouraging free users to upgrade to premium plans. The automation of playlist curation and notifications has been key to delivering a seamless and enjoyable user experience.

The bottom line: learning from the masters of automation

These companies—Airbnb, HubSpot, Netflix, Amazon, and Spotify—demonstrate the power of marketing automation in driving engagement, enhancing customer experiences, and achieving scalable growth. By implementing automation strategies like personalized email campaigns, behavior-based recommendations, and dynamic segmentation, they have streamlined their marketing efforts and built stronger relationships with their customers. The success of these companies highlights the importance of leveraging automation to not only simplify processes but also to deliver meaningful, tailored experiences that foster loyalty and long-term success.

CHAPTER 11

AI-powered growth: the future is now

Understanding AI's role in marketing: from chatbots to analytics

Artificial intelligence (AI) is reshaping the marketing landscape, enabling businesses to enhance customer experiences, optimize campaigns, and make data-driven decisions. By harnessing AI-powered tools, companies can automate repetitive tasks, analyze vast amounts of data, personalize interactions, and even predict customer behavior. From **chatbots** that provide instant customer support to **analytics** tools that deliver actionable insights, AI has become a pivotal component of modern marketing strategies.

The transformative power of AI in marketing

AI's role in marketing extends far beyond simple automation. Its true power lies in its ability to **learn** from data, adapt to changing customer behaviors, and provide real-time responses. This transformative capability empowers businesses to:

1.   **Enhance customer engagement:** AI enables instant, personalized interactions through chatbots, recommendation engines, and targeted content delivery, resulting in higher engagement and satisfaction.

2. **Optimize marketing efforts:** AI-driven analytics provide deep insights into customer behavior, campaign performance, and market trends, enabling marketers to refine their strategies and maximize ROI.

3. **Drive growth with personalization:** AI analyzes customer data to understand preferences and behaviors, allowing marketers to deliver highly personalized experiences at scale, which drives conversions and customer loyalty.

AI applications in marketing

Here's how AI is being applied in key areas of marketing, from customer interaction to analytics:

1.   Chatbots for instant customer support

AI-powered chatbots have revolutionized customer service by providing instant, 24/7 support through websites, social media, and messaging apps. Using natural language processing (NLP) and machine learning, chatbots can understand customer queries, provide relevant responses, and perform tasks like booking appointments or processing orders.

Benefits of AI chatbots:

- **Instant responses:** Chatbots can handle multiple customer interactions simultaneously, providing immediate answers to common questions and reducing wait times.

- **Cost-effective:** By automating routine customer support tasks, chatbots free up human agents to focus on more complex inquiries, reducing overall support costs.

- **Personalization:** Advanced chatbots can access customer data, such as purchase history or preferences, to deliver tailored responses and product recommendations.

Example: H&M's chatbot on the messaging app Kik engages customers by offering style suggestions, helping them find specific clothing items, and providing fashion advice based on the user's preferences. This interactive experience not only aids in product discovery but also strengthens customer relationships.

2. AI-driven content personalization

AI-powered content personalization uses customer data and behavior analysis to tailor marketing content, product recommendations, and messages for individual users. AI can dynamically adjust website content, emails, and ads to match each user's interests, enhancing the relevance and impact of the marketing.

How AI personalizes content:

- **Dynamic website content:** AI algorithms analyze user behavior on websites and adjust content accordingly. For instance, an e-commerce site may highlight products that a returning visitor has previously browsed or purchased, increasing the likelihood of conversion.

- **Product recommendations:** AI recommendation engines, like those used by Netflix and Amazon, analyze customer preferences and suggest products, movies, or services that align with their tastes. This targeted approach boosts user engagement and encourages additional purchases.

- **Targeted emails:** AI tools segment customers based on behavior, demographics, and purchase history, enabling marketers to send personalized emails with tailored offers, content, and product suggestions.

Example: Spotify uses AI to create personalized playlists, such as "Discover Weekly," which recommends songs based on a user's listening habits. This tailored content keeps users engaged with the platform, leading to increased customer retention and satisfaction.

3.   Predictive analytics for customer insights

Predictive analytics is the use of AI and machine learning to analyze historical data, identify patterns, and predict future customer behavior. Marketers use predictive analytics to gain insights into customer preferences, forecast trends, and make data-driven decisions about campaigns, product development, and customer targeting.

Applications of predictive analytics in marketing:

- **Customer segmentation:** AI can analyze customer data to identify distinct segments based on behavior, interests, and purchasing patterns. This segmentation helps marketers create targeted campaigns that resonate with each group.

- **Churn prediction:** AI models can predict which customers are at risk of churning by analyzing factors like engagement levels, purchase frequency, and customer support interactions. With this insight, marketers can take proactive steps, such as offering loyalty incentives or personalized re-engagement campaigns.

- **Sales forecasting:** AI-driven predictive analytics assess historical sales data, market trends, and external factors to forecast future sales, enabling businesses to optimize inventory management, pricing strategies, and marketing spend.

Example: Amazon uses predictive analytics to anticipate what products customers are likely to buy next based on their browsing and purchasing history. This insight informs product recommendations, personalized ads, and inventory planning, driving both customer satisfaction and sales.

4. Programmatic advertising

Programmatic advertising leverages AI to automate the buying and placement of online ads. By using machine learning algorithms, programmatic platforms analyze vast datasets, including customer behavior, demographics, and real-time bidding data, to deliver highly targeted ads to the right audience at the right time.

Key benefits of programmatic advertising:

- **Precision targeting:** AI algorithms evaluate multiple data points, such as browsing behavior, location, and purchase history, to target ads to the most relevant audience segments, increasing the chances of conversion.

- **Real-time optimization:** AI continuously analyzes campaign performance and adjusts bidding strategies in real-time to maximize ad effectiveness and ROI.

- **Reduced costs:** Automated ad placement reduces the need for manual intervention and optimizes ad spend, ensuring budget is allocated to the most impactful placements.

Example: Coca-Cola uses programmatic advertising to target different customer segments with personalized ads. The company leverages AI to analyze consumer data and deliver dynamic content tailored to the user's preferences, location, and behavior, resulting in more effective and engaging campaigns.

5. AI-enhanced customer segmentation

Effective marketing relies on understanding your audience and delivering relevant messages to the right people. **AI-enhanced customer segmentation** uses machine learning to analyze vast amounts of data and identify patterns that may not be apparent through traditional methods. This advanced segmentation allows marketers to create more precise and effective campaigns.

How AI enhances customer segmentation:

- **Behavioral clustering:** AI algorithms group customers based on behaviors, such as purchase frequency, product preferences, or browsing habits. These clusters help marketers tailor campaigns and offers to each group's specific characteristics.

- **Dynamic segmentation:** AI-driven segmentation is dynamic, continuously updating segments as new data becomes available. This ensures that marketing efforts remain relevant and aligned with evolving customer behaviors and preferences.

- **Predictive segmentation:** AI can predict how customers are likely to behave in the future, allowing marketers to identify high-value segments, such as potential loyal customers or those most likely to respond to an upsell.

Example: Sephora uses AI to analyze customer behavior, purchase history, and product preferences to create detailed customer segments. These segments receive personalized product recommendations, tailored emails, and targeted promotions, resulting in increased customer engagement and loyalty.

6.   Automated content creation and optimization

AI-powered tools are increasingly being used for **content creation** and **optimization**. AI can assist marketers in generating text, curating content, and even optimizing visuals to enhance engagement across websites, social media, and advertising platforms.

AI applications in content creation:

- **Copywriting:** AI tools like **Jasper** and **ChatGPT** can generate marketing copy for emails, social media posts, product descriptions, and blog articles. These tools use natural language processing to create content that aligns with brand voice and messaging.

- **Content curation:** AI curates content by analyzing trends, keywords, and customer interests to recommend topics, headlines, and formats that resonate with the target audience. This helps marketers maintain a steady flow of relevant content.

- **Ad optimization:** AI analyzes the performance of digital ads and provides recommendations for optimizing headlines, images, and calls-to-action based on real-time data and user interactions.

Example: The Associated Press (AP) uses AI-powered content generation to automatically write financial reports and news articles. This automation allows AP to produce a high volume of data-driven content quickly and accurately, freeing up journalists to focus on more complex stories.

The future of AI in marketing

AI's role in marketing is constantly evolving, with advancements in natural language processing, machine learning, and predictive analytics driving new applications. The future of AI in marketing will likely involve even more sophisticated personalization, real-time decision-making, and interactive customer experiences, such as voice-activated shopping and virtual assistants.

The bottom line: AI as a growth catalyst

AI is no longer a futuristic concept but a practical, essential tool for modern marketing. By leveraging AI for chatbots, content personalization, predictive analytics, programmatic advertising, customer segmentation, and content creation, businesses can enhance customer interactions, optimize campaigns, and drive growth. The companies that effectively harness the power of AI will be well-positioned to outperform competitors and deliver exceptional customer experiences in the rapidly changing digital landscape.

How machine learning personalizes user experiences

In an era where consumers expect tailored interactions, **machine learning (ML)** has become a cornerstone of personalized marketing. By analyzing vast amounts of data and learning from user behavior, machine learning algorithms can dynamically adjust content, recommendations, and communication to suit individual preferences. This level of personalization creates a seamless and engaging user experience, fostering loyalty, boosting conversions, and maximizing customer lifetime value.

What is machine learning in the context of marketing?

Machine learning is a subset of artificial intelligence that enables computers to learn from data, identify patterns, and make decisions with minimal human intervention. In marketing, ML analyzes customer data—such as browsing behavior, purchase history, and engagement metrics—to predict future actions and deliver personalized experiences.

Unlike traditional rule-based systems, ML continuously learns and adapts based on new data, allowing for real-time adjustments that enhance the customer journey. Whether it's through personalized product recommendations, dynamic content delivery, or targeted messaging, ML-driven marketing creates a more relevant and meaningful interaction for each user.

Applications of machine learning in user personalization

Here are some key ways in which machine learning is used to personalize user experiences:

1.   Personalized product recommendations

One of the most common applications of ML in marketing is **product recommendations**. By analyzing user behavior, purchase history, and interactions, ML algorithms can predict which products a customer is most likely to be interested in, and display those recommendations at the right moment.

How it works:

- **Collaborative filtering:** ML algorithms use collaborative filtering to identify patterns in user behavior. By analyzing what similar users have purchased or interacted with, the system recommends products that align with the preferences of individuals in that group.

- **Content-based filtering:** This method involves analyzing the features of products a user has shown interest in and recommending similar products based on those attributes. For example, if a user frequently buys eco-friendly skincare products, the system will suggest other items with similar characteristics.

- **Hybrid systems:** Advanced ML recommendation engines combine collaborative and content-based filtering to provide more accurate and diverse suggestions.

Example: Amazon's recommendation engine is a prime example of ML in action. The platform analyzes a customer's browsing history, past purchases, and items in their cart to recommend products they might be interested in. This personalized shopping experience not only increases the likelihood of additional purchases but also enhances customer satisfaction.

2. Dynamic website and app content

Dynamic content personalization involves using ML to adjust website or app content in real-time based on user behavior, preferences, and profile data. This ensures that visitors see content that is most relevant to their interests, improving engagement and conversion rates.

How it works:

- **Behavioral analysis:** ML algorithms track user interactions, such as pages visited, time spent on each page, and clicks. Based on this behavior, the system modifies content to match the user's apparent interests.

- **A/B and multivariate testing:** Machine learning can automatically run A/B or multivariate tests to determine which content variations perform best for different audience segments, and then adapt the website to show the most effective versions to each user.

- **Predictive modeling:** By analyzing historical data, ML predicts what type of content (e.g., product highlights, blog articles, promotional banners) is likely to resonate with a particular user and displays it accordingly.

Example: Netflix employs ML to personalize its homepage for each user. The system analyzes viewing habits, genre preferences, and ratings to highlight shows and movies that match the user's taste. It even personalizes the cover art for titles, selecting the image that is most likely to entice the individual viewer based on their interaction history.

3. Customer segmentation and targeted marketing

Machine learning enhances customer segmentation by analyzing data to identify unique patterns and behaviors within your customer base. This segmentation allows marketers to create highly targeted campaigns that address the specific needs and preferences of different groups.

How it works:

- **Behavioral clustering:** ML algorithms group users based on similar behaviors, such as purchasing patterns, frequency of interactions, or responses to past marketing efforts. This clustering helps marketers identify segments like "frequent buyers," "discount seekers," or "loyal advocates."

- **Dynamic segmentation:** Traditional segmentation relies on predefined rules (e.g., age, location), but ML creates dynamic segments that evolve as customer behavior changes. This adaptability ensures that marketing efforts stay relevant over time.

- **Lookalike modeling:** ML identifies characteristics of high-value customers and searches for similar prospects, allowing marketers to target individuals who are likely to convert.

Example: Spotify uses ML to segment its users based on listening habits, preferred genres, and interaction frequency. This segmentation informs personalized marketing messages, such as playlist recommendations and event promotions, increasing user engagement and satisfaction.

4. Personalized email marketing

Email marketing remains a highly effective channel for customer engagement, and machine learning takes it to the next level by personalizing content, timing, and messaging to align with each recipient's preferences.

How it works:

- **Content optimization:** ML analyzes user interactions, such as email opens, clicks, and website behavior, to tailor email content. For instance, a user who frequently clicks on product updates may receive emails featuring the latest product launches, while another user might receive how-to guides or tips.

- **Send time optimization:** Machine learning algorithms determine the optimal time to send emails to each recipient based on their past behavior. By sending emails when the user is most likely to engage, marketers can increase open and click-through rates.

- **Predictive engagement:** ML predicts which email content and offers are most likely to resonate with each segment, allowing marketers to craft targeted messages that drive conversions.

Example: E-commerce brands like ASOS use ML to send personalized emails featuring product recommendations based on the recipient's browsing history, past purchases, and style preferences. This tailored approach results in higher engagement rates and encourages repeat purchases.

5. Predictive customer support

Machine learning enhances **customer support** by predicting customer needs and providing personalized assistance. AI-driven chatbots, virtual assistants, and predictive support tools use ML to understand customer queries, anticipate issues, and recommend solutions tailored to the individual.

How it works:

- **AI chatbots:** ML-powered chatbots use natural language processing (NLP) to understand customer inquiries and provide relevant responses. They can access customer data, such as recent orders or account information, to offer personalized support.

- **Proactive support:** ML analyzes customer behavior to identify patterns that might indicate an issue, such as a sudden drop in product usage. The system can then trigger proactive support actions, such as sending a helpful email or offering a live chat session.

- **Self-service recommendations:** Machine learning helps identify common customer questions and issues, providing automated recommendations for self-service resources, such as FAQs or knowledge base articles, based on the user's profile and interaction history.

Example: Zendesk uses ML in its customer support platform to provide predictive insights, automatically routing tickets to the most appropriate support agent based on the nature of the query and past interactions. This intelligent routing speeds up resolution times and enhances the overall support experience.

6.   Automated content creation and curation

Machine learning is also making strides in content creation and curation. AI-powered tools can generate written content, such as product descriptions, social media posts, and even news articles, based on predefined parameters and user data.

How it works:

- **Content generation:** Tools like GPT-3 (which powers ChatGPT) use natural language processing to generate content that aligns with specific guidelines, such as tone, format, and key messages. Marketers can use this AI-generated content for blog posts, emails, and social media.

- **Content curation:** ML algorithms analyze trending topics, user interests, and engagement data to recommend content for curation. This approach ensures that content shared with users is both relevant and timely.

- **Visual content adaptation:** Some advanced ML tools can automatically edit visual content, such as resizing images or generating dynamic ad creatives based on user preferences and engagement data.

Example: The Washington Post's AI tool, Heliograf, generates news stories on topics like sports scores, election results, and financial updates. By automating content creation, the newspaper provides timely and data-driven reports while freeing up journalists to focus on more complex reporting.

The bottom line: machine learning as a personalization engine

Machine learning is at the heart of personalization in modern marketing. By analyzing customer behavior, preferences, and interactions, ML enables marketers to tailor product recommendations, website content, email messaging, and customer support in real-time. This level of personalization not only improves user experiences but also drives engagement, loyalty, and revenue growth. As machine learning technology continues to advance, businesses that leverage its capabilities will gain a competitive edge in delivering seamless and meaningful customer experiences.

AI-driven marketing tools like Jasper, ChatGPT, and OpenAI

The advent of **AI-driven marketing tools** has revolutionized how businesses approach content creation, customer interaction, and data analysis. Tools like **Jasper**, **ChatGPT**, and **OpenAI** are making it easier for marketers to create high-quality content, personalize customer experiences, and optimize marketing strategies efficiently. By automating repetitive tasks and providing intelligent insights, these tools free up time for marketers to focus on creativity, strategy, and innovation.

1. Jasper: AI-powered content creation

Jasper (formerly Jarvis) is an AI-powered content generation tool designed to assist marketers, writers, and businesses in creating compelling and engaging copy. Leveraging advanced language models, Jasper can write blogs, product descriptions, social media posts, emails, and more in a variety of tones and styles.

Key features of Jasper:

- **Content generation:** Jasper uses natural language processing (NLP) to generate text based on prompts provided by the user. Marketers can input details such as tone, target audience, and key points, and Jasper produces content that aligns with these guidelines.

- **Multiple templates:** The platform offers a variety of pre-built templates for different types of content, such as blog introductions, ad copy, social media posts, product descriptions, and email subject lines. This feature simplifies content creation and ensures consistency across channels.

- **SEO optimization:** Jasper integrates with SEO tools, allowing users to optimize content for keywords, readability, and engagement. This ensures that the AI-generated copy not only resonates with readers but also ranks well in search engine results.

Use cases for Jasper:

- **Blog writing:** Marketers can use Jasper to draft blog articles by providing a brief overview or headline. The AI generates a detailed and structured article, which can then be edited and refined to meet specific content goals.

- **Ad copy creation:** Jasper's templates enable quick generation of catchy ad copy for platforms like Facebook, Google Ads, and Instagram, helping marketers craft compelling messages that drive clicks and conversions.

- **Email marketing:** Jasper assists in writing personalized email copy for various campaigns, such as promotional emails, newsletters, and follow-ups. By specifying the tone and audience, marketers can produce targeted messages that resonate with recipients.

Example: A digital marketing agency uses Jasper to create blog posts for multiple clients across different industries. By providing Jasper with industry-specific keywords and topics, the agency can quickly generate high-quality content that aligns with each client's voice and messaging.

2. ChatGPT: conversational AI for customer engagement

ChatGPT, powered by OpenAI, is an advanced conversational AI model designed to understand and generate human-like responses in natural language. This tool is widely used in customer support, chatbots, content generation, and other applications where interactive, contextual communication is essential.

Key features of ChatGPT:

- **Natural language understanding:** ChatGPT can comprehend complex queries, detect context, and provide relevant responses. This makes it an ideal tool for automating customer interactions in a way that feels personalized and conversational.

- **Content creation:** Beyond chat interactions, ChatGPT is capable of generating written content for blogs, social media, FAQs, product descriptions, and more. Marketers can use it to draft and refine various forms of copy.

- **Customizability:** ChatGPT can be fine-tuned to match a brand's voice and style. Businesses can train the model with specific data or guidelines to ensure that responses align with brand messaging.

Use cases for ChatGPT:

- **Chatbots:** Integrating ChatGPT into customer support chatbots enables businesses to provide instant, 24/7 assistance. The AI can handle a wide range of customer inquiries, from answering product questions to assisting with troubleshooting, enhancing the overall customer experience.

- **Lead qualification:** ChatGPT-powered chatbots can engage with website visitors, qualify leads by asking relevant questions, and guide prospects through the sales funnel. When leads meet specific criteria, they can be handed off to a human sales representative for further interaction.

- **Social media engagement:** Marketers can use ChatGPT to draft social media responses, create engaging posts, and generate content ideas that align with current trends and audience preferences.

Example: A SaaS company uses ChatGPT to power its website chatbot, which answers customer questions, provides product recommendations, and collects information for lead qualification. The AI-driven chatbot improves customer engagement by providing immediate, relevant responses, thereby enhancing the user experience and driving conversions.

3. OpenAI: the platform behind AI-driven innovation

OpenAI is the research organization that developed the GPT-3 language model, which powers both Jasper and ChatGPT. OpenAI's models are known for their ability to generate human-like text based on inputs, making them valuable tools for a wide range of marketing applications.

Key capabilities of OpenAI models:

- **Language generation:** OpenAI's language models can generate coherent, contextually appropriate text across various formats, including articles, product descriptions, customer support responses, and more.

- **Sentiment analysis:** OpenAI's models can analyze the sentiment of customer feedback, reviews, and social media comments, helping businesses understand customer opinions and refine their marketing strategies.

- **Creative assistance:** In addition to structured content, OpenAI can assist in brainstorming ideas, crafting creative copy, and providing suggestions for slogans, taglines, and campaign themes.

Use cases for OpenAI:

- **Content moderation:** OpenAI's models can be used to moderate user-generated content, such as comments, reviews, and forum posts. By automatically flagging inappropriate or off-topic content, businesses can maintain a positive brand image and foster a healthy online community.

- **Email automation:** OpenAI can be integrated into email marketing platforms to generate personalized email copy based on customer behavior, preferences, and engagement history. This automation enables marketers to scale their email campaigns while maintaining a personalized touch.

- **Customer feedback analysis:** OpenAI's sentiment analysis capabilities allow businesses to analyze large volumes of customer feedback, identifying trends and insights that inform product development, marketing strategies, and customer support improvements.

Example: An e-commerce company uses OpenAI's API to automatically generate product descriptions for its online store. By feeding product specifications and features into the AI model, the company can quickly produce compelling, SEO-optimized descriptions that enhance the shopping experience.

How to leverage AI-driven tools for growth

Using tools like Jasper, ChatGPT, and OpenAI, marketers can enhance their strategies in the following ways:

1. **Automate content creation:** Use Jasper and OpenAI for drafting blog posts, product descriptions, and email campaigns. This automation speeds up the content creation process while ensuring consistency and quality across different channels.

2. **Enhance customer interactions:** Integrate ChatGPT into chatbots and customer support systems to provide instant, personalized responses. This improves customer satisfaction and frees up human agents to handle more complex inquiries.

3. **Personalize marketing efforts:** Utilize AI's natural language processing to analyze customer data, preferences, and interactions. With this insight, you can create targeted campaigns, tailored content, and personalized product recommendations that resonate with your audience.

4. **Gain actionable insights:** Use OpenAI's sentiment analysis to monitor customer feedback and social media conversations. This data-driven approach allows you to understand customer sentiments, track emerging trends, and refine your marketing strategies accordingly.

The bottom line: leveraging AI-driven tools for smarter marketing

AI-driven marketing tools like Jasper, ChatGPT, and OpenAI are transforming the way businesses approach content creation, customer engagement, and data analysis. By automating routine tasks, enhancing personalization, and providing actionable insights, these tools enable marketers to optimize their efforts, increase efficiency, and drive growth. The companies that embrace AI-driven marketing will be better equipped to meet customer expectations, stay ahead of market trends, and achieve sustainable success.

Predictive analytics and customer segmentation powered by AI

Predictive analytics and **customer segmentation** are fundamental components of modern marketing strategies, enabling businesses to anticipate customer behavior, tailor campaigns, and make data-driven decisions. With the integration of **artificial intelligence (AI)**, these practices have evolved to be more accurate, dynamic, and actionable. AI-powered tools analyze vast amounts of customer data, identify patterns, and generate insights that help marketers understand their audience, optimize campaigns, and drive revenue growth.

What is predictive analytics in marketing?

Predictive analytics in marketing involves using data analysis, machine learning, and statistical algorithms to predict future outcomes based on historical data. AI-driven predictive analytics can forecast customer behavior, market trends, and campaign performance, allowing marketers to make informed decisions and proactively address potential challenges.

By incorporating AI into predictive analytics, businesses gain a deeper understanding of their customers and can fine-tune their marketing strategies to align with predicted behaviors. This level of foresight enables personalized marketing, optimized resource allocation, and improved ROI.

AI-powered customer segmentation: understanding your audience

Customer segmentation is the process of dividing a customer base into distinct groups based on shared characteristics such as demographics, behavior, or preferences. Traditional segmentation methods rely on static data, but AI-powered segmentation dynamically adapts to changing customer behaviors, providing a more nuanced understanding of the audience.

How AI enhances customer segmentation:

1. **Behavioral clustering:** AI algorithms analyze customer behavior, including browsing habits, purchase history, interaction frequency, and content engagement, to identify clusters or segments. This behavioral-based segmentation helps marketers target groups more effectively with relevant messaging.

2. **Dynamic updates:** AI-powered segmentation automatically updates as new customer data is collected, ensuring that marketing efforts remain aligned with the most current customer profiles. This continuous adaptation

allows businesses to respond quickly to changes in customer preferences.

3. **Predictive segmentation:** By using predictive analytics, AI can segment customers based on predicted future behaviors, such as likelihood to purchase, risk of churn, or response to specific promotions. This proactive segmentation supports personalized marketing initiatives and customer retention strategies.

Example: A subscription-based streaming service uses AI to segment its user base into groups such as "casual viewers," "binge-watchers," and "genre enthusiasts." These segments receive tailored recommendations, content suggestions, and marketing messages that match their viewing habits and preferences, resulting in higher engagement and retention rates.

Applications of AI-powered predictive analytics and segmentation

Here are some key applications of AI in predictive analytics and customer segmentation that marketers can leverage to drive growth:

1. Churn prediction and retention strategies

Churn prediction is a critical aspect of customer retention. By using AI-powered predictive analytics, businesses can identify customers at risk of churning and take proactive measures to retain them.

How it works:

- **Behavioral analysis:** AI models analyze customer behaviors, such as decreased engagement, reduced purchasing frequency, or negative interactions with customer support, to identify patterns associated with churn.

- **Risk scoring:** The system assigns a churn risk score to each customer, indicating the likelihood that they may stop using the product or service. This scoring allows marketers to prioritize retention efforts.

- **Personalized retention campaigns:** With this insight, businesses can create targeted campaigns to re-engage at-risk customers. These campaigns may include special offers, personalized messages, or loyalty incentives aimed at restoring the customer's interest.

Example: A fitness app uses AI to monitor user activity, identifying subscribers who have not engaged with workout plans or logged activity in the past month. The system assigns a high churn risk score to these users and triggers an automated re-engagement campaign offering a discount on a personal training session, encouraging them to return to the app.

2.   Sales forecasting and inventory optimization

Sales forecasting is essential for effective inventory management, marketing planning, and revenue growth. AI-driven predictive analytics analyze historical sales data, market trends, seasonal factors, and external variables to forecast future sales with greater accuracy.

How it works:

- **Data integration:** AI models integrate various data sources, including past sales performance, customer demographics, website traffic, social media trends, and economic indicators, to generate comprehensive sales forecasts.

- **Seasonal adjustments:** AI automatically identifies seasonal patterns and adjusts forecasts accordingly, helping businesses anticipate demand fluctuations and optimize inventory levels.

- **Scenario analysis:** Predictive analytics enable businesses to simulate different scenarios, such as the impact of a new product launch or promotional campaign on sales, allowing marketers to plan more effectively.

Example: A clothing retailer uses AI-powered predictive analytics to forecast sales for its upcoming winter collection. By analyzing historical sales data, weather patterns, and fashion trends, the retailer optimizes its inventory levels and plans a targeted marketing campaign to promote key items, reducing overstock and enhancing sales performance.

3.   Customer lifetime value (CLV) prediction

Customer lifetime value (CLV) is a critical metric that represents the total revenue a business can expect from a customer over the entire duration of their relationship. AI-powered predictive analytics can accurately estimate CLV by analyzing customer behavior, purchasing habits, and engagement levels.

How it works:

- **Behavioral tracking:** AI tracks customer interactions, purchase frequency, average order value, and product preferences to calculate CLV.

- **Segmentation based on CLV:** Customers are segmented into different groups based on their predicted lifetime value, such as high-value, moderate-value, or low-value customers. This segmentation informs marketing strategies and resource allocation.

- **Targeted marketing:** Businesses can tailor their marketing efforts to maximize CLV by offering personalized experiences, upselling opportunities, loyalty programs, and retention initiatives for high-value customers.

Example: An online retailer uses AI to predict the CLV of its customer base. High-CLV customers are automatically enrolled in a VIP loyalty program, where they receive exclusive promotions, early access to sales, and personalized recommendations, strengthening their loyalty and increasing their long-term value to the company.

4. Campaign performance prediction and optimization
AI-powered predictive analytics enhance **campaign performance** by forecasting potential outcomes, enabling marketers to adjust strategies before launching full-scale campaigns.

How it works:

- **Historical data analysis:** AI analyzes past campaign performance data, including engagement rates, conversions, ad spend, and customer responses, to predict the success of future campaigns.

- **Real-time adjustments:** Predictive models provide real-time insights during ongoing campaigns, allowing marketers to adjust elements such as targeting, messaging, or budget allocation for optimal performance.

- **A/B testing recommendations:** AI recommends which campaign variations are likely to perform best based on historical testing data, streamlining the A/B testing process and maximizing ROI.

Example: A software company uses AI to predict the performance of its upcoming email marketing campaign. By analyzing previous email data, including open rates, click-through rates, and customer segments, the AI model suggests personalized subject lines, optimal send times, and target audience groups, resulting in higher engagement and conversion rates.

5.   Personalized product recommendations

AI-driven **product recommendation engines** leverage predictive analytics to suggest products that customers are most likely to purchase. These personalized recommendations enhance the user experience and increase cross-selling and upselling opportunities.

How it works:

- **Data-driven predictions:** AI analyzes a customer's browsing history, past purchases, and interactions with similar products to predict their preferences.

- **Collaborative filtering:** The system identifies patterns in the behaviors of similar customers and recommends products based on what others with similar preferences have purchased.

- **Continuous learning:** The recommendation engine continuously learns from customer interactions and adjusts its predictions to provide more relevant suggestions over time.

Example: An e-commerce platform uses AI to display personalized product recommendations on its homepage and within marketing emails. When a customer views a product, the system suggests related items or "customers also bought" recommendations, increasing the likelihood of additional purchases and boosting average order value.

The bottom line: data-driven growth through AI-powered insights

AI-powered predictive analytics and customer segmentation are game changers for businesses seeking to optimize their marketing strategies and drive growth. By analyzing customer behavior, predicting future actions, and dynamically segmenting audiences, AI enables marketers to create personalized experiences, improve retention, and maximize customer lifetime value.

C H A P T E R   1 2

Scaling growth: what got you here won't get you there

Identifying new channels and opportunities for scaling

As businesses grow, they often reach a point where their existing channels and strategies plateau. What worked to get you to your current stage won't necessarily be enough to push you further. To break through this growth ceiling, companies must **identify new channels and opportunities** that can drive the next wave of expansion. Scaling effectively requires a blend of creativity, experimentation, and data-driven decision-making to uncover the right growth levers for your business.

Why exploring new channels is crucial for scaling

Focusing solely on existing marketing channels can lead to stagnation. For instance, if most of your traffic and conversions come from organic search, you may find it increasingly difficult to achieve incremental gains in that channel alone. By exploring new opportunities, you diversify your marketing mix, reach new audiences, and reduce dependency on a single growth source. Additionally, new channels often present unique benefits, such as lower customer acquisition costs, access to niche markets, or the potential for viral growth.

How to identify new channels for growth

Identifying new channels requires a mix of market research, customer insights, and continuous testing. Here's how to approach this process:

1. Conduct a customer journey analysis

Understanding the **customer journey** is critical to identifying new touchpoints where you can engage potential customers. By analyzing how customers discover, interact with, and purchase from your business, you can pinpoint gaps and opportunities for new channels.

How to conduct customer journey analysis:

- **Map out the journey:** Create a customer journey map that outlines the stages your customers go through, from awareness and consideration to decision and post-purchase. Identify the touchpoints at each stage, such as website visits, social media interactions, or email campaigns.

- **Gather customer insights:** Use tools like Google Analytics, Hotjar, and Mixpanel to collect data on customer behavior and interactions. Conduct surveys, interviews, and feedback sessions to gain deeper insights into how customers find and engage with your brand.

- **Identify gaps:** Look for stages in the journey where engagement drops or where customers encounter friction. These gaps may indicate opportunities to introduce new channels or optimize existing ones.

Example: A fitness app conducts a customer journey analysis and discovers that most users first learn about the app through social media but drop off during the sign-up process. To address this, the company identifies partnerships with fitness influencers and launches a referral program to drive sign-ups and enhance customer acquisition efforts.

2. Leverage customer feedback and market research

Customer feedback and **market research** provide valuable insights into potential new channels. Your customers can reveal where they spend their time, how they prefer to engage with brands, and what unmet needs they have, which can inform your strategy for entering new markets or channels.

How to gather insights:

- **Survey your audience:** Use survey tools like SurveyMonkey or Typeform to ask your customers about their preferred platforms, media consumption habits, and interests. Identify emerging trends or platforms that your audience uses but where your brand has minimal presence.

- **Analyze competitors:** Study your competitors to identify channels they're using successfully. Look at where they advertise, how they engage with customers, and which platforms drive the most traffic to their website. Competitor analysis can uncover new opportunities for you to explore.

- **Explore market trends:** Keep an eye on industry reports, market research, and emerging technologies. Tools like Google Trends and social listening platforms like Hootsuite or Sprout Social can help you track what's trending in your industry and identify potential channels.

Example: A cosmetics brand surveys its customers and finds that many of them discover new beauty products through YouTube tutorials and TikTok challenges. In response, the brand collaborates with beauty influencers on these platforms, launching makeup tutorials and product showcases to tap into a new, younger audience segment.

3. Test new advertising platforms

Paid advertising can be a quick way to test new channels and measure their potential for customer acquisition. Expanding to new advertising platforms can help you reach a different audience or engage with your existing audience in new ways.

Channels to consider:

- **Social media advertising:** If your business has primarily focused on one or two social platforms, experiment with others like TikTok, Snapchat, or Pinterest. These platforms offer unique ways to interact with users through short-form videos, visual content, and storytelling.

- **Native advertising:** Use native ads on platforms like Taboola or Outbrain to promote content and products in a way that blends seamlessly with the platform's environment. Native ads often reach audiences in content-rich contexts, such as news sites, blogs, and online magazines.

- **Podcast and streaming ads:** Advertising on podcasts, music streaming services (e.g., Spotify), or video platforms (e.g., YouTube) can expose your brand to engaged, niche audiences. Creating audio or video ads tailored to these mediums can be an effective way to connect with listeners and viewers.

Example: An online learning platform primarily using Facebook Ads for customer acquisition decides to test advertising on TikTok. By creating short, engaging video content showcasing quick learning tips and course highlights, the platform successfully reaches a younger demographic, resulting in an increase in new sign-ups.

4. Explore content partnerships and collaborations

Content partnerships and **collaborations** allow you to tap into new audiences through partnerships with complementary brands, influencers, or industry experts. This approach can broaden your reach and build credibility within your target market.

How to approach collaborations:

- **Influencer marketing:** Partner with influencers who align with your brand values and have a strong following within your target demographic. Collaborate on content that showcases your products, offers discounts, or shares testimonials.

- **Co-branded content:** Create joint content with complementary brands, such as webinars, podcasts, or e-books. Co-branded content not only provides value to both brands' audiences but also exposes each brand to new potential customers.

- **Guest blogging:** Write guest posts for reputable blogs in your industry or invite industry experts to contribute to your blog. This strategy increases your brand's visibility and positions your business as a thought leader.

Example: A meal-kit delivery service partners with popular food bloggers to create a series of recipe videos featuring their products. These collaborations allow the brand to reach the bloggers' followers, introduce new recipes, and highlight the convenience of their meal kits, ultimately driving traffic to the brand's website.

5. Leverage emerging technologies

Emerging technologies like AI, virtual reality (VR), augmented reality (AR), and blockchain are creating new opportunities for customer engagement and marketing. Exploring these technologies can set your brand apart and attract tech-savvy audiences.

How to leverage emerging tech:

- **AR and VR experiences:** Use AR or VR to create interactive product experiences. For example, a furniture retailer can use AR to allow customers to visualize how furniture pieces would look in their homes, enhancing the shopping experience.

- **AI chatbots:** Implement AI-powered chatbots on your website or social media channels to provide instant, personalized customer support. Chatbots enhance user experiences, answer questions, and guide visitors through the sales funnel, increasing conversions.

- **Voice search optimization:** Optimize your website and content for voice search to capture traffic from users who search for products or services through voice-activated devices like Alexa, Google Home, and Siri.

Example: A skincare brand integrates an AI-powered virtual skincare consultant into its website. The consultant asks users about their skin type, concerns, and preferences, then provides personalized product recommendations. This interactive experience increases user engagement and leads to higher conversion rates.

6. Experiment with new product offerings and services

New product offerings or services can open up entirely new channels for growth. By identifying gaps in the market or listening to customer feedback, businesses can introduce new products that appeal to different customer segments or fulfill unmet needs.

How to experiment:

- **Limited-time launches:** Test new products, features, or services through limited-time launches or beta versions. This allows you to gauge customer interest and gather feedback before committing to a full-scale launch.

- **Subscription models:** If your business currently sells products on a one-time basis, consider introducing subscription models to create a steady revenue stream and improve customer retention.

- **Cross-selling and bundling:** Offer product bundles or complementary services to encourage customers to try additional items. Cross-selling can increase average order value and introduce customers to new aspects of your product line.

Example: An online fitness platform that traditionally offers individual workout plans launches a subscription service that includes live classes, meal plans, and community support. The new service attracts a broader audience seeking comprehensive fitness solutions, driving recurring revenue growth.

The bottom line: continually expanding your growth channels

Identifying new channels and opportunities is essential for scaling your business beyond its current growth ceiling. By conducting customer journey analysis, gathering market insights, exploring new advertising platforms, leveraging content collaborations, adopting emerging technologies, and experimenting with new offerings, you can diversify your marketing efforts and reach new audiences. The key to successful scaling is ongoing experimentation, data-driven decision-making, and adapting your strategies to capitalize on new opportunities as they arise.

International expansion: how to grow beyond borders

For many businesses, **international expansion** represents a significant opportunity to access new customer bases, diversify revenue streams, and increase market share. However, expanding beyond borders comes with its unique set of challenges, including cultural differences, legal regulations, localization needs, and logistical complexities. To successfully navigate this process, companies need a strategic approach that considers market research, cultural understanding, product adaptation, and robust marketing efforts.

Why consider international expansion?

Going global opens up new growth prospects and offers several key benefits:

1.   **Access to larger markets:** Expanding into international markets increases your potential customer base, offering new opportunities for sales, revenue, and brand recognition.

2.   **Revenue diversification:** International expansion allows you to diversify revenue sources, reducing reliance on a single market and mitigating risks associated with local economic fluctuations.

3.   **Competitive advantage:** Entering new markets early can give you a first-mover advantage, helping you establish brand presence and customer loyalty before competitors.

Steps to successful international expansion

Here's a comprehensive guide to expanding your business beyond borders:

1.   Conduct thorough market research

The first step in any successful international expansion is **market research**. Understanding the target market's demand, competitive landscape, consumer behavior, and regulatory environment is critical for making informed decisions.

How to conduct market research:

- **Identify target markets:** Use data-driven analysis to identify countries or regions where there is high demand for your products or services. Look for indicators such as market size, growth potential, purchasing power, and cultural fit.

- **Analyze competitors:** Study local and international competitors operating in the target market to understand their strengths, weaknesses, pricing strategies, and market positioning. This analysis will help you identify gaps and opportunities for differentiation.

- **Understand local regulations:** Research legal, tax, and regulatory requirements, including import/export restrictions, labeling and packaging laws, data privacy regulations, and intellectual property rights. Ensuring compliance with local laws is crucial for avoiding costly setbacks.

- **Assess cultural nuances:** Understand the cultural norms, values, and preferences of the target market. Cultural awareness will guide your marketing messaging, product adaptations, and customer engagement strategies.

Example: A beauty brand considering expansion into the Asian market conducts extensive research and discovers a strong preference for skincare products with natural ingredients. The brand adapts its product line to include herbal and plant-based formulas, appealing to local consumer preferences and gaining a competitive edge.

2. Localize your product and marketing efforts

Localization is key to resonating with international audiences. It involves adapting your products, marketing content, and customer experiences to align with the cultural and linguistic nuances of each target market.

How to localize effectively:

- **Language adaptation:** Translate your website, product descriptions, packaging, and marketing materials into the local language. Ensure that translations are culturally sensitive and convey the intended message accurately. Using professional localization services or native speakers is recommended to avoid misinterpretations.

- **Cultural adaptation:** Tailor your product and messaging to reflect cultural norms, values, and preferences. This may include adjusting product features, colors, symbols, imagery, and marketing messages to align with local customs and avoid cultural faux pas.

- **Payment methods:** Offer local payment options that are widely used and trusted in the target market. In some countries, credit cards may not be the preferred payment method, and alternative options like mobile payments, digital wallets, or cash on delivery may be necessary.

- **Customer support:** Provide customer support in the local language through multiple channels, including phone, chat, email, and social media. Localizing customer support enhances user experience and builds trust with new customers.

Example: Netflix has successfully expanded internationally by localizing its content library, marketing materials, and user interface for each market. The platform offers subtitles and dubbed versions in various languages, promotes region-specific shows, and features payment options suited to local preferences, enabling it to attract and retain a global audience.

3. Develop a market entry strategy

Your **market entry strategy** defines how you will introduce your products or services into the new market. Different approaches have varying levels of risk, investment, and potential rewards, so it's important to choose a strategy that aligns with your business goals and resources.

Common market entry strategies:

- **Exporting:** Exporting involves selling your products directly to customers in the foreign market. This approach is relatively low-risk and cost-effective but requires managing logistics, shipping, and compliance with local import regulations.

- **E-commerce:** Setting up an online store that caters to international customers is a practical way to test market demand before establishing a physical presence. Consider using global e-commerce platforms like Shopify, Amazon, or Alibaba, which offer built-in features for international transactions, shipping, and localization.

- **Local partnerships:** Partnering with local businesses, distributors, or agents can facilitate market entry by leveraging their existing networks, market knowledge, and distribution channels. This approach can help you navigate regulatory complexities and build brand credibility more quickly.

- **Direct investment:** Establishing a local presence through a subsidiary, branch office, or manufacturing facility provides full control over operations but requires significant investment and carries higher risk. This strategy is often used when there is a strong long-term market potential.

Example: A US-based coffee chain decides to enter the Japanese market by partnering with a local distributor. The partnership allows the brand to leverage the distributor's knowledge of local consumer preferences, regulatory environment, and retail network, facilitating a smoother market entry.

4. Adapt pricing and business models

Pricing strategies and business models that work in your home market may not be effective in a different country due to varying purchasing power, market expectations, and competitive landscapes. It's essential to **adapt your pricing** and models to match the target market's economic conditions and consumer behavior.

How to adapt pricing and models:

- **Market-based pricing:** Research local market pricing for similar products and services to set competitive prices that reflect the market's purchasing power. Adjust your pricing to account for costs related to taxes, tariffs, import duties, and shipping.

- **Flexible business models:** Consider introducing different business models to suit the target market, such as subscription services, freemium models, or tiered pricing. Offering flexible options can appeal to a wider range of customers and increase market penetration.

- **Local promotions:** Use localized promotions, discounts, and loyalty programs to attract new customers and drive initial sales. Promotional tactics that resonate with local customs, holidays, and shopping habits can boost your brand's visibility in the new market.

Example: Spotify adjusts its subscription pricing in different countries based on local purchasing power and market conditions. By offering student discounts, family plans, and free ad-supported tiers, Spotify makes its services accessible to a broad range of international customers, driving user acquisition and market growth.

5. Establish a global logistics and supply chain

International expansion requires a well-structured **logistics and supply chain** system to ensure efficient distribution and customer satisfaction. Factors like shipping costs, delivery times, customs regulations, and inventory management play a crucial role in providing a seamless customer experience.

How to establish a global logistics network:

- **Partner with local logistics providers:** Collaborate with local shipping and fulfillment companies that understand the market's logistics challenges, customs procedures, and delivery preferences. This partnership can enhance shipping efficiency and reduce costs.

- **Warehousing:** Consider setting up regional warehouses or using third-party fulfillment centers to store products closer to the target market. This approach shortens delivery times, reduces shipping costs, and improves customer satisfaction.

- **Customs and compliance:** Ensure compliance with international trade regulations, customs requirements, and import/export documentation. Work with customs brokers and legal advisors to navigate the complexities of cross-border trade and avoid delays.

Example: An apparel retailer expanding to Europe sets up a fulfillment center in Germany to manage inventory and streamline distribution across the European Union. This regional warehousing approach reduces shipping times, lowers costs, and enables the retailer to provide customers with a smooth shopping experience.

6. Monitor, measure, and adapt your strategy

Continuous monitoring and **adaptation** are essential for a successful international expansion. Markets evolve, consumer preferences change, and competitors enter, so businesses need to stay agile and responsive to new developments.

How to monitor and adapt:

- **Track performance metrics:** Use analytics tools to monitor key performance indicators (KPIs) in the new market, such as sales growth, customer acquisition cost (CAC), customer lifetime value (CLV), website traffic, and engagement rates.

- **Gather customer feedback:** Collect feedback from local customers to understand their experiences, identify pain points, and assess the effectiveness of your localization efforts. Use surveys, reviews, and social media listening to gather insights.

- **Adjust strategies:** Based on performance data and customer feedback, make data-driven adjustments to your marketing campaigns, product offerings, pricing, and customer support. Adaptation is key to building a loyal customer base and maintaining a competitive edge in the market.

Example: A tech company expanding into Latin America closely monitors its customer support interactions to identify common issues faced by local users. The company then adapts its user interface and support materials to address these challenges, resulting in improved customer satisfaction and increased retention rates.

The bottom line: expanding beyond borders for sustainable growth

International expansion presents a wealth of opportunities for businesses to grow, diversify, and establish a global presence. By conducting thorough market research, localizing products and marketing efforts, developing a robust market entry strategy, adapting pricing, managing logistics efficiently, and continuously monitoring performance, businesses can navigate the complexities of global markets and achieve long-term success. The journey to international growth requires a strategic approach, cultural awareness, and the agility to adapt, but the rewards can be substantial for those who execute it well.

Avoiding growth plateaus: common pitfalls and how to overcome them

As businesses grow, they often reach a point where their revenue, customer acquisition, and market penetration slow down—a phenomenon known as a **growth plateau**. Hitting a plateau can be frustrating, especially when previous strategies that fueled rapid growth no longer seem effective. To reignite momentum, businesses must identify common pitfalls that lead to stagnation and implement strategies to adapt, innovate, and continue expanding.

Why do growth plateaus happen?

Growth plateaus occur for several reasons:

1. **Market saturation:** As you capture more market share, the pool of potential new customers shrinks, making it harder to maintain the same growth rate.

2. **Strategy fatigue:** The marketing tactics and growth strategies that once delivered results become less effective over time, either due to market changes, increased competition, or changing consumer behavior.

3. **Operational bottlenecks:** As a company scales, operational inefficiencies, process gaps, and resource limitations can create bottlenecks that hinder further growth.

4. **Lack of innovation:** Failing to adapt products, services, or marketing strategies to meet evolving customer needs can result in lost market relevance and customer interest.

Recognizing these factors is the first step toward avoiding and overcoming growth plateaus. The key lies in staying agile, innovative, and data-driven.

Strategies to avoid and overcome growth plateaus

Here's how to identify growth plateaus and implement strategies to sustain growth:

1. Diversify your marketing channels

One common cause of a growth plateau is **over-reliance on a single marketing channel**. For example, if your customer acquisition largely depends on paid search ads, rising costs and diminishing returns can slow down growth over time. To avoid this, it's crucial to **diversify your marketing mix** by exploring new channels.

How to diversify effectively:

- **Experiment with emerging platforms:** Test new social media platforms, content channels, and advertising networks to reach different audience segments. For example, if you've been primarily using Facebook and Instagram for advertising, consider experimenting with TikTok, Pinterest, or LinkedIn to connect with new demographics.

- **Implement content marketing:** Develop a robust content marketing strategy that includes blogging, video content, podcasts, webinars, and e-books. Content marketing not only drives organic traffic but also positions your brand as an industry authority.

- **Leverage influencer marketing:** Collaborate with influencers who align with your brand values and audience. Influencer partnerships can help you tap into new communities, build trust, and generate word-of-mouth promotion.

Example: An e-commerce clothing brand that initially relied on Instagram ads to drive sales reaches a plateau in customer acquisition. To diversify, the brand launches a TikTok campaign featuring fashion influencers, creates a YouTube channel with styling tips, and starts a blog covering the latest fashion trends. These new channels attract a broader audience and boost website traffic, breaking through the plateau.

2. Introduce new products or services

A stagnant product offering can contribute to a growth plateau, as existing customers may have already purchased what they need. **Introducing new products or services** can revitalize interest in your brand, attract new customer segments, and encourage repeat purchases from existing customers.

How to approach product expansion:

- **Conduct customer research:** Gather feedback from your current customers to understand their pain points, needs, and preferences. Use this data to develop products or services that address these needs and align with market demand.

- **Test with limited releases:** Before a full-scale launch, test new products with limited-time or region-specific releases. Collect feedback, refine offerings, and gauge market demand to ensure a successful rollout.

- **Expand complementary offerings:** Identify opportunities to introduce complementary products or services that align with your core offerings. For example, a fitness equipment retailer can expand into nutritional supplements or online workout classes to provide a holistic solution for fitness enthusiasts.

Example: A software company offering project management tools reaches a plateau in user growth. Through customer feedback, the company learns that its users need a more integrated solution. In response, the company introduces a new suite of tools that includes time tracking, team communication, and file management. The expanded product line attracts new users and boosts customer retention, driving renewed growth.

3. Optimize operational efficiency

As companies scale, **operational inefficiencies** can become a significant barrier to growth. Bottlenecks in processes, communication gaps, and resource constraints can slow down customer acquisition, service delivery, and product development.

Optimizing internal operations is key to sustaining momentum and scaling effectively.

How to optimize operations:

- **Automate processes:** Implement automation tools for repetitive tasks such as email marketing, customer follow-ups, CRM updates, and order processing. Marketing automation tools like HubSpot, ActiveCampaign, and Zapier can streamline workflows and free up time for strategic activities.

- **Improve team collaboration:** Use project management and communication tools like Slack, Asana, or Trello to enhance team collaboration and streamline project execution. Clear communication and alignment across departments reduce delays and improve overall efficiency.

- **Scale customer support:** Implement AI-powered chatbots and self-service options to handle routine customer inquiries, allowing your support team to focus on more complex issues. This approach enhances customer satisfaction while maintaining manageable support costs as you scale.

Example: An online retailer facing fulfillment delays and customer service bottlenecks adopts an inventory management system integrated with its e-commerce platform. The system automates order processing, tracks stock levels, and provides real-time updates to customers. This operational overhaul reduces delivery times, improves customer satisfaction, and frees up resources to focus on marketing and expansion initiatives.

4. Focus on customer retention and loyalty programs

A focus solely on **customer acquisition** can lead to neglecting the existing customer base. Retaining current customers and nurturing loyalty are essential for sustainable growth, as acquiring new customers is often more expensive than retaining existing ones.

How to enhance customer retention:

- **Implement loyalty programs:** Introduce a loyalty program that rewards repeat purchases, referrals, or social media engagement. Offer exclusive discounts, early access to new products, or special perks to encourage customers to stay engaged and make repeat purchases.

- **Provide exceptional customer support:** Invest in customer support to address issues promptly, provide valuable assistance, and create positive experiences. A happy customer is more likely to become a repeat buyer and brand advocate.

- **Nurture post-purchase relationships:** Use email marketing to follow up with customers after a purchase, offer product care tips, and recommend complementary products. Engaging with customers beyond the point of sale fosters a lasting relationship and increases the likelihood of future purchases.

Example: A beauty subscription box company introduces a points-based loyalty program that rewards subscribers for referrals, product reviews, and social media shares. Subscribers can redeem points for discounts on future boxes or exclusive products, incentivizing ongoing engagement and increasing customer lifetime value.

5. Invest in data analytics and experimentation

A lack of data-driven decision-making and experimentation can lead to stagnant growth. Regularly analyzing performance metrics and testing new ideas is vital for identifying areas of improvement and discovering untapped opportunities.

How to implement data-driven strategies:

- **Use analytics tools:** Utilize tools like Google Analytics, Mixpanel, and Hotjar to track key performance indicators (KPIs) such as conversion rates, customer acquisition costs, website traffic, and customer behavior. Analyze this data to understand what's working and where there are gaps.

- **Run A/B tests:** Continuously run A/B tests on marketing assets, website elements, email campaigns, and product features to identify which variations drive better engagement and conversions. Use tools like Optimizely or Google Optimize to conduct experiments and implement the winning changes.

- **Experiment with new tactics:** Allocate a portion of your marketing budget to test new growth tactics, such as influencer partnerships, video content, or new ad formats. Experimenting allows you to adapt to market changes, explore new channels, and find innovative ways to reach your audience.

Example: A SaaS company hits a growth plateau in user acquisition. By analyzing its website data, the company discovers that many visitors drop off at the pricing page. The team runs A/B tests with different pricing page layouts, messaging, and CTA buttons. The test results reveal that a simplified pricing structure and a clear value proposition increase conversions, helping the company overcome the plateau.

6. Keep innovating and staying agile

Stagnation often occurs when businesses become too comfortable with their current strategies and stop innovating. To maintain growth, it's crucial to **stay agile, adapt to market trends**, and continuously innovate.

How to drive innovation:

- **Stay informed:** Keep up with industry trends, emerging technologies, and changing consumer behaviors. Subscribe to industry publications, attend conferences, and participate in webinars to stay ahead of market shifts.

- **Encourage a growth mindset:** Foster a company culture that encourages experimentation, learning from failures, and taking calculated risks. A growth mindset empowers teams to explore new ideas and pivot when needed.

- **Iterate based on feedback:** Actively seek feedback from customers, employees, and partners. Use these insights to improve products, services, and marketing strategies, ensuring that your business evolves to meet changing market demands.

Example: A fitness app continuously releases new features and content, such as virtual workout classes, nutrition guides, and community challenges. By regularly innovating and responding to user feedback, the app keeps its user base engaged and attracts new customers, sustaining growth over time.

The bottom line: sustaining growth through adaptability

Growth plateaus are a natural part of the business lifecycle, but they don't have to signal the end of progress. By diversifying marketing channels, introducing new products, optimizing operations, focusing on customer retention, investing in data-driven experimentation, and fostering a culture of innovation, businesses can overcome growth plateaus and unlock new opportunities for expansion. The key is to remain agile, continuously adapt strategies, and stay focused on delivering value to your customers in an ever-evolving market.

CHAPTER 13

Measuring success: the growth marketer's dashboard

Key metrics and KPIs for growth

Measuring success in growth marketing requires a deep understanding of which **metrics** and **KPIs** accurately reflect your business performance and customer engagement. By tracking these indicators, growth marketers can make data-driven decisions, refine strategies, and ultimately drive sustainable growth. Here, we'll delve into the most crucial metrics and KPIs that every growth marketer should have on their dashboard, categorized by various stages of the customer journey.

Why tracking the right metrics matters

Without tracking the right metrics, it's challenging to gauge the effectiveness of your growth strategies or identify areas for improvement. By focusing on KPIs that align with your business goals, you can:

1. **Assess campaign performance:** Understand which marketing campaigns and channels are delivering the best ROI and adjust your budget accordingly.

2.   **Optimize customer acquisition:** Identify the most cost-effective ways to acquire new customers and streamline your marketing funnel.

3.   **Drive retention and loyalty:** Measure customer satisfaction and engagement to implement strategies that enhance customer lifetime value (CLV).

The essential growth marketing metrics and KPIs

Below are the key metrics and KPIs to track at each stage of the customer journey, including acquisition, activation, retention, revenue, and referral.

1. Customer acquisition metrics

Customer acquisition is the process of attracting new customers to your business. The following metrics provide insights into how effectively your marketing efforts are driving traffic, generating leads, and converting prospects into customers.

Key acquisition metrics:

1.   **Customer Acquisition Cost (CAC)**

   o   **Definition:** The total cost of acquiring a new customer, including marketing and sales expenses. It's calculated by dividing the total marketing and sales costs by the number of new customers acquired within a specific period.

   o   **Why it matters:** CAC helps you understand how much you're spending to gain each customer. Lowering CAC while maintaining or increasing customer quality is crucial for sustainable growth.

   o   **Example:** If you spend $10,000 on marketing in a month and acquire 100 new customers, your CAC is $100.

2. Cost Per Lead (CPL)

   o   **Definition:** The cost incurred to generate a new lead, calculated by dividing total marketing spend by the number of leads generated.

   o   **Why it matters:** CPL provides insights into the efficiency of your lead generation efforts. A lower CPL indicates that your marketing campaigns are effectively attracting potential customers.

   o   **Example:** If a business spends $5,000 on a Google Ads campaign and generates 250 leads, the CPL is $20.

3. Conversion Rate

   o   **Definition:** The percentage of visitors who take a desired action, such as signing up for a newsletter, filling out a form, or making a purchase. It's calculated by dividing the number of conversions by the total number of visitors and multiplying by 100.

   o   **Why it matters:** Conversion rate indicates how well your marketing funnel is performing. A higher conversion rate means more prospects are successfully moving through your funnel, leading to increased customer acquisition.

   o   **Example:** If 500 people visit your landing page and 50 sign up for your service, the conversion rate is 10%.

4. **Traffic Sources**

- **Definition:** The channels through which visitors arrive at your website, such as organic search, social media, direct traffic, or paid advertising.

- **Why it matters:** Understanding which traffic sources drive the most visitors and conversions helps you allocate resources to the most effective channels and optimize your marketing strategy.

- **Example:** Google Analytics shows that 60% of your website traffic comes from organic search, while 20% comes from social media and 10% from paid ads.

2. Activation metrics

Activation refers to the moment when a customer experiences the value of your product or service for the first time. Activation metrics indicate how effectively you're onboarding new customers and engaging them early in their journey.

Key activation metrics:

1. **Activation Rate**

- **Definition:** The percentage of new users who reach a key milestone that indicates they've experienced the core value of your product. The milestone could be completing a sign-up process, using a key feature, or making an initial purchase.

- **Why it matters:** A higher activation rate indicates that your onboarding process is effective in demonstrating your product's value and setting the stage for long-term engagement and retention.

o   **Example:** If 1,000 users sign up for a free trial and 300 use a key feature within the first week, your activation rate is 30%.

2.   Time to Value (TTV)

o   **Definition:** The time it takes for a new customer to realize the value of your product or service after their first interaction.

o   **Why it matters:** Shortening TTV enhances the customer experience and increases the likelihood of retention. The quicker customers see the value, the more likely they are to continue using your product.

o   **Example:** If it typically takes a new user three days to use a core feature and experience the product's benefits, your TTV is three days.

3. Retention metrics

Retention measures how well you keep customers engaged and returning over time. High retention rates are crucial for building a loyal customer base and increasing customer lifetime value (CLV).

Key retention metrics:

1.   Customer Retention Rate (CRR)

o   **Definition:** The percentage of customers who continue to use your product or service over a specific period. It's calculated by taking the number of customers at the end of the period, subtracting the number of new customers acquired during that period, and dividing by the number of customers at the start of the period.

- o **Why it matters:** A high CRR indicates that customers find value in your product, leading to repeat business and long-term loyalty. Improving retention is often more cost-effective than acquiring new customers.

- o **Example:** If you had 500 customers at the start of the quarter, acquired 100 new customers, and ended with 550, your retention rate is 90% [(550 - 100) / 500].

2. Churn Rate

- o **Definition:** The percentage of customers who stop using your product or service within a given period. It's calculated by dividing the number of customers lost during that period by the total number of customers at the start of the period.

- o **Why it matters:** Churn rate is a direct indicator of customer satisfaction and product-market fit. Reducing churn is key to improving CLV and overall business growth.

- o **Example:** If you start the month with 1,000 customers and lose 50, your churn rate is 5%.

3. Repeat Purchase Rate

- o **Definition:** The percentage of customers who make more than one purchase over a specific time frame. It's calculated by dividing the number of returning customers by the total number of customers.

- o **Why it matters:** A higher repeat purchase rate indicates strong customer loyalty and satisfaction.

Repeat customers often have a higher CLV and are more likely to refer others.

- o **Example:** If you have 200 customers, and 60 of them make a second purchase, your repeat purchase rate is 30%.

4. Revenue metrics

Revenue metrics provide insights into the financial performance of your business and help you understand how customer acquisition, retention, and pricing strategies contribute to overall profitability.

Key revenue metrics:

1. **Customer Lifetime Value (CLV)**

   - o **Definition:** The total revenue a business can expect from a customer over the entire duration of their relationship. It's calculated by multiplying the average purchase value, purchase frequency, and average customer lifespan.

   - o **Why it matters:** CLV helps you determine how much you can spend on customer acquisition while maintaining profitability. A high CLV indicates that your customers are valuable, loyal, and provide recurring revenue.

   - o **Example:** If the average customer spends $100 per month and stays with your business for 12 months, the CLV is $1,200.

2.   Monthly Recurring Revenue (MRR)

- o   **Definition:** The total predictable revenue generated by your customers each month. MRR is a key metric for subscription-based businesses.

- o   **Why it matters:** MRR provides a clear picture of your company's revenue health and growth trajectory. Tracking MRR helps you measure the impact of new customer acquisition, upgrades, downgrades, and churn on your revenue.

- o   **Example:** If you have 100 customers paying $50 per month, your MRR is $5,000.

3.   Average Revenue Per User (ARPU)

- o   **Definition:** The average revenue generated per user or customer over a specific time period. It's calculated by dividing total revenue by the number of customers.

- o   **Why it matters:** ARPU helps you evaluate the effectiveness of your pricing strategy and identify opportunities to upsell or cross-sell to increase revenue.

- o   **Example:** If your business generates $10,000 in revenue with 200 customers, the ARPU is $50.

5. Referral metrics

Referral metrics measure how effectively your customers are promoting your business to others, driving organic growth through word-of-mouth marketing.

Key referral metrics:

1. **Net Promoter Score (NPS)**

   o **Definition:** A measure of customer satisfaction and loyalty based on the likelihood that customers would recommend your product to others. NPS is calculated using a survey that asks customers to rate, on a scale of 0-10, how likely they are to recommend your product.

   o **Why it matters:** A high NPS indicates strong customer advocacy, leading to organic referrals and lower acquisition costs. NPS feedback can also provide insights into areas for improvement.

   o **Example:** If 50% of respondents are promoters (9-10 scores) and 20% are detractors (0-6 scores), the NPS is 30.

2. **Referral Rate**

   o **Definition:** The percentage of new customers acquired through referrals from existing customers. It's calculated by dividing the number of referred customers by the total number of new customers.

   o **Why it matters:** A high referral rate indicates that your customers are satisfied and willing to advocate for your brand, which can significantly reduce CAC and drive growth organically.

   o **Example:** If you acquire 200 new customers in a month and 40 of them are referred by existing customers, your referral rate is 20%.

The bottom line: building your growth dashboard

Tracking the right metrics and KPIs is essential for understanding the effectiveness of your growth strategies and making data-driven decisions. By focusing on key metrics related to acquisition, activation, retention, revenue, and referral, growth marketers can optimize their campaigns, enhance customer experiences, and drive sustainable growth. Remember, the metrics you prioritize should align with your specific business model, goals, and stage of growth.

How to build a data-driven growth marketing dashboard

A **growth marketing dashboard** is a centralized platform that consolidates your key metrics and KPIs, offering a comprehensive view of your marketing performance. Building a data-driven dashboard allows marketers to quickly identify trends, spot areas for improvement, and make agile, data-backed decisions. By monitoring metrics in real-time, businesses can optimize their strategies to maximize ROI, customer acquisition, and overall growth.

Why a growth marketing dashboard is essential

A well-designed dashboard provides several benefits:

1. **Real-time insights:** Having all your key metrics in one place enables you to monitor performance in real-time and respond swiftly to market changes, customer behavior, and campaign results.

2. **Data-driven decision-making:** Visualizing your KPIs helps you identify successful strategies and areas needing

adjustment, ensuring your marketing efforts are continuously optimized.

3.   **Team alignment:** A dashboard serves as a single source of truth for your team, promoting transparency and aligning everyone on the key goals and metrics driving growth.

Steps to build a data-driven marketing dashboard

Here's a step-by-step guide to creating a growth marketing dashboard that provides actionable insights:

1. Define your goals and KPIs

Before building your dashboard, **define your marketing goals** and identify the **key metrics** that align with those goals. Focus on metrics that will help you measure progress and success at each stage of the customer journey, such as acquisition, activation, retention, revenue, and referral.

How to define KPIs:

- **Align with business objectives:** Choose KPIs that directly support your business objectives. For example, if your goal is to increase customer retention, relevant KPIs might include customer retention rate, churn rate, and customer lifetime value (CLV).

- **Prioritize actionable metrics:** Select metrics that provide actionable insights and inform strategic adjustments. Avoid vanity metrics (e.g., total followers) that don't directly impact growth.

- **Break down KPIs by funnel stage:** Identify specific KPIs for each stage of your marketing funnel, such as customer acquisition cost (CAC) for acquisition, activation rate for onboarding, and repeat purchase rate for retention.

Example: A SaaS company looking to increase monthly recurring revenue (MRR) might track metrics like new customer acquisition rate, customer retention rate, upsell conversion rate, and average revenue per user (ARPU) on their dashboard.

2. Choose the right tools for data collection and visualization

Your dashboard's effectiveness depends on the tools you use for **data collection, integration, and visualization**. Several marketing analytics platforms and dashboard tools allow you to aggregate data from multiple sources and present it in an easy-to-understand format.

Popular tools for building dashboards:

1. **Google Looker Studio**

   - **Overview:** A free data visualization tool that integrates with various data sources, including Google Analytics, Google Ads, Google Sheets, and more. It allows you to create customizable reports and dashboards.

   - **How to use:** Connect your marketing data sources to Google Looker Studio and use its drag-and-drop interface to create charts, tables, and graphs that display your key metrics. Customize the dashboard layout to highlight your most important KPIs.

   - **Pros:** User-friendly, highly customizable, free, and integrates seamlessly with other Google products.

2. **Tableau**

   - **Overview:** A powerful data visualization tool that connects to a wide range of data sources, offering advanced analytics capabilities and interactive dashboards.

- o   **How to use:** Import your data into Tableau from sources like CRMs, marketing automation tools, spreadsheets, and databases. Use Tableau's visual builder to create dynamic, interactive dashboards that provide detailed insights into your marketing performance.

- o   **Pros:** Highly flexible, advanced analytics features, suitable for complex data sets, interactive visualizations.

3.   HubSpot

- o   **Overview:** A comprehensive marketing, sales, and service platform with built-in analytics and reporting tools. HubSpot's dashboard capabilities are particularly useful for tracking customer acquisition, engagement, and conversion metrics.

- o   **How to use:** Use HubSpot's reporting dashboard to create custom reports based on data from email campaigns, lead generation forms, website traffic, social media, and CRM. Set up automated reporting to keep your team informed of key performance metrics.

- o   **Pros:** Integrates with HubSpot's marketing, sales, and service tools, provides end-to-end insights into customer journeys, and allows for custom report creation.

3. Collect and integrate your data sources

To build a comprehensive dashboard, **collect data** from various sources that represent your marketing ecosystem. Your dashboard should integrate with data from tools like Google Analytics, CRM platforms, marketing automation systems, ad platforms, and social media channels.

Steps to integrate data sources:

- **Connect analytics tools:** Use API integrations or third-party connectors to link tools like Google Analytics, Facebook Ads, Google Ads, Mixpanel, HubSpot, and Mailchimp to your dashboard. This integration allows you to pull data from multiple channels into a centralized view.

- **Set up data automation:** Automate data collection to ensure that your dashboard displays real-time or regularly updated metrics. Many dashboard tools, such as Google Looker Studio and Tableau, offer connectors that automate data syncing at scheduled intervals.

- **Consolidate data:** Use data aggregation tools like Supermetrics or Zapier to combine data from different sources into a single spreadsheet or database. Import this consolidated data into your dashboard to create a unified view of your marketing performance.

Example: A retail business integrates data from Google Analytics, Shopify, Facebook Ads, and Mailchimp into its dashboard. This integration provides a complete picture of website traffic, sales performance, ad campaign effectiveness, and email engagement, all in one place.

4. Design your dashboard layout

The design of your dashboard plays a crucial role in its usability. A well-organized layout enables you to quickly understand your performance metrics and identify trends or anomalies.

Dashboard design best practices:

- **Prioritize key metrics:** Place your most important KPIs at the top of the dashboard for easy access. These should be the metrics that directly align with your business goals, such as MRR, CAC, or conversion rate.

- **Use visual elements:** Utilize charts, graphs, and gauges to visualize data in an intuitive way. Line charts are great for showing trends over time, while pie charts and bar graphs are useful for comparing segments or categories.

- **Segment by funnel stages:** Organize your dashboard into sections that represent different stages of the customer journey, such as acquisition, activation, retention, and revenue. This segmentation helps you quickly assess performance across your entire funnel.

- **Incorporate filters:** Add filters to allow users to drill down into specific data, such as time periods, traffic sources, campaign types, or customer segments. This flexibility enables more detailed analysis and insights.

Example: A B2B software company designs its dashboard with the following layout:

- **Top section:** Key business KPIs, including monthly recurring revenue (MRR), customer acquisition cost (CAC), and customer retention rate.

- **Middle section:** Acquisition metrics, such as website traffic, conversion rates, and lead sources.

- **Bottom section:** Engagement and retention metrics, including user activation rate, churn rate, and net promoter score (NPS).

5. Set up automated reporting

Automated reporting ensures that your dashboard stays up-to-date and provides timely insights to your team. Many dashboard tools offer automation features that allow you to schedule reports and set up alerts for specific metric thresholds.

How to automate reporting:

- **Schedule data refresh:** Configure your dashboard to automatically refresh data at regular intervals (e.g., daily, weekly, or monthly) to ensure that you're always working with the latest information.

- **Set up alerts:** Use built-in alert features in tools like Google Analytics, HubSpot, or Tableau to receive notifications when key metrics reach specific thresholds. For example, you might set an alert to trigger if your website conversion rate drops below a certain percentage.

- **Share reports:** Enable automated report sharing with your team via email or direct access to the dashboard. Regularly sharing insights fosters collaboration and keeps everyone aligned with growth objectives.

Example: A marketing agency sets up automated weekly reports in Google Data Studio that summarize client campaign performance, including ad spend, click-through rates, and lead generation. These reports are automatically emailed to clients every Monday, providing transparency and fostering data-driven discussions.

6. Continuously refine your dashboard

A **growth marketing dashboard** is not a static tool. As your business evolves, so will your goals, strategies, and key metrics. Continuously refine your dashboard to reflect these changes and ensure it remains a valuable decision-making resource.

How to refine your dashboard:

- **Review regularly:** Schedule regular reviews (e.g., monthly or quarterly) to assess the relevance of the metrics on your dashboard. Remove metrics that are no longer useful and add new ones that align with your current objectives.

- **Incorporate feedback:** Gather feedback from your team on the dashboard's usability and the insights it provides. Use this input to improve the dashboard's layout, visualizations, and data sources.

- **Experiment and iterate:** Test different visualization methods, filters, and data segments to enhance your dashboard's effectiveness. Experimentation helps you uncover deeper insights and optimize how you track performance.

Example: An e-commerce store regularly reviews its dashboard to align with seasonal marketing campaigns. During holiday seasons, the dashboard is updated to include metrics like holiday-specific sales, promotional campaign performance, and average order value, providing focused insights for the period.

The bottom line: driving growth with a well-crafted dashboard

Building a data-driven growth marketing dashboard is essential for tracking performance, making informed decisions, and optimizing strategies. By defining your goals, choosing the right tools, integrating data sources, designing an intuitive layout, automating reporting, and continuously refining your dashboard, you can create a powerful tool that empowers your team to drive growth effectively. The insights gained from a comprehensive dashboard will guide your marketing efforts, highlight successes, and pinpoint areas for improvement, ensuring that your business stays on the path to sustainable growth.

Analyzing and refining your growth strategy over time

Achieving sustainable growth requires more than just setting up a dashboard and monitoring metrics. It involves a **continuous cycle of analysis, learning, and refinement**. By regularly examining performance data, testing new ideas, and making iterative improvements, you can optimize your strategies, address challenges, and maintain growth momentum. The process of analyzing and refining your growth strategy is essential to staying adaptable and competitive in a constantly evolving market.

Why continuous analysis and refinement matter

Regularly analyzing your growth strategy and refining it based on data-driven insights offers several benefits:

1. **Adaptability:** Markets, consumer behaviors, and technologies change rapidly. Continuous analysis helps you stay agile and adjust your strategies to align with new trends and shifts in the market.

2. **Maximized ROI:** By identifying what's working and what isn't, you can allocate resources more effectively, invest in high-performing channels, and eliminate underperforming tactics.

3. **Learning and innovation:** Ongoing experimentation and refinement lead to new learnings and innovations that drive business growth and keep your brand relevant.

Steps to analyze and refine your growth strategy

Here's a step-by-step guide to systematically analyze and optimize your growth strategy over time:

1. Regularly review performance data

The first step in refining your growth strategy is to **regularly review the performance data** from your marketing dashboard. A consistent review schedule (e.g., weekly, monthly, quarterly) enables you to stay informed about trends, track progress toward goals, and quickly identify issues or opportunities.

How to conduct a performance review:

- **Focus on key metrics:** Start by reviewing your key performance indicators (KPIs) and metrics that align with your business objectives. Analyze metrics related to customer acquisition, activation, retention, revenue, and referrals to get a holistic view of your marketing funnel's health.

- **Identify trends:** Look for trends in your data, such as a steady increase in customer acquisition cost (CAC), a drop in conversion rates, or a spike in customer churn. Understanding these trends helps you identify areas that require attention and optimization.

- **Compare against benchmarks:** Compare your current metrics to historical data, industry benchmarks, and your predefined goals. This comparison provides context, helping you assess whether your growth strategy is on track or if adjustments are needed.

Example: An e-commerce business reviews its dashboard at the end of each month and notices that its customer retention rate has dropped by 10% over the past quarter. The team investigates further to identify the root cause and develop strategies to address the issue.

2. Identify areas for improvement

After reviewing your performance data, the next step is to **identify specific areas that need improvement**. Look for bottlenecks, inefficiencies, or gaps in your marketing funnel that may be hindering growth.

How to identify areas for improvement:

- **Pinpoint underperforming channels:** If certain marketing channels are not delivering the desired ROI, analyze the data to understand why. It could be due to poor targeting, low-quality content, or a mismatch between the channel and your audience.

- **Assess user behavior:** Use tools like Google Analytics, Hotjar, or Mixpanel to analyze user behavior on your website or app. Identify points in the customer journey where users drop off or fail to convert, such as a lengthy sign-up process or an unclear value proposition.

- **Examine customer feedback:** Collect and review customer feedback from surveys, reviews, social media comments, and support interactions. Customer insights can reveal pain points, unmet needs, and opportunities for product or service improvements.

Example: A SaaS company identifies that its free trial sign-up process has a high abandonment rate. Upon further analysis, they discover that the process is too lengthy and requires too much information. This insight prompts the company to simplify the sign-up form, reducing the number of required fields and improving the user experience.

3. Test new strategies and tactics

Experimentation is at the core of refining your growth strategy. By testing new strategies and tactics, you can discover what resonates with your audience, optimize marketing efforts, and continuously improve performance.

How to run effective tests:

- **A/B testing:** Use A/B testing to experiment with different variations of marketing assets, such as landing pages, email subject lines, CTAs, and ad copy. Compare performance data to identify which variations drive the best results and implement the winning changes.

- **Pilot new channels:** Test new marketing channels, such as TikTok, podcasts, or influencer partnerships, on a small scale before committing to larger investments. Measure the effectiveness of these channels in terms of reach, engagement, and conversions.

- **Refine messaging:** Experiment with different value propositions, messaging, and content formats to see which resonate most with your target audience. Testing different approaches helps you refine your brand voice and tailor your marketing communications.

Example: A subscription box company notices that its email open rates are declining. The team runs an A/B test with different subject lines, experimenting with personalized messaging versus general announcements. The test reveals that personalized subject lines, including the recipient's name and preferences, significantly increase open rates. The company then applies this approach across its email campaigns.

4. Measure the impact of changes

After implementing new strategies or optimizations, **measure the impact** to understand their effectiveness. Analyze how these changes influence your key metrics and overall growth.

How to measure impact:

- **Set clear objectives:** Define what success looks like before implementing changes. For example, if you're simplifying the sign-up process, your objective might be to increase the activation rate by 20% within the next month.

- **Use control groups:** When testing new strategies, use control groups to isolate the impact of changes. For instance, if you're testing a new referral program, compare the behavior of users who received the referral incentive with those who didn't.

- **Monitor short-term and long-term effects:** Track both immediate and long-term impacts of your changes. Some strategies, such as content marketing or SEO improvements, may take time to show results, so it's important to monitor performance over an extended period.

Example: An online learning platform introduces a new onboarding flow designed to guide users through the first steps of the platform. After one month, the team compares the activation rates between users who experienced the new onboarding flow and those who went through the old one. The new flow shows a 25% improvement in activation rate, validating the effectiveness of the change.

5. Iterate based on insights

The insights gained from your analyses and experiments should inform the next steps in your growth strategy. **Iteration**involves making continuous, data-driven adjustments to optimize performance and capitalize on new opportunities.

How to iterate effectively:

- **Make incremental changes:** Focus on making small, incremental changes based on your findings. Gradual improvements can lead to significant gains over time without disrupting your overall strategy.

- **Document learnings:** Keep a record of your experiments, including the changes made, results, and key takeaways. Documenting your learnings creates a knowledge base that guides future decision-making and prevents repeating past mistakes.

- **Adopt a growth mindset:** Encourage a culture of learning and agility within your team. Embrace failures as learning opportunities, and be open to testing new ideas and approaches that challenge the status quo.

Example: A fitness app iteratively improves its user engagement strategy by testing various in-app notifications and content recommendations. By analyzing user responses to different notification styles, the app discovers that short, motivational messages yield higher engagement than longer, instructional content. The app then adopts this approach across its user communication efforts.

6. Scale successful strategies

When an experiment or optimization proves successful, **scale the strategy** to maximize its impact on your growth objectives. Scaling involves increasing investment, expanding reach, or replicating the approach across different channels.

How to scale effectively:

- **Increase budget:** Allocate more budget to high-performing campaigns or channels that deliver a positive return on investment (ROI). For example, if a particular social media ad campaign consistently generates leads at a low cost, increase ad spend to reach a larger audience.

- **Expand to new markets:** If a product or service enhancement resonates with your current audience, consider expanding to new geographic markets or customer segments with a similar offering.

- **Automate processes:** Use automation tools to streamline repetitive tasks and processes, such as lead nurturing, customer onboarding, or content distribution. Automation allows you to scale successful strategies without overburdening your team.

Example: An online retailer runs a successful A/B test on a new product recommendation engine that significantly boosts average order value (AOV). To scale the strategy, the retailer integrates the recommendation engine across all product pages, email campaigns, and the checkout process, resulting in a sustained increase in revenue.

The bottom line: refining for continuous growth

Continuous analysis and refinement are crucial for maintaining growth and staying competitive in an ever-changing market landscape. By regularly reviewing performance data, identifying areas for improvement, testing new strategies, measuring impact, iterating based on insights, and scaling successful tactics, businesses can optimize their growth strategies for maximum effectiveness. This ongoing cycle of learning and adaptation not only helps overcome challenges and plateaus but also drives sustainable, long-term success.

CHAPTER 1 4
The future of Growth Marketing

Emerging trends: Web3, blockchain, and decentralized marketing

The digital marketing world is experiencing a significant shift with the rise of **Web3, blockchain**, and **decentralized marketing**. These emerging technologies are changing how businesses interact with consumers, manage data, and conduct transactions online. For growth marketers, understanding and embracing these trends is essential to staying ahead of the curve and unlocking new opportunities for customer engagement, loyalty, and revenue generation.

What is Web3, and why does it matter?

Web3 refers to the next evolution of the internet, where decentralization, blockchain, and user ownership are central. Unlike Web2, which is characterized by centralized platforms like Google, Facebook, and Amazon, Web3 promotes a more open, user-controlled internet powered by blockchain technology and decentralized applications (dApps).

Key aspects of Web3 include:

- **Decentralization:** In Web3, power is shifted away from centralized authorities (such as tech giants) and toward a network of users. This structure creates more transparency, security, and user control over data.

- **Blockchain technology:** Blockchain is the underlying technology of Web3, providing a secure, immutable ledger for transactions. It enables peer-to-peer interactions, eliminating the need for intermediaries in various processes, including payments, contracts, and data storage.

- **Tokenization and digital assets:** Web3 introduces digital assets like cryptocurrencies and non-fungible tokens (NFTs), enabling new models of value exchange, ownership, and community participation.

Why it matters for growth marketing: Web3 represents a fundamental shift in how brands and consumers interact online. With a focus on decentralization and user control, Web3 technologies empower consumers to take charge of their data, engage in peer-to-peer transactions, and participate in decentralized communities. For marketers, this shift opens up new opportunities for innovative customer experiences, loyalty programs, and marketing strategies that resonate with a tech-savvy audience.

How blockchain is transforming marketing

Blockchain technology is at the heart of Web3 and is transforming marketing by providing solutions for transparency, data privacy, and direct value exchange. Here's how blockchain is reshaping marketing practices:

1. Decentralized data ownership and privacy

One of the key challenges in the current marketing landscape is **data privacy**. Traditional Web2 marketing relies heavily on collecting and analyzing consumer data, often without full transparency or user consent. Blockchain offers a decentralized approach to data ownership, giving users more control over their personal information.

How it works:

- **Self-sovereign identities:** In Web3, users can create decentralized identities using blockchain-based wallets. These wallets store user data in an encrypted, self-owned manner, allowing users to control what information they share with brands and platforms.

- **Permissioned data sharing:** With blockchain, users can selectively share their data with companies in exchange for value, such as discounts, rewards, or access to premium content. Smart contracts on the blockchain automate and enforce these data-sharing agreements, ensuring transparency and security.

Example: Brave, a privacy-focused web browser, uses blockchain to enable users to control their data and online advertising experience. Users can opt into viewing ads and are rewarded with Basic Attention Tokens (BAT) for their attention. This approach gives users autonomy over their data and creates a more transparent, value-driven interaction between brands and consumers.

2. Cryptocurrency and token-based marketing

Cryptocurrencies and **tokens** are central to Web3, allowing for new models of customer engagement, loyalty, and value exchange. Brands can use cryptocurrencies and tokens to incentivize specific behaviors, reward customer loyalty, and even co-create with their communities.

How it works:

- **Loyalty and rewards programs:** Businesses can create their own branded tokens to reward customers for actions like making purchases, sharing content, or participating in community events. These tokens can be used for discounts, exclusive access, or exchanged for other cryptocurrencies.

- **Token-gated experiences:** Brands can use tokens as a form of digital access pass, granting holders entry to exclusive events, content, or communities. This model encourages users to hold and use branded tokens, increasing engagement and brand loyalty.

- **Decentralized finance (DeFi) integration:** By integrating with decentralized finance (DeFi) protocols, brands can offer new ways for customers to pay, save, or earn interest using cryptocurrencies, enhancing the customer experience.

Example: A fashion brand launches a tokenized loyalty program where customers earn brand tokens for every purchase. These tokens can be redeemed for exclusive merchandise, early access to new collections, or traded on decentralized exchanges. The brand fosters a sense of community and ownership, incentivizing repeat purchases and engagement.

3. NFTs and the creator economy

Non-fungible tokens (NFTs) are unique digital assets stored on the blockchain. NFTs have gained popularity in the art, gaming, and entertainment industries and offer brands new ways to engage with consumers through digital collectibles, experiences, and membership programs.

How it works:

- **Digital collectibles:** Brands can create limited-edition NFTs, such as virtual collectibles, artwork, or digital fashion items, that fans can purchase, trade, or showcase. The scarcity and uniqueness of NFTs make them valuable and desirable, fostering deeper brand engagement.

- **Access and memberships:** NFTs can serve as digital passes that grant holders access to exclusive content, events, or communities. This use case creates a sense of exclusivity and rewards loyal customers or early adopters.

- **Co-creation with consumers:** NFTs empower consumers to co-create with brands. For example, brands can collaborate with their communities to design NFT collections or involve NFT holders in decision-making processes, building a stronger connection between the brand and its audience.

Example: A music artist launches a limited-edition NFT collection of album artwork and behind-the-scenes content. Fans who purchase the NFTs gain access to a private virtual concert and voting rights on future album releases. This NFT-based experience not only generates revenue but also strengthens the artist-fan relationship through interactive participation.

4. Decentralized communities and social tokens

In Web3, **decentralized communities** are emerging as powerful ecosystems where users have a direct say in the direction and governance of projects. Social tokens represent a new way for brands and creators to build and monetize their communities.

How it works:

- **Social tokens:** Creators, brands, or communities can issue social tokens that represent a stake in their ecosystem.

Holders of these tokens gain access to exclusive content, voting rights, and the ability to participate in community decisions. Social tokens incentivize community members to engage, contribute, and grow the brand.

- **Decentralized autonomous organizations (DAOs):** Brands can establish DAOs—decentralized, blockchain-based organizations that allow members to propose, vote, and execute decisions democratically. This structure creates a sense of shared ownership and empowers community members to shape the brand's future.

Example: A fitness brand creates a social token that members can earn by participating in fitness challenges, sharing progress on social media, or attending community events. Token holders receive exclusive benefits, such as access to premium workout programs, branded merchandise, and voting rights on future product lines. This model turns customers into active participants in the brand's journey.

5. Transparent and secure advertising with blockchain

Blockchain technology addresses many of the challenges associated with **digital advertising**, including ad fraud, lack of transparency, and data privacy concerns. By leveraging blockchain, marketers can create a more secure, efficient, and trustworthy advertising ecosystem.

How it works:

- **Ad verification:** Blockchain provides an immutable ledger of advertising transactions, enabling advertisers to verify that their ads are being displayed to the intended audience and receiving genuine clicks or impressions. This transparency reduces ad fraud and ensures that advertising budgets are spent effectively.

- **Smart contracts for ad placement:** Advertisers can use smart contracts to automate ad placement and payment processes. Payments are only released when specific conditions, such as verified impressions or clicks, are met, ensuring accountability and performance-based advertising.

- **Privacy-centric targeting:** Blockchain enables privacy-centric advertising by allowing users to control their data. Brands can use permissioned blockchain networks to target users who have explicitly opted into sharing their data, creating a more ethical and user-friendly approach to advertising.

Example: A digital ad network uses blockchain to verify ad impressions and clicks, reducing fraudulent activity and improving trust between advertisers and publishers. Advertisers can track their campaigns in real-time through a transparent blockchain ledger, ensuring that they reach their desired audience efficiently.

The bottom line: preparing for the Web3 future

The rise of Web3, blockchain, and decentralized marketing is transforming how brands connect with consumers, manage data, and build communities. These technologies empower users, foster transparency, and open new avenues for customer engagement and loyalty. For growth marketers, embracing Web3 means exploring innovative strategies like tokenized loyalty programs, NFT-based experiences, and decentralized communities to create value and deepen customer relationships.

As we move into the Web3 era, staying informed about emerging trends and experimenting with blockchain-based marketing initiatives will be crucial for building a forward-thinking, future-ready growth strategy.

The role of AI and automation in the future of growth

Artificial intelligence (AI) and **automation** have become central to growth marketing, offering powerful tools to enhance decision-making, streamline processes, and deliver personalized customer experiences at scale. As these technologies continue to evolve, they promise even more transformative capabilities for growth marketers. From predictive analytics to personalized recommendations and marketing automation, AI is not just a tool — it's the driving force behind the future of growth.

How AI is transforming growth marketing

AI's ability to analyze large volumes of data, identify patterns, and make predictions enables growth marketers to move beyond traditional methods and adopt a more data-driven, customer-centric approach. Here's how AI is revolutionizing key aspects of growth marketing:

1. Hyper-personalization at scale

Personalization has become a critical component of successful marketing strategies, and AI takes it to a whole new level by delivering hyper-personalized experiences at every touchpoint. AI algorithms analyze customer behavior, preferences, and interactions to provide tailored content, product recommendations, and offers in real-time.

How it works:

- **Dynamic content:** AI-driven tools like **Dynamic Yield** and **Monetate** use machine learning to deliver personalized website content based on user behavior, demographics, location, and past interactions. This dynamic approach creates a unique experience for each visitor, improving engagement and conversion rates.

- **Product recommendations:** E-commerce platforms use AI algorithms to analyze customer browsing and purchase history, enabling them to offer personalized product recommendations. This strategy not only increases sales but also enhances customer satisfaction by providing relevant suggestions.

- **Personalized email campaigns:** AI-powered email marketing tools like **ActiveCampaign** and **Mailchimp** use customer data to craft personalized email content, timing, and frequency. These tools can segment audiences based on behavior, past purchases, and preferences, sending tailored messages that resonate with recipients.

Example: Amazon leverages AI to provide personalized product recommendations on its website and in follow-up emails. By analyzing user behavior, search queries, and purchase history, Amazon offers product suggestions that align with each customer's interests, driving cross-selling and increasing average order value.

2. Predictive analytics and customer segmentation

Predictive analytics powered by AI allows marketers to forecast future customer behavior, trends, and market changes. This predictive power enables businesses to optimize their marketing strategies, improve customer targeting, and allocate resources more effectively.

How it works:

- **Customer segmentation:** AI algorithms analyze customer data, including purchase behavior, engagement levels, and demographics, to create dynamic customer segments. These segments are updated in real-time based on changing customer behavior, allowing marketers to tailor campaigns to each group's specific needs.

- **Churn prediction:** AI models identify patterns associated with customer churn, such as reduced engagement, negative feedback, or changes in purchasing behavior. Marketers can use these insights to proactively engage at-risk customers with personalized retention campaigns, such as exclusive offers or loyalty rewards.

- **Sales forecasting:** AI-driven predictive analytics tools, like **Salesforce Einstein** and **HubSpot**, analyze historical sales data, market trends, and seasonal variations to forecast future sales. This foresight enables businesses to plan inventory, optimize pricing strategies, and launch timely marketing campaigns.

Example: A subscription-based SaaS company uses AI-powered predictive analytics to segment its user base into categories like "high-value," "at-risk," and "new users." Based on these segments, the company deploys targeted retention strategies, offering personalized incentives to high-value users and re-engagement campaigns to at-risk customers. This data-driven approach reduces churn and maximizes customer lifetime value (CLV).

3. Automating marketing campaigns and workflows

Marketing automation powered by AI is redefining how businesses interact with customers, enabling them to deliver the right message to the right audience at the right time. Automation streamlines repetitive tasks, allowing marketers to focus on strategic planning and creative initiatives.

How it works:

- **Email automation:** AI-driven tools like **HubSpot**, **Marketo**, and **Mailchimp** automate email marketing by sending targeted messages based on customer behavior, such as abandoned cart reminders, welcome sequences, and post-purchase follow-ups. AI can also optimize email content and subject lines to maximize open and click-through rates.

- **Ad optimization:** AI algorithms in advertising platforms like **Google Ads** and **Facebook Ads** automatically adjust bids, target audience segments, and optimize ad placements in real-time to achieve the best ROI. These platforms use machine learning to analyze performance data and adapt campaigns to changing market conditions.

- **Lead nurturing:** AI-powered chatbots and CRM systems automate lead nurturing by engaging prospects in real-time on websites, social media, and messaging apps. Chatbots can answer questions, qualify leads, and provide personalized recommendations, accelerating the buyer's journey.

Example: An online retailer uses AI-driven marketing automation to send personalized product recommendations and follow-up emails based on each customer's browsing and purchase history. The automation platform tracks customer interactions and sends targeted emails, such as reminding customers of items left in their cart or suggesting complementary products. This automated approach increases engagement and conversion rates while reducing manual effort.

4. AI-enhanced content creation

AI is transforming **content creation**, making it faster and more efficient to produce high-quality, relevant content tailored to audience preferences. Tools like **Jasper**, **Grammarly**, and **ChatGPT** are empowering marketers to create engaging copy, blog posts, social media updates, and more.

How it works:

- **Content generation:** AI content generation tools like **Jasper** and **ChatGPT** use natural language processing

(NLP) to create content based on prompts, keywords, and style guidelines. Marketers can quickly generate blogs, product descriptions, ad copy, and emails that resonate with their audience.

- **Content optimization:** AI tools like **Clearscope** and **Surfer SEO** analyze top-ranking content for specific keywords and provide recommendations to optimize content for SEO, readability, and engagement. This optimization increases the chances of content ranking higher in search engine results and attracting organic traffic.

- **Automated social media posting:** AI-powered social media tools like **Buffer** and **Hootsuite** automatically schedule and post content at optimal times based on audience engagement patterns. AI algorithms analyze past performance data to suggest the best posting times and content formats for maximum reach.

Example: A digital marketing agency uses AI-driven content creation tools to generate initial drafts of blog posts and social media updates. The AI suggests topics based on trending keywords and provides outlines tailored to the target audience. The agency then refines and edits the AI-generated content, speeding up production while maintaining quality and relevance.

5. AI-powered customer service and support

AI-powered customer service is enhancing the customer experience by providing instant, personalized support across various channels. AI chatbots, virtual assistants, and automated help desks handle routine inquiries, allowing human support teams to focus on more complex issues.

How it works:

- **Chatbots:** AI chatbots integrated into websites, messaging apps, and social media platforms provide 24/7 customer support. They can answer common questions, guide users through product features, and even assist with order processing. Advanced chatbots like **ChatGPT** learn from interactions to improve their responses over time.

- **Sentiment analysis:** AI analyzes customer feedback, reviews, and social media comments to detect sentiment and identify areas for improvement. This real-time sentiment analysis helps businesses address issues proactively and improve customer satisfaction.

- **Automated ticketing:** AI-driven CRM systems like **Zendesk** and **Salesforce** automatically categorize, prioritize, and route support tickets based on customer queries, ensuring efficient and timely resolution.

Example: A travel booking platform uses an AI chatbot to handle customer inquiries about flight schedules, hotel reservations, and cancellation policies. The chatbot provides instant, accurate responses and guides customers through booking changes, enhancing the overall customer experience and reducing the workload on human support agents.

6. AI-driven insights and decision-making

AI's advanced data analysis capabilities enable growth marketers to gain deeper insights into customer behavior, market trends, and campaign performance. These insights support **data-driven decision-making**, optimizing marketing strategies and improving ROI.

How it works:

- **Customer journey analysis:** AI tracks customer interactions across multiple touchpoints to create a holistic view of the customer journey. By understanding how customers move through the funnel, marketers can identify pain points and opportunities for optimization.

- **Real-time performance monitoring:** AI analytics tools provide real-time insights into campaign performance, including engagement, conversions, and ROI. Marketers can use these insights to make adjustments on the fly, such as reallocating ad spend or modifying messaging based on current market dynamics.

- **Sales and revenue forecasting:** AI models use historical data and market trends to forecast future sales, revenue, and customer behavior. These forecasts inform marketing strategies, budgeting, and resource allocation.

Example: An e-commerce business uses AI-powered analytics to monitor customer behavior on its website in real-time. The AI identifies patterns, such as an increase in product page views for a specific category, prompting the business to launch a targeted promotion. This data-driven decision-making approach maximizes sales opportunities and enhances marketing efficiency.

The bottom line: embracing AI and automation for future growth

AI and automation are reshaping the growth marketing landscape, offering unparalleled opportunities to personalize customer experiences, optimize campaigns, and scale operations efficiently. By leveraging AI-driven tools for hyper-personalization, predictive analytics, automated workflows, content creation, customer support, and real-time insights, marketers can stay ahead in a competitive market and drive sustainable growth.

As AI technologies continue to advance, growth marketers who embrace these innovations will be well-positioned to navigate the complexities of modern marketing, deliver exceptional customer value, and achieve long-term success.

Predictions and opportunities for the next wave of marketers

The marketing world is in the midst of a technological revolution, with advancements in artificial intelligence (AI), blockchain, Web3, and other cutting-edge technologies setting the stage for a new era of growth marketing. As we look to the future, several key trends are poised to redefine how marketers connect with audiences, build brands, and drive business growth. Understanding these trends and embracing the opportunities they present will be critical for the next wave of growth marketers.

Prediction 1: Hyper-personalization will be the standard

As AI and machine learning continue to evolve, **hyper-personalization** will become the new norm in marketing. Consumers increasingly expect brands to deliver tailored experiences that reflect their preferences, behavior, and unique needs. Growth marketers will need to move beyond traditional segmentation and embrace AI-driven solutions to offer real-time, individualized interactions at every touchpoint.

Opportunity: Dynamic content and real-time marketing

- **How to seize it:** Use AI-powered tools to create dynamic content that adapts in real-time based on user behavior, location, and interactions. Implement AI algorithms to deliver personalized product recommendations, emails, ads, and website content that resonate with each customer.

- **Future tools:** Expect the rise of more advanced personalization platforms that leverage natural language processing (NLP) and predictive analytics to automate customer interactions and enhance user experiences.

Example: A streaming service uses AI to analyze each user's viewing habits, preferences, and ratings. The platform then dynamically curates personalized recommendations and creates tailored playlists that keep users engaged, enhancing retention and loyalty.

Prediction 2: The growth of Web3 and community-driven marketing

Web3 technologies, including blockchain, decentralized applications (dApps), and non-fungible tokens (NFTs), are creating new models for marketing based on transparency, user ownership, and community participation. Brands will increasingly leverage Web3 to build decentralized, community-driven ecosystems where users have a direct stake in the brand's success.

Opportunity: Tokenized loyalty programs and DAOs

- **How to seize it:** Develop tokenized loyalty programs using cryptocurrencies and NFTs to incentivize and reward customer engagement. Consider forming a decentralized autonomous organization (DAO) where your community members have a say in brand decisions, creating a sense of ownership and shared purpose.

- **Future tools:** Expect growth in Web3 marketing platforms that facilitate NFT creation, token distribution, and DAO management, making it easier for marketers to implement these decentralized initiatives.

Example: A fashion brand launches a tokenized loyalty program using its own cryptocurrency. Customers earn tokens for purchases, social media engagement, and attending virtual fashion events. The brand also establishes a DAO, allowing token holders to vote on future product designs and collaborations, fostering community involvement and loyalty.

Prediction 3: AI-powered creativity will redefine content marketing

AI's role in content marketing is expanding, enabling marketers to **automate creative processes** such as writing, video production, and graphic design. As AI tools become more sophisticated, marketers will be able to produce high-quality, tailored content at scale, freeing up time for strategy and innovation.

Opportunity: AI-generated content and interactive experiences

- **How to seize it:** Use AI-powered content creation tools to generate blog posts, social media updates, video scripts, and visual assets. Experiment with interactive experiences like chatbots, virtual reality (VR), and augmented reality (AR) to create immersive content that captivates your audience.

- **Future tools:** The next wave of AI tools will be capable of generating highly complex and interactive content, such as personalized videos, virtual events, and dynamic storytelling experiences.

Example: A travel company uses AI to create personalized travel itineraries and destination guides for its customers. The AI-generated content is tailored to each user's preferences, travel history, and budget, providing a unique experience that boosts customer engagement and conversion rates.

Prediction 4: Privacy-centric marketing will gain prominence

With increasing concerns over data privacy and new regulations like GDPR and CCPA, **privacy-centric marketing** will become a critical focus. Consumers are becoming more aware of how their data is used and are demanding greater transparency and control. As a result, marketers will need to adopt strategies that respect user privacy while still delivering personalized experiences.

Opportunity: First-party data and permission-based marketing

- **How to seize it:** Shift focus to collecting and leveraging first-party data—information that customers willingly share with your brand, such as purchase history, preferences, and interactions. Implement permission-based marketing practices that give users control over their data and how it's used.

- **Future tools:** Look for the emergence of privacy-focused analytics tools that anonymize and aggregate data while still providing actionable insights for personalized marketing.

Example: A fitness app adopts a privacy-centric approach by allowing users to control what data they share. The app uses first-party data collected through user consent to provide personalized workout plans and nutrition tips. This transparency builds trust and encourages users to engage more deeply with the app's services.

Prediction 5: The rise of voice search and conversational AI

Voice search and **conversational AI** are becoming increasingly popular as consumers use voice assistants like Alexa, Siri, and Google Assistant to find information, shop online, and interact with brands. This trend will create new marketing opportunities that focus on natural language processing and voice-activated experiences.

Opportunity: Voice-optimized content and conversational marketing

- **How to seize it:** Optimize your website content and product descriptions for voice search by using conversational keywords, natural language, and featured snippets. Integrate AI-driven chatbots on your website and messaging apps to provide instant, conversational support that enhances customer engagement.

- **Future tools:** Advanced voice AI tools will enable marketers to create sophisticated voice-activated campaigns, virtual assistants, and interactive voice-based experiences tailored to user queries.

Example: A home services company optimizes its website for voice search by including conversational FAQs and how-to guides. It also integrates a voice-activated chatbot on its mobile app, allowing customers to schedule appointments, ask questions, and receive instant support through simple voice commands.

Prediction 6: Data analytics will become more predictive and proactive

The future of marketing analytics lies in **predictive and proactive analytics**, where AI models forecast customer behavior, market trends, and campaign outcomes. This shift from reactive to proactive decision-making will empower marketers to optimize their strategies based on real-time insights and predictive modeling.

Opportunity: Predictive customer journey mapping and scenario planning

- **How to seize it:** Use AI-driven analytics tools to map customer journeys and predict future behavior, such as purchasing patterns, churn risk, and engagement trends. Implement scenario planning to forecast the impact of different marketing strategies, enabling you to allocate resources more effectively.

- **Future tools:** Expect the development of more advanced predictive analytics platforms that provide detailed forecasts, customer lifetime value (CLV) predictions, and automated optimization recommendations.

Example: A subscription-based media service uses AI analytics to forecast customer churn and identify high-value segments for targeted retention campaigns. By analyzing user behavior and engagement trends, the company proactively offers personalized content recommendations and loyalty rewards, reducing churn and increasing customer lifetime value.

Prediction 7: Ethical AI and responsible marketing practices

As AI becomes more integrated into marketing strategies, **ethical AI** practices and responsible marketing will gain importance. Consumers expect brands to use AI in ways that are fair, transparent, and respectful of privacy. Future growth marketers will need to adopt ethical guidelines and frameworks to build trust and foster positive customer relationships.

Opportunity: Transparent AI usage and value-driven marketing

- **How to seize it:** Be transparent about how you use AI in marketing, especially when it involves customer data and personalization. Implement ethical guidelines that prioritize customer consent, data privacy, and unbiased algorithms. Use AI to support value-driven marketing that aligns with your brand's mission and values.

- **Future tools:** Look out for tools that help monitor AI ethics, detect biases in algorithms, and ensure compliance with privacy regulations, helping marketers maintain ethical standards in their practices.

Example: A financial services app adopts an ethical AI policy, ensuring that its AI-driven investment recommendations are free from bias and tailored to each user's financial goals. The app provides clear explanations of how AI influences its suggestions, empowering users to make informed decisions and building trust in the brand.

The bottom line: embracing the future of growth marketing

The future of growth marketing is dynamic, driven by technological innovation, changing consumer behaviors, and a heightened focus on personalization, privacy, and ethical practices. As we move into this new era, marketers who embrace emerging trends such as Web3, AI-driven personalization, privacy-centric marketing, and predictive analytics will be well-positioned to succeed.

To thrive in the next wave of marketing, it's essential to:

- Stay informed about technological advancements and consumer trends.

- Experiment with new tools and strategies, leveraging AI, blockchain, and decentralized technologies.

- Adopt an ethical and customer-centric approach that respects privacy and builds long-term trust.

By harnessing these opportunities, the next generation of growth marketers can drive impactful, sustainable growth and create meaningful, lasting connections with their customers.

CONCLUSION
Your growth marketing playbook in action

You've now journeyed through the dynamic world of growth marketing, exploring strategies, tools, and emerging trends that drive sustainable business success. From building a solid foundation and adopting a growth mindset to leveraging AI, automation, and Web3 technologies, each chapter has provided insights and actionable steps to help you unlock your business's growth potential.

But reading about growth marketing is just the first step. Now, it's time to put these strategies into action and transform your marketing efforts into a finely-tuned, data-driven playbook that fuels ongoing success.

Tying it all together: from strategy to execution

Growth marketing is not a one-size-fits-all approach. It's a mindset—a relentless focus on experimentation, data-driven decision-making, and customer-centric strategies. As you begin implementing your growth marketing playbook, keep these key principles in mind:

1. **Lay a strong foundation:** Before diving into campaigns, establish a deep understanding of your target audience and product-market fit. Set clear, growth-driven goals using

metrics like North Star metrics, OKRs, and KPIs to guide your efforts.

2. **Adopt a data-driven mindset:** Collect, analyze, and act on data at every stage of the customer journey. Use analytics to identify trends, measure performance, and refine strategies. Let data—not assumptions—drive your decisions.

3. **Test, learn, and iterate:** Embrace experimentation as a core part of your growth strategy. Run A/B tests, pilot new channels, and explore creative tactics. Whether it's tweaking your website's call-to-action or launching a new ad campaign, test and learn continuously.

4. **Focus on the entire funnel:** Growth marketing is not just about acquisition; it's about optimizing every stage of the funnel. From attracting the right audience to activating users, nurturing retention, driving referrals, and maximizing revenue, each stage requires a tailored approach.

5. **Leverage technology and automation:** Utilize AI, automation, and growth marketing tools to streamline processes, personalize customer interactions, and scale your efforts. Automation frees up your team to focus on strategic, creative initiatives that drive growth.

6. **Adapt to emerging trends:** Stay ahead of the curve by embracing emerging trends such as Web3, blockchain, AI, and privacy-centric marketing. Adopting these technologies and practices will keep your brand relevant and competitive in an ever-changing digital landscape.

Case studies of startups and companies who mastered growth marketing

To inspire your journey, let's look at a few examples of companies that successfully implemented growth marketing strategies:

1. Dropbox: Building viral loops for organic growth Dropbox leveraged a viral referral program to drive exponential growth. By offering free additional storage space to users who referred friends, Dropbox created a viral loop that significantly lowered customer acquisition costs and accelerated user growth. This simple yet powerful strategy turned Dropbox into a household name in the cloud storage industry.

> **Key takeaway:** Viral referral programs can be a cost-effective way to scale customer acquisition. Consider offering incentives that align with your product's value to encourage users to promote your brand organically.

2. Spotify: Personalized experiences through data-driven insights Spotify harnessed the power of data and AI to create hyper-personalized user experiences. From curated playlists like "Discover Weekly" to real-time music recommendations, Spotify continuously used customer behavior data to enhance user engagement and retention, setting a benchmark for personalization in the music streaming industry.

> **Key takeaway:** Use customer data to deliver tailored experiences that resonate with individual preferences. Personalization drives engagement, satisfaction, and loyalty, leading to increased customer lifetime value (CLV).

3. HubSpot: Inbound marketing and educational content HubSpot pioneered the inbound marketing movement by providing valuable, educational content to attract, engage, and delight potential customers. Through its extensive blog, e-books, webinars, and certification courses, HubSpot established itself as an industry authority and built a loyal user community.

> **Key takeaway:** Content marketing is a powerful tool for building brand authority and nurturing leads. Create valuable, educational content that addresses your audience's pain points and positions your brand as a trusted resource.

Next steps: implementing your growth marketing playbook

Here's a step-by-step guide to help you kickstart your growth marketing playbook:

1. **Assess your current state:** Conduct a thorough analysis of your current marketing efforts, customer journey, and performance metrics. Identify your strengths, weaknesses, and areas of opportunity.

2. **Set growth-driven goals:** Define your short-term and long-term growth objectives. Use these goals to select relevant KPIs and create a roadmap for your growth marketing initiatives.

3. **Build your growth marketing stack:** Invest in the right tools and technologies to support your strategy. Consider tools for analytics, marketing automation, CRM, content creation, and AI-powered personalization.

4. **Experiment and iterate:** Develop an experimentation framework that allows you to test new strategies, measure results, and iterate based on data insights. Start with small-scale experiments before committing significant resources.

5. **Focus on customer-centric growth:** Put your customers at the heart of your strategy. Listen to their feedback, address their pain points, and build meaningful relationships through personalized, value-driven interactions.

6. **Monitor and refine:** Use your growth marketing dashboard to track performance, identify trends, and make data-driven adjustments. Regularly review your strategy to ensure it aligns with evolving market trends and customer needs.

Final thoughts: your growth marketing journey

Growth marketing is a dynamic, ever-evolving field that requires a blend of creativity, data analysis, technological savvy, and customer empathy. The strategies, tools, and trends discussed in this playbook are designed to empower you to navigate the complexities of growth marketing, drive sustainable success, and build a brand that resonates with your audience.

As you put this playbook into action, remember that growth is not a linear process. It involves experimentation, adaptation, and a relentless focus on delivering value to your customers. Stay curious, embrace change, and keep refining your strategies to unlock new growth opportunities.

Your growth marketing journey has just begun. Now, it's time to take the insights and strategies you've learned and turn them into actionable plans that drive your business forward. Here's to your growth and the exciting possibilities that lie ahead!

References

Anderson, C. (2009). **Free: The future of a radical price**. Hyperion.

Batra, R., & Keller, K. L. (2016). **Integrating marketing communications: New findings, new lessons, and new ideas**. *Journal of Marketing*, 80(6), 122-145.

Baumgartner, J., & Quigley, E. (2019). **Smart marketing with artificial intelligence**. In K. G. Wilson & J. McCarthy (Eds.), *AI in marketing: Transforming customer engagement and marketing strategy* (pp. 45-67). Marketing Profs Press.

Berman, S. J. (2012). **Digital transformation: Opportunities to create new business models**. *Strategy & Leadership*, 40(2), 16-24.

Brinker, S., & McLellan, K. (2020). **Hacking marketing: Agile practices to make marketing smarter, faster, and more innovative**. John Wiley & Sons.

Brown, T. (2019). **Unlocking innovation with a growth mindset**. *Harvard Business Review*. https://hbr.org/2019/10/unlocking-innovation-with-a-growth-mindset

Brynjolfsson, E., & McAfee, A. (2014). **The second machine age: Work, progress, and prosperity in a time of brilliant technologies**. W.W. Norton & Company.

Cialdini, R. B. (2006). **Influence: The psychology of persuasion**. Harper Business.

Clifton, B. (2012). **Advanced web metrics with Google Analytics** (3rd ed.). Sybex.

Collins, J. (2001). **Good to great: Why some companies make the leap and others don't**. Harper Business.

Covey, S. R. (1989). **The 7 habits of highly effective people**. Free Press.

Dolgin, A. (2012). **The economics of symbolic exchange**. Springer.

Donnelly, C., & Scaff, R. (2013). **Who are the millennial shoppers? And what do they really want?** *Accenture Report*. https://www.accenture.com

Eisenmann, T. R., Ries, E., & Dillard, J. F. (2012). **Hypothesis-driven entrepreneurship: The lean startup methodology**. Harvard Business School.

Gladwell, M. (2000). **The tipping point: How little things can make a big difference**. Little, Brown and Company.

Guerini, M., & Rossi-Lamastra, C. (2013). **Success factors of crowdfunding campaigns**. *Journal of Business Venturing Insights*, 2(1), 63-70.

Gupta, S., & Lehmann, D. R. (2005). **Managing customers as investments: The strategic value of customers in the long run**. Wharton School Publishing.

Holloman, C. (2016). **The social media MBA in practice: An essential collection of inspirational case studies to influence your social media strategy**. John Wiley & Sons.

Järvinen, J., & Karjaluoto, H. (2015). **The use of web analytics for digital marketing performance measurement**. *Industrial Marketing Management*, 50, 117-127.

Kahneman, D. (2011). **Thinking, fast and slow**. Farrar, Straus and Giroux.

Kawasaki, G. (2015). **The art of the start 2.0: The time-tested, battle-hardened guide for anyone starting anything**. Penguin Books.

Kotler, P., Kartajaya, H., & Setiawan, I. (2017). **Marketing 4.0: Moving from traditional to digital**. John Wiley & Sons.

Lindstrom, M. (2016). **Small data: The tiny clues that uncover huge trends**. St. Martin's Press.

McKinsey & Company. (2019). **The future of personalization — and how to get ready for it**. https://www.mckinsey.com

Newlands, M. (2016). **The ultimate guide to growth hacking: Digital marketing for startups**. Entrepreneur Press.

Pereira, F., & Romero, D. (2020). **The rise of predictive analytics in marketing: A systematic literature review**. *Marketing Intelligence & Planning*, 38(7), 867-883.

Pine, B. J., & Gilmore, J. H. (2011). **The experience economy**. Harvard Business Review Press.

Ries, E. (2011). **The lean startup: How today's entrepreneurs use continuous innovation to create radically successful businesses**. Crown Business.

Rogers, D. L. (2016). **The digital transformation playbook: Rethink your business for the digital age**. Columbia University Press.

Rogers, E. M. (2003). **Diffusion of innovations** (5th ed.). Free Press.

Rose, S., Spinks, N., & Canhoto, A. I. (2015). **Management research: Applying the principles**. Routledge.

Scott, D. M. (2017). **The new rules of marketing and PR: How to use social media, online video, mobile applications, blogs, news releases, and viral marketing to reach buyers directly** (6th ed.). John Wiley & Sons.

Solis, B. (2018). **X: The experience when business meets design**. John Wiley & Sons.

Stukent, Inc. (2018). **Digital marketing essentials**. Stukent, Inc.

Sunstein, C. R., & Thaler, R. H. (2008). **Nudge: Improving decisions about health, wealth, and happiness**. Yale University Press.

Sutton, R. I. (2010). **Scaling up excellence: Getting to more without settling for less**. Crown Business.

Sweeney, S., & Craig, L. (2011). **Social media for business: 101 ways to grow your business without wasting your time**. Maximum Press.

Taneja, H., & Maney, K. (2018). **Unscaled: How AI and a new generation of upstarts are creating the economy of the future**. PublicAffairs.

Turban, E., King, D., & Lang, J. (2017). **Introduction to electronic commerce** (4th ed.). Springer.

Webster, F. E., Malter, A. J., & Ganesan, S. (2005). **The decline and dispersion of marketing competence**. *California Management Review*, 48(4), 13-28.

Westerman, G., Bonnet, D., & McAfee, A. (2014). **Leading digital: Turning technology into business transformation**. Harvard Business Review Press.

Wuebben, J. (2017). **Future marketing: Winning in the prosumer age**. Content Marketing Institute.

Glossary of Terms

Account-Based Marketing (ABM): A strategic approach to marketing that focuses on creating highly personalized campaigns targeted at specific high-value accounts rather than a broader audience.

Acquisition: The process of attracting and converting new customers to your product or service, often through marketing channels like social media, paid advertising, SEO, or email marketing.

A/B Testing: A method of comparing two versions of a webpage, email, or ad to determine which one performs better based on metrics such as conversion rate, click-through rate, or user engagement.

Artificial Intelligence (AI): The simulation of human intelligence processes by machines, especially computer systems. In marketing, AI is used for predictive analytics, personalization, content creation, and customer service automation.

Average Revenue Per User (ARPU): A metric that calculates the average revenue generated per user over a specified period. It helps assess the revenue contribution of individual users or customers.

Blockchain: A decentralized, digital ledger technology that records transactions across many computers in a secure, immutable manner. In marketing, blockchain is used for data privacy, ad verification, and creating decentralized loyalty programs.

Churn Rate: The percentage of customers who stop using a product or service during a specific period. It's an important metric for understanding customer retention and identifying areas for improvement in the customer journey.

Content Marketing: The practice of creating and sharing valuable, relevant content to attract and engage a target audience, with the goal of driving profitable customer action.

Conversion Rate: The percentage of visitors to a website, landing page, or ad who complete a desired action, such as making a purchase, signing up for a newsletter, or filling out a form.

Cost Per Lead (CPL): The total marketing cost divided by the number of new leads generated during a campaign. It measures the efficiency of lead generation efforts.

Customer Acquisition Cost (CAC): The total cost incurred to acquire a new customer, including marketing, sales, and advertising expenses. It's calculated by dividing the total marketing spend by the number of new customers acquired.

Customer Journey: The complete experience a customer has with a brand, from the initial awareness and consideration stages to the post-purchase experience. Mapping the customer journey helps identify touchpoints for marketing optimization.

Customer Lifetime Value (CLV): The total revenue a business can expect from a customer throughout their entire relationship with the brand. CLV helps marketers determine how much they can spend on customer acquisition while remaining profitable.

Decentralized Autonomous Organization (DAO): An organization governed by smart contracts on a blockchain, allowing members to propose, vote, and execute decisions democratically. DAOs foster community-driven decision-making in marketing strategies.

Demand Generation: Marketing activities aimed at creating awareness, interest, and demand for a product or service. It involves educating potential customers about the value and benefits of the offering to stimulate demand.

Dynamic Content: Website or email content that automatically changes based on user behavior, preferences, or demographics, providing a personalized experience for each visitor.

Experimentation: The practice of testing different marketing strategies, tactics, or hypotheses to find the most effective methods for driving growth. It includes techniques like A/B testing, multivariate testing, and controlled trials.

First-Party Data: Data collected directly by a company from its customers or users, including information from website interactions, purchase history, and surveys. It is valuable for creating personalized marketing campaigns.

Freemium Model: A business model in which a basic version of a product is offered for free, while additional features or services are available through paid upgrades.

Growth Hacking: A data-driven, experimental approach to marketing focused on finding innovative, low-cost strategies to drive rapid business growth, often involving creative use of technology and analytics.

Growth Marketing: A holistic, data-driven marketing approach that optimizes every stage of the customer journey—from acquisition to retention—through continuous experimentation and iteration.

Hyper-Personalization: An advanced form of personalization that uses AI, real-time data, and machine learning to deliver highly customized content, recommendations, and experiences tailored to individual customer preferences.

Inbound Marketing: A strategy that focuses on attracting customers through valuable content and experiences tailored to their needs, drawing them in naturally rather than using interruptive advertising methods.

Key Performance Indicators (KPIs): Metrics used to evaluate the success of a marketing campaign or business strategy. Common KPIs include conversion rate, customer acquisition cost, customer lifetime value, and monthly recurring revenue.

Lookalike Audience: A group of potential customers who share similar characteristics or behaviors with an existing customer segment. Platforms like Facebook and Google Ads use lookalike audiences for targeted advertising.

Marketing Automation: The use of software and technology to automate repetitive marketing tasks, such as email campaigns, social media posting, and ad targeting, allowing marketers to focus on strategic activities.

Monthly Recurring Revenue (MRR): A measure of the predictable monthly revenue generated from subscription-based products or services. MRR helps assess the health and growth of a business, especially in SaaS companies.

Multivariate Testing: A testing method that involves experimenting with multiple variables (e.g., headlines, images, CTA buttons) on a webpage or ad to determine the best-performing combination.

Net Promoter Score (NPS): A metric that measures customer loyalty and satisfaction based on how likely customers are to recommend a product or service to others, on a scale of 0-10.

Non-Fungible Tokens (NFTs): Unique digital assets stored on the blockchain that represent ownership of a specific item or piece of content, such as digital art, collectibles, or access passes.

North Star Metric: The key metric that best captures the core value your product delivers to customers. It guides strategic decisions and focuses on driving sustainable, long-term growth.

Organic Growth: Growth achieved through non-paid channels, such as content marketing, SEO, social media engagement, and word-of-mouth referrals.

Paid Acquisition: The use of paid advertising channels, such as PPC (Pay-Per-Click), display ads, and social media ads, to attract and convert new customers.

Predictive Analytics: The use of data, statistical algorithms, and machine learning techniques to identify the likelihood of future outcomes based on historical data. In marketing, predictive analytics help forecast customer behavior, optimize campaigns, and improve decision-making.

Product-Market Fit: The degree to which a product meets the needs and preferences of a specific market. Achieving product-market fit is essential for driving sustainable growth and retaining customers.

Referral Rate: The percentage of new customers acquired through referrals from existing customers. A high referral rate indicates strong customer advocacy and word-of-mouth marketing.

Retention: The process of keeping existing customers engaged, satisfied, and loyal to the brand. Retention strategies include loyalty programs, personalized experiences, and ongoing customer support.

Sales Funnel: A visual representation of the stages customers go through, from initial awareness to final purchase. The funnel typically includes stages like awareness, consideration, decision, and retention.

SEO (Search Engine Optimization): The practice of optimizing a website's content, structure, and technical aspects to rank higher in search engine results and attract organic traffic.

Smart Contracts: Self-executing contracts with terms and conditions directly written into lines of code on the blockchain. They enable automated, transparent transactions and agreements without the need for intermediaries.

Social Tokens: Digital assets issued by creators, brands, or communities that represent a stake in their ecosystem. Holders of social tokens often receive access to exclusive content, voting rights, or rewards.

Subscription Model: A business model in which customers pay a recurring fee (monthly or yearly) to access a product or service. It creates a steady revenue stream and improves customer retention.

User Experience (UX): The overall experience a user has while interacting with a product, website, or app. Good UX is characterized by ease of use, accessibility, and positive emotional impact.

Viral Loop: A self-perpetuating cycle where users refer new customers, who in turn refer more customers, creating exponential growth. Viral loops are often driven by incentives, social sharing, and word-of-mouth marketing.

Web3: The next phase of the internet, characterized by decentralized, blockchain-based technologies that promote user ownership, transparency, and peer-to-peer interactions. Web3 offers new marketing opportunities through tokenization, NFTs, and decentralized communities.

Thank You

Marcos G. Figueira

Instagram
@marcosfigueira
LinkedIn
@marcosfigueira
https://marcosfigueira.com

—

Marcia Berardinelli

Instagram
@marciaberardinellidefreitas
LinkedIn
@marcia-berardinelli

—

https://wyse.com.br